studies in jazz

Institute of Jazz Studies
Rutgers—The State University of New Jersey
General Editors: Dan Morgenstern and Edward Berger

1. BENNY CARTER: A Life in American Music, *by Morroe Berger, Edward Berger, and James Patrick, 2 vols., 1982* [see no. 40 for 2nd ed.]
2. ART TATUM: A Guide to His Recorded Music, *by Arnold Laubich and Ray Spencer, 1982*
3. ERROLL GARNER: The Most Happy Piano, *by James M. Doran, 1985*
4. JAMES P. JOHNSON: A Case of Mistaken Identity, *by Scott E. Brown;* Discography 1917–1950, *by Robert Hilbert, 1986*
5. PEE WEE ERWIN: This Horn for Hire, *as told to Warren W. Vaché Sr., 1987*
6. BENNY GOODMAN: Listen to His Legacy, *by D. Russell Connor, 1988*
7. ELLINGTONIA: The Recorded Music of Duke Ellington and His Sidemen, *by W. E. Timner, 1988; 4th ed., 1996*
8. THE GLENN MILLER ARMY AIR FORCE BAND: Sustineo Alas / I Sustain the Wings, *by Edward F. Polic;* Foreword *by George T. Simon, 1989*
9. SWING LEGACY, *by Chip Deffaa, 1989*
10. REMINISCING IN TEMPO: The Life and Times of a Jazz Hustler, *by Teddy Reig, with Edward Berger, 1990*
11. IN THE MAINSTREAM: 18 Portraits in Jazz, *by Chip Deffaa, 1992*
12. BUDDY DeFRANCO: A Biographical Portrait and Discography, *by John Kuehn and Arne Astrup, 1993*
13. PEE WEE SPEAKS: A Discography of Pee Wee Russell, *by Robert Hilbert, with David Niven, 1992*
14. SYLVESTER AHOLA: The Gloucester Gabriel, *by Dick Hill, 1993*
15. THE POLICE CARD DISCORD, *by Maxwell T. Cohen, 1993*
16. TRADITIONALISTS AND REVIVALISTS IN JAZZ, *by Chip Deffaa, 1993*
17. BASSICALLY SPEAKING: An Oral History of George Duvivier, *by Edward Berger;* Musical Analysis *by David Chevan, 1993*
18. TRAM: The Frank Trumbauer Story, *by Philip R. Evans and Larry F. Kiner, with William Trumbauer, 1994*
19. TOMMY DORSEY: On the Side, *by Robert L. Stockdale, 1995*
20. JOHN COLTRANE: A Discography and Musical Biography, *by Yasuhiro Fujioka, with Lewis Porter and Yoh-ichi Hamada, 1995*
21. RED HEAD: A Chronological Survey of "Red" Nichols and His Five Pennies, *by Stephen M. Stroff, 1996*
22. THE RED NICHOLS STORY: After Intermission 1942–1965, *by Philip R. Evans, Stanley Hester, Stephen Hester, and Linda Evans, 1997*
23. BENNY GOODMAN: Wrappin' It Up, *by D. Russell Connor, 1996*
24. CHARLIE PARKER AND THEMATIC IMPROVISATION, *by Henry Martin, 1996*

The *Annual Review of Jazz Studies* is published by Scarecrow Press and the Institute of Jazz Studies at Rutgers, The State University of New Jersey. Authors should address manuscripts and editorial correspondence to:

The Editors, Annual Review of Jazz Studies
Institute of Jazz Studies
Dana Library, Rutgers, The State University
185 University Avenue
Newark, New Jersey 07102

Publishers should send review copies of books to this address, marked to the attention of the Book Review Editor.

Authors preparing manuscripts for consideration should follow *The Chicago Manual of Style*, 15th Edition. In particular: (1) manuscripts should be original word-processed copy; (2) except for foreign-language quotations, manuscripts must be in English; (3) *all* material (text, quotations, endnotes, author's biographical note) must be neat, *double-spaced*, left-aligned, and with adequate margins; (4) notes must be grouped together at the end of the manuscript, *not as footnotes* at page bottoms, following either of the two documentation styles (chapters 16 and 17 in *The Chicago Manual of Style*, 15th Edition); (5) authors should append a two- or three-sentence biographical note, including current affiliation; (6) each music sample or complex table must be on a separate sheet in computer-copied, camera-ready form; in formatting examples and tables, authors should take into account that each item may have to be reduced to fit, with a caption, on a page of this size (4 x 6 inches; 10.5 x 16 cm.); (8) all text materials (but not the camera-ready examples) should be submitted both in hard copy and on a 3.5-inch computer diskette in Word for PC or Macintosh; (9) a cassette tape or CD of any examples transcribed or reproduced from recordings must be included to facilitate reading the paper and checking accuracy of transcriptions (a cassette is not necessary for printed music or examples composed by the author).

Authors alone are responsible for the contents of their articles and for obtaining permission for use of material under copyright protection.

ANNUAL REVIEW OF JAZZ STUDIES 12
2002

Edited by
Edward Berger
David Cayer
Henry Martin
Dan Morgenstern

Assistant Editor
George Bassett

The Scarecrow Press, Inc.
Lanham, Maryland • Toronto • Oxford
and
Institute of Jazz Studies
Rutgers—The State University of
New Jersey
2004

SCARECROW PRESS, INC.

Published in the United States of America
by Scarecrow Press, Inc.
A wholly owned subsidary of
The Rowman & Littlefield Publishing Group, Inc.
4501 Forbes Boulevard, Suite 200, Lanham, Maryland 20706
www.scarecrowpress.com

PO Box 317
Oxford
OX2 9RU, UK

ISSN 0731-0641
ISBN 0-8108-5005-2

∞™ The paper used in this publication meets the minimum requirements of
American National Standard for Information Sciences—Permanence of
Paper for Printed Library Materials, ANSI/NISO Z39.48-1992.
Manufactured in the United States of America.

CONTENTS

BOOK REVIEWS

CD-ROM REVIEW

PREFACE

This twelfth volume of the *Annual Review of Jazz Studies*, covering the year 2002, celebrates the fiftieth anniversary of the Institute of Jazz Studies. A half-century ago, Marshall Stearns and a number of devoted colleagues created IJS in a New York City apartment. Our photo gallery in this issue illustrates some of the persons and locations in its history, both in New York and at the Institute's present home at the Newark campus of Rutgers, The State University of New Jersey.

As usual, articles in this issue deal with major jazz figures from widely separated eras. Some of them, despite their undisputed importance, have not been the central subjects of past articles in *ARJS,* so we are pleased to present studies of Gil Evans, Django Reinhardt, Lucky Thompson, and Paul Bley. Other articles include an analysis of John Coltrane's harmonics and its impact on later compositions, and a survey of recordings based on Charlie Green's classic 1924 trombone solo on "The Gouge of Armour Avenue." A memorial salutes the contributions of a notable Danish scholar, Erik Wiedemann (a small part of whose work on Ellington appeared in *ARJS* some years ago).

Once again, the impact of computers and the internet are felt in our contents. *ARJS 10* contained a survey of internet sources useful for discographical research. This issue contains a review of a discography on CD-ROM, following book reviews of a volume covering jazz recordings from "modernism to postmodernism" and books devoted to saxophonist Gigi Gryce and three trumpet giants: Louis Armstrong, Roy Eldridge, and Miles Davis.

Our special thanks go to George Bassett, who assumed responsibility for copyediting with this issue of *ARJS*. Some years ago, George was the expert editor who helped produce several issues of our predecessor periodical, *Journal of Jazz Studies,* so his return is particularly welcome.

This issue also continues two features recently introduced to benefit jazz researchers. We again thank Keith Waters and Jason R. Titus—and the many individuals who assisted them—for compiling the many scholarly articles on jazz which appeared in other journals during the 2000–2001 period. Vincent Pelote of the Institute of Jazz Studies has again compiled a list of books, both new and republished, recently received at IJS.

Finally, we note that this is the last issue of *ARJS* to bear the name of David Cayer on the cover. For over thirty years, beginning with the *Journal of Jazz Studies*, which he cofounded in 1973, Dave has been the driving force behind this publication. His superb editorial sense, knowledge of the music, thorough grasp of the intricacies of *The Chicago Manual of Style*, not to mention his sense of humor have guided dozens of authors over these three decades through the publication process. While we will miss him as a coeditor, we are pleased that Dave will continue to contribute to *ARJS* from time to time as well as to our *Studies in Jazz* series. He remains an important member of the IJS family.

The Editors

GIL EVANS:
THE ART OF MUSICAL TRANSFORMATION

Scott D. Reeves

When we consider the exponential growth of the jazz vocabulary since the beginning of the twentieth century, the work of a few artists stands out as having the broadest and most decisive influence over its decade-to-decade development, particularly the innovations of Louis Armstrong, Duke Ellington, Lester Young, Charlie Parker, Miles Davis, John Coltrane, and Ornette Coleman. Although these seminal figures are composers, with the exception of Ellington, it is largely through their efforts as jazz improvisers that the harmonic-melodic-rhythmic vocabulary of jazz evolved. This is not to undervalue the significant work of such composers as Fletcher Henderson, Don Redman, Billy Strayhorn, Thelonious Monk, Horace Silver, Wayne Shorter, Bob Brookmeyer, and Jim McNeely, but their compositions often serve to formalize, consolidate, and extend many of the innovations first introduced by improvisers. Indeed, in the jazz tradition, the distinction between improviser and composer is often blurred—most jazz soloists are also composers, and vice versa. Improvisation may be viewed as a spontaneously created composition, even as the songs of many jazz composers, especially those of Parker and Monk, often display many commonalities with their improvised solos, as if their written themes are but improvisations frozen in time. Accordingly, it has also become standard practice in the field of jazz studies to transcribe improvised solos and analyze them as if they were formal compositions.

Gil Evans stands in marked contrast to this tradition of the jazz improviser-composer. He infrequently appears on recordings as a pianist, often favoring the sparser texture of a pianoless rhythm section in his orchestrations (particularly those for Miles Davis) where the trombones and French horns "comp" in the manner of a jazz pianist.[1] In addition, although he composed several fine themes, most notably "Miles Ahead," "Eleven," and "Time of the Barracudas" (all three cowritten with Davis), his theme song, "La Nevada Blues," the moody and evocative "Sunken Treasure," "Variation on the Misery," and "Proclamation," the New Orleans-inspired "Jambangle," his paean to bebop, "Bud and Bird," and Spanish-influenced pieces such as "Blues for

Pablo" and "Solea," his entire oeuvre as a composer is rather small.[2] It may
be argued that Evans's major contribution is that of an arranger of other composers' music, but to dismiss Evans's efforts as being limited to orchestration
would be missing the fresh perspective and depth of transformation with
which he imbues each arrangement. Evans states that "orchestration is one of
the elements of composition. You might say that it is the choice of sound units
and their manipulation as part of expressing a musical idea" (Gitler 1989).
Joe Muccioli, who has transcribed Evans, aptly summarizes that "it is often
difficult to find that fine line between the original music and where Evans'
own compositional ideas take over. Similarly, in his original music after
1959, it is difficult to define the point where composition ends and improvisation begins" (Muccioli 1997, 4–5).

Evans's ability to create arrangements that blur the line between composed music and improvisation, his judicious use of dissonance and
unique chord voicings, as well as the fresh timbres he elicits from the jazz
orchestra, are legendary among jazz musicians, if not the general public.
Evans was an unassuming, gentle individual who eschewed the spotlight
and fame that often focused on better-known musicians. He was not prone
to discuss the inner workings of his music and left little in the way of a
school of imitators upon his death in 1988.[3] Although his place in jazz
history is significant, before 2001 the only published research on Evans
consisted of two out-of-print biographies (one in English, one in French),
two dissertations on selected pieces written for Claude Thornhill and
Davis, respectively, and a short article in *Down Beat* on the voicings used
in his arrangement of "My Ship." Sketch scores (without analysis) were
published in 1997 in *The Gil Evans Collection,* and some of the scores
and parts written for Davis recently became available in rental form.[4]
Since this article was written, two new biographies, *Gil Evans—Out of
the Cool: His Life and Music* and *Castles Made of Sound: The Story of
Gil Evans,* as well as a book containing analyses of selected scores written for Davis, *Gil Evans & Miles Davis—Historic Collaborations,* and a
collection of scores from *The Birth of the Cool* (which includes Evans's
arrangement of "Boplicity") have been published. These welcome addi-
tions should help address this paucity of information on his arranging
techniques.[5] Although a complete examination of his body of work is beyond the scope of this article, an overview of Evans's choice of material,
his manipulation of musical elements such as timbre, form, melody, harmony, and rhythm, as well as an extended discussion of his recomposition
of Tchaikovsky's "Danse Arabe" and Gershwin's "Gone, Gone, Gone,"
will follow.

While researching Evans's methods, I was also struck by the many parallels between Evans's and Ellington's writing, although Evans's output as a composer pales in comparison with Ellington's prodigious body of work. Both men drew on sources of material and rhythms not typically associated with the jazz idiom. Each in his own way combined traditional instruments in innovative ways and expanded the tonal spectrum of the jazz orchestra. Both wrote melodies of an improvisational character and developed personal means of incorporating dissonance within a traditional harmonic context. Consequently, although their styles are superficially dissimilar, it may be argued that Evans's writing can be viewed as a logical outgrowth of Ellington's and the next step in the evolution of jazz arranging. Ellington himself recognized Evans's gifts, once telephoning Evans to tell him that "he [Evans] was his favorite jazz orchestrator" (Sidran). For his part, Evans commented that "there has never been . . . and never will be another Duke Ellington. I love him and his men and his music madly and I owe them all plenty" (Stein 1986,12). This connection to Ellington also extended to Ellington's collaborator and musical alter ego, Billy Strayhorn, of whom Evans said, "that's all I ever did—try to do what Billy Strayhorn did" (Hajdu 1997, 87).

GRIST FOR THE ARRANGER'S MILL

Evans drew on extremely diverse sources for inspiration, ranging from jazz, folk and world music, pop music and the European "classical" genre. Not surprisingly, works from the jazz idiom form the core of Evans's work, but even here his choices are uncharacteristic of a musician of his generation. Juxtaposed alongside standards by bebop masters such as Charlie Parker, Dizzy Gillespie, and Thelonious Monk are contemporary settings of songs by early jazz and blues composers like W.C. Handy, Jelly Roll Morton, Don Redman, Bix Beiderbecke, and Lillian Hardin Armstrong.[6]

Evans also had a keen interest in folk and world music, especially that from Spain and Latin America. *Sketches of Spain* and *Quiet Nights* contain arrangements of tunes based on Andalusian, Peruvian, and flamenco folk melodies (Hentoff 1996, 129–130).[7] He also had a great affinity for the African American blues tradition. "Where Flamingos Fly," while credited jointly to Courlander, Peale, and Brooks, is according to Evans "actually a field song. A man just leaned up against a fence in a field somewhere in Alabama and sang that melody" (Sidran). The songs of rural blues artists such Huddie "Leadbelly" Ledbetter and Willie Dixon also serve as sources of inspiration for Evans.[8]

Towards the end of his career, pop and rock music began to influence the direction of Evans's work, as evidenced by the *Gil Evans Plays the Music of Jimi Hendrix* and *Svengali* recordings. This development parallels the direction his musical soul mate, Davis, was taking at the time and gives credence to Evans's statement that "usually the rhythm I've had in my music has been whatever the contemporary rhythms were . . . . [and as for] rock rhythms . . . you can superimpose almost anything over them" Palmer 1974, 13).

Atypical of most jazz composers-arrangers is Evans's penchant for transforming classical repertoire by composers such as Claude Debussy, Frédéric Chopin, Leo Delibes, Manuel de Falla, and Joaquin Rodrigo into convincing jazz vehicles.[9] He was also attracted to works of American composers who drew on both the symphonic and Broadway traditions, such as Bernstein and Gershwin, as well as the German émigré Kurt Weill.[10] An analysis of his methodology in transforming this material to the jazz vernacular is discussed later in this article.

TIMBRE

The employment of instruments not normally found in large jazz ensembles is arguably the most striking aspect of Evans's style. In the mid– to late 1920s, the makeup of the big band, which evolved largely out the formative work of Don Redman, Fletcher Henderson, and Duke Ellington, typically consisted of three or four saxophones (doubling on B-flat clarinet), two or three trumpets, one or two trombones, and a rhythm section consisting of piano, bass, drums, and frequently guitar. During the Swing Era of the late 1930s, the ensemble grew to embrace five saxophones, four trumpets, and three or four trombones. Notwithstanding Stan Kenton's experiments with a section of four mellophoniums and the addition of a fifth trumpet and trombone, the big band instrumentation became standardized. Furthermore, with a few notable exceptions (such as the collaborative efforts of Redman and Henderson, Ellington and Strayhorn, and Eddie Sauter and Bill Finnegan), most big band arrangers of the 1930s and 1940s typically juxtaposed the brass against the reeds, eschewing the color possibilities inherent in cross section voicings.

Evans's interest in enlarging the timbre of the jazz orchestra dates to his 1941–48 stint as arranger for Claude Thornhill, a visionary Swing Era big band leader-pianist-arranger who typically employed two French horns and tuba in his band. Evans expanded Thornhill's tonal palette and modernized the harmonic and rhythmic underpinnings, prompting jazz historian-saxophonist

Bill Kirchner to comment that Evans presented "a new way of looking at the jazz orchestra, one of the few since Ellington" (1996, 57). Davis remarked that "he [Gil] and Duke Ellington are the same way. They can use four instruments when others need eight" (Crawford 1961, 18–19).

Although it was common for saxophonists to double on B-flat clarinet and sometimes C flute, other woodwinds were largely nonexistent in big bands (with the exceptions of the Thornhill and Paul Whiteman orchestras). Evans frequently used woodwinds more characteristic of the classical idiom, including double reeds (oboe, English horn, bassoon), bass clarinet, and the entire flute family (piccolo, C, alto, and bass). In lieu of five saxophones, Evans's scores are likely to call for three woodwinds and no more than two saxophones. The saxophone may also be used in unconventional ways, as exemplified by the slap-tongue melody on "Stratusphunk."[11]

Alto flute seems to have been a particularly favored color for Evans, as the top voice in the trombone section ("My Man's Gone" and "Lotus Land"), in combination with lighter timbres (as in "Gone, Gone, Gone," where two alto flutes play a unison lead over three French horns and a bass clarinet), or in a solo role, as in his composition "Flute Song."[12] In this passage, Evans explores the dark, mysterious quality of the instrument, compensating for its lack of volume by accompanying it lightly with acoustic guitar and bass during the introduction (Example 1).

Example 1: Evans, "Flute Song": Evans's notated flute introduction

When Evans employs C flutes, they are frequently combined with trumpets in Harmon mutes—the Harmon imparting to the trumpet a soft, metallic buzz that blends with the flute's crystalline character.

One of Evans's earliest recorded use of double reeds occurs on the 1959 album *Sketches of Spain*, where the bassoon, heard throughout, is featured in a prominent solo on "Saeta." The bassoon is also employed in "Time of the Barracudas" and "Greensleeves," where it has a prominent countermelody.[13] Evans wrote for oboe in his arrangements of "Spring Is Here" and "Las Vegas Tango" and for a choir of oboe, English horn, and bassoon in "Lotus Land."[14]

Bass clarinet, and to a lesser extent B-flat and E-flat clarinets, are featured in many of Evans's scores. In his arrangement of Gershwin's "There's a Boat That's Leaving Soon for New York," he uses three bass clarinets simultaneously, and in "Chant of the Weed," a composition by Don Redman, Evans combines a B-flat clarinet lead with a choir of four trombones (Sturm 1995, 44–45).[15] In Evans's version, the melody has been transposed down a minor seventh to bring out the woody lower register character of the clarinet, accompanied by dramatically reharmonized trombone voicings. Note that at times the melody conflicts with the reharmonization, yet the contour of each is so strong that listener does not perceive it as incorrect (Examples 2 and 3).

Example 2: Don Redman, "Chant of the Weed": C section of 1931 arrangement

Example 3: "Chant of the Weed": Evans's reharmonization of C section

Evans's use of brass is also atypical, relying on conical brass (flugelhorn, French horn, tuba) or muted trumpets, or sometimes omitting the trumpets entirely.[16] However, Evans is not averse to writing technically demanding trumpet parts when the music calls for it. Lead trumpeter Ernie Royal commented during the recording of *Sketches of Spain*: "'These look like flute parts we're playing,' shaking his head in respect and exasperation" (Hentoff 1996, 129).

Evans typically uses French horns in combination with alto flutes ("The Buzzard Song"), as the top voice of the trombone section, or to "comp" behind a soloist in lieu of the piano, as in his arrangements of "Manteca," "I Don't Wanna Be Kissed," "Struttin' with Some Barbecue," and the subsequent excerpt from "It Ain't Necessarily So" (Example 4).[17]

Example 4: Gershwin, *Porgy and Bess*: Evans's scoring for French horns in "It Ain't Necessarily So"

Although the tuba was frequently the bass rhythm instrument in New Orleans early jazz, its role had largely been usurped by the string bass after 1930. Evans was a pioneer in exploring new melodic possibilities for the tuba in jazz. Whereas he frequently uses it as the bottom of the French horn or trombone sections, Evans also scores it in contrary motion to the ensemble, as in the transcription from "Moondreams" (Example 5). In an unexpected role reversal, the tuba line is decidedly more active than the melody.[18]

Example 5: MacGregor, "Moondreams": Evans's scoring for tuba

He also casts the tuba in the role of a solo instrument, as in "Struttin' with Some Barbecue" and the coda of "The Buzzard Song," where it is doubled by acoustic bass. The rhythmic complexity of this latter passage, with its reliance on eighth notes and triplets, as well as the angularity created by the use of wide intervals and chord arpeggios makes the tuba a surprisingly creative choice (Example 6).[19]

Example 6: Gershwin, *Porgy and Bess*: Evans's coda for "The Buzzard Song"

Evans sought out and wrote for rare and unusual instruments such as the tenor violin (his arrangement of John Lewis's "Concorde") and a unique five-note mallet instrument similar in timbre to a bass marimba or a log drum, which is featured in "Bilbao Song" (Example 7).[20] He also experimented with the configuration of the rhythm section, including the aforementioned piano-less texture and experiments with the simultaneous use of three bassists.[21] Harp appears throughout the *Quiet Nights* and *Sketches of Spain* recordings (where it has a prominent solo on "Pan Piper") and "Time of the Barracudas." With the addition of percussionists Sue Evans (no relation) and Warren Smith to the working band in the 1970s, Evans's use of orchestral percussion becomes ubiquitous. He employs marimba on "Up from the Skies," timpani on "Proclamation," and chimes on "General Assembly."[22] During this same period, guitar also appears regularly in his band. Rather than simply give the guitar player chord symbols, Evans meticulously scores the guitar part, giving it melodic roles, using it to reinforce wind voicings, and writing tremolos

Example 7: Weill, "Bilbao Song": with Evans's 5-note bass marimba fills

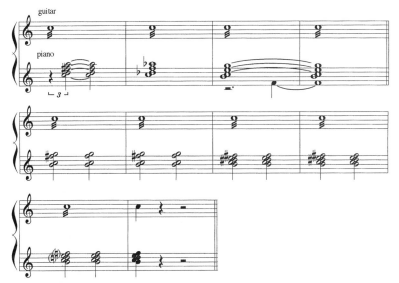

Example 8: "Bilbao Song": Evans's scoring for guitar and piano

to convey drama. At one point in "Bilbao Song," a tremolo C in the guitar acts as a pedal point, anchoring dense piano harmonies (Example 8).[23]

In the early 1970s, Evans also explored the use of electronic instruments and synthesizers. Inspired by hearing Morton Subotnik's electronic composition "The Wild Bull," he decided to "find out what they are all about," feeling that "the synthesizer is like any other instrument . . . you simply find out their capacity and use them" (Smith 1976, 15). The dilemma of combining electronic with acoustic instruments is revealed in Evans's comment "I have to divide it up so that the electronics and the acoustics don't have to compete with one another" (Smith 1976, 15). Despite his interest in this new color, Evans felt that "you don't have to be electrified to produce energy. . . . If you can't play an instrument the way you feel it, or if it isn't going to respond the way you feel, you either make adjustments, or quit playing it" (Smith 1976, 15).

Occasionally Evans employs unusual instrumental textures to convey nonmusical images, as evidenced by the deep, undulating timbres of "Sunken Treasure," the processional parade band that "marches in" on one stereo channel and "leaves" on the other in "Saeta," his portrayal of an African American church choir in Gershwin's "Prayer, Oh Doctor Jesus," and an ascending flute ostinato in "Where Flamingos Fly," which conjures up images of birds in flight (Example 9).[24]

Example 9: Courlander, Peale, Brooks, "Where Flamingos Fly": Evans's flute ostinato

Although his ensembles fluctuated with regard to personnel, Evans nonetheless tended to write parts with a specific musician in mind. Joe Muccioli (1997, 7-8) notes that

> in "Jambangle," the high concert "C" for the alto sax at the beginning is not a mistake; even today, the note is rarely found in published music for the instrument. Gil knew that Lee Konitz would be on the session, so he wrote for his specific sound and capability. . . . [Evans] often specified certain passages to be played by a specific instrumentalist (part-crossing in Evans's music occurs with great frequency). Evidence even suggests that he rewrote woodwind parts for the *Quiet Nights* album because of soprano saxophonist Steve Lacy's availability.

FORM

The standard format for many big band arrangements consists of the presentation of the melody, development of the theme through improvised solos with backgrounds, an instrumental soli (often by the saxophones), a climactic tutti "shout chorus," followed by a recapitulation of the theme, which is often a literal return by means of a dal segno or da capo.

Evans typically rescores the reappearance of thematic material. In his arrangement of the Clifford Brown composition "Joy Spring," Evans saves the complete statement of the melody for the end.

> *First chorus* (a 32-measure A–A^1–B–A structure; the A^1 section being a half step higher than the other A sections): an Evans piano solo with rhythm section accompaniment in which the guitar plays call-and-response figures against the piano.
>
> *Second chorus*: The ensemble plays a 6-measure sendoff, followed by a 2-measure guitar break by Ray Crawford. This idea is repeated a half step higher in A^1. The guitar solo continues with rhythm section accompaniment over the remainder of the form.
>
> *Third chorus*: The ensemble plays the entire 32 measures in octaves. An abrupt cutoff provides a return to unaccompanied guitar for the last two chords.[25]

Evans greatly expands the scope of otherwise standard forms. Frequently his introductions and codas contain original material more profound than the song itself. "Aos Pes Da Cruz," a short folk-like tune, contains an extended coda of shifting colors over which Davis "sails above the winds and harp, playing the tag as though it were "Bye Bye Blackbird" (Belden 1996, 79–80).[26] The coda of Chummy MacGregor's rather ordinary ballad, "Moondreams," dissolves into a complex texture of contrary motion and bitonal implications. In particular, note the opening ascending line played in stretto fashion, the upper pedal F# in the alto saxophone, the chromatically descending harmonies and general independence of each part (Example 10).[27]

Example 10: MacGregor, "Moondreams": Evans's original coda

Evans occasionally used connecting or cyclic elements to tie songs together into a larger entity. On *Miles Ahead*, Evans "not only planned the sequence of the two LP sides, but also scored bridges between each composition so that the final effect would be that of a continuous suite" (Avakian 1996, 33). In *Porgy and Bess*, an interlude connects "Bess, You

Is My Woman Now" with "Gone." Later in the work, a transposed, re-orchestrated, and expanded version of the interlude links "My Man's Gone" with "It Ain't Necessarily So" (Examples 11 and 12).[28] Upon careful listening, one can hear another unifying ingredient in *Porgy and Bess* in Evans's two subtle quotes of "Gone" during "There's a Boat That's Leaving Soon for New York."[29]

Example 11: Gershwin, *Porgy and Bess*: Evans's original interlude connecting "Bess, You Is My Woman Now" with "Gone"

Example 12: Gershwin, Porgy and Bess: Evans's original interlude connecting "My Man's Gone Now" with "It Ain't Necessarily So"

Much of Evans's music serves to frame the work of a featured soloist. His best known efforts in this genre are the collaborations with Davis, including the 1949 and 1950 recordings of "Moondreams" and "Boplicity" from the *Birth of the Cool*, the four masterworks recorded between 1957 and 1962 (*Miles Ahead*, *Porgy and Bess*, *Sketches of Spain,* and *Quiet Nights*), and the incomplete or aborted efforts such as the 1963 project for the play "Time of the Barracudas" and the 1968 recording of "Falling Water." In particular,

Miles Ahead was unique in that "it was the first concept album built on the sound of the soloist, not the composer" (Belden 1996, 72). In addition to his arrangements for Davis, Evans also wrote music for several albums that highlighted the talents of a featured soloist, such as guitarist Kenny Burrell (*Guitar Forms*), alto saxophonist Cannonball Adderley (*New Bottle, Old Wine*), and singers Astrud Gilberto (*Look to the Rainbow*) and Helen Merrill (*Dream of You*). For his own band, he frequently wrote pieces that showcased sidemen such as tenor saxophonist Wayne Shorter ("Time of the Barracudas"), trombonist Jimmy Knepper ("Where Flamingos Fly"), soprano saxophonist Steve Lacy ("Just One of Those Things"), trumpeter Johnny Coles ("Davenport Blues"), and tenor saxophonist Billy Harper ("So Long").[30]

MELODY

Evans was fond of writing melodies of an instrumental nature, particularly those characteristic of the post-1940 bebop vocabulary, with its predominant reliance on eighth notes as the basic rhythmic unit. Baritone saxophonist Gerry Mulligan once remarked, "Gil is the one arranger I've ever played who can really notate the thing the way the soloist would blow it," as his line to the bridge of Lester Young's "Lester Leaps In" aptly demonstrates (Hentoff 1957). In the first four bars, Evans mimics the type of lines Lester Young used in his improvisations, whereas the last four measures take on attributes of bebop vocabulary, with its emphasis on the flat ninth, sharp ninth, and flat fifth of the chord (Example 13).[31]

Example 13: Lester Young, "Lester Leaps In": Evans's recomposition of the bridge

Frequently Evans writes passages that begin as unison or octave lines and branch into harmony as they reach their peak, a technique heard in his arrangements of "Joy Spring," "St. Louis Blues," "Springsville," "Bird Feathers," and "Struttin' with Some Barbecue," as well as Jelly Roll Morton's "King Porter Stomp" (Sturm 1995, 197; shown in Example 14).[32]

Example 14: Jelly Roll Morton, "King Porter Stomp": Evans's tutti interlude

Towards the end of his career, Evans followed his predilection for lines with an improvisatory character to an occasionally chaotic conclusion, in which he allowed large sections of his arrangements to be collectively improvised by his musicians. Compositions such as "Spaced," "Anita's Dance," and "Makes Her Move" all contain considerable amounts of controlled group improvisation.[33] Evans described his thoughts about free improvisation within the context of the big band:

> I tell the players not to be terrified by the vagueness . . . something's going to come out of it. . . . [I]f it looks like we're teetering on the edge of formlessness, someone's going to be so panicked they'll do something about it (Mandel 1984, 21).

Even as he permitted improvisations by his band members to shape his arrangements, conversely he wrote ensemble passages that were often thought to be improvised; for example, the alto flute solo in "Flute Song" is entirely written out (Muccioli 1997, 7).

Evans also drew on transcriptions of improvised solos as a basis for ensemble tuttis, a facet of his arranging that has been largely overlooked. His arrangement of "So What" includes an orchestration of Bill Evans's (no relation) improvised piano introduction from the now-classic *Kind of Blue* recording, while his arrangement of "Spring Is Here" is based on the Bill Evans piano trio arrangement (Priestly 1978, 27). Likewise, "New Rhumba" (from *Miles Ahead*) is modeled on the Ahmad Jamal Trio's recording of the song and includes quotes from guitarist Ray Crawford's improvised solo (Kirchner 1996, 56). In 1963, Davis and Evans collaborated on a series of musical cues for the play *Time of the Barracudas*, portions of which eventually ended up being utilized as the themes for "Hotel Me" and "Waltz of the Barracudas" (also known as "General Assembly"). Both songs were recorded subsequently by Evans, most notably on his 1964 album, *The Individualism of Gil Evans*. However, the original music from the play was not released until 1996 as part of *The Complete Columbia Studio Recordings*. Only after that time did a comparative analysis by the author reveal that the ensemble chorus on "Hotel Me" from *The Individualism of Gil Evans* was actually Evans's recreation of Davis's improvisation from the

Time of the Barracudas project, performed in unison by the entire trumpet section.[34]

HARMONY

A feature common to Evans's arranging is the controlled used of dissonance in his chord voicings. Evans had a fondness for altered tones, or "blue" notes, in his chord voicings, and the judicious use of instrumental color was intrinsic to his placement of those notes in the orchestration. As saxophonist Ray Downey has noted:

> A lot of his voicings are standard harmonies with tension notes added for flavoring. . . . [F]or example, down low in a voicing, he may add a bass clarinet a half-step below the trombone, placing the flat fifth against the perfect fifth. What makes this mysterious is the balance of the orchestration. In this example the trombone would cut through, making it hard for the ear to discern where the dissonance is coming from.[35]

In the first measure of this excerpt from "Where Flamingos Fly," the augmented, perfect, and diminished fifths of the chord occur simultaneously in the top three trumpets, the major sixth is placed adjacent to the minor seventh in the second and third trombones, while the major ninth (used as a lower neighbor in the fourth trumpet) "crunches" against the minor third in the first trombone (Example 15).[36] In the second example from this arrangement, the trumpet voicings contain the diminished and perfect fifths of the chord in the first measure and the major sixth and minor seventh in the second measure, while in the third bar, the augmented eleventh in the lowest trombone lies a minor ninth below the perfect fifth in the lead trumpet. Although many arrangers use half-step "grinds," very few would expose them by placing them on the top of the chord or drop the lower voice to form the interval of a minor ninth (Example 16). Most arranging students are taught to avoid the interval of the minor ninth (with the exception of the root to the minor ninth of an altered dominant chord). Jazz arranger Clyde Cortright notes that

> by writing strong melodic lines, Evans makes the dissonant harmonies sound inevitable. We hear where the lines are going so clearly that the vertical structures he finally arrives at sound O.K. because the lines logically lead to those notes. He also uses precise orchestration to soften intervals that might leap out if written by less experienced writers (Cortright 1998, 62).

Example 15: "Where Flamingos Fly": Evans's use of dissonance in mm. 17–20

Example 16: "Where Flamingos Fly": Evans's use of dissonance in mm. 41–44

In the passage from Evans's arrangement of Kurt Weill's "My Ship" given in Example 17, the use of the minor ninth between the bass and melody on beat two of the second measure is mitigated by the contrary motion, as well as the timbres of the instruments involved (tuba, clarinet, French horn). In the third measure an augmented ninth occurs over the passing Emaj7(#11) chord but sounds acceptable because the sustained G in the melody is perceived as a pedal tone. During the D7 chord in the fifth measure, both the natural and flat fifth of the chord occur, but at metrically different times. The third beat of the seventh bar contains three instances of minor ninths: between the second trombone and third trumpet, the tuba and second trumpet, and French horn and first trumpet. Here the shimmering quality of trumpets in Harmon mutes mitigates the dissonance, along with the pedal implications of the sustained A in the second trombone (Cortright 1998, 62).

Example 17: Weill, "My Ship": Evans's score, mm. 12–19

In Evans's "Variation on the Misery" (Example 18) dissonances of minor seconds result from shifting triads over a pedal B♭.[37] In describing the effect, Evans stated:

> That little spice is a thing that I learned from the flamenco guitar players. It takes away the blandness. I played a B♭ all the way through... it gives it a tortured sound (Sidran).

In "Las Vegas Tango" (Example 19), Evans creates minor ninth intervals by superimposing triads above the dissonant interval, while the excerpted chordal voicing from "Proclamation" (Example 20) combines D and D♭ tonalities.[38]

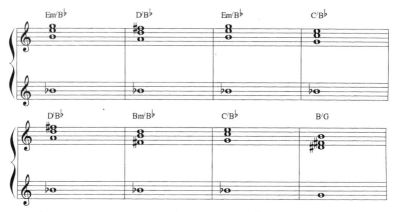

Example 18: Evans, "Variations on the Misery": pedal point

Example 19: Evans, "Las Vegas Tango": bitonal chords

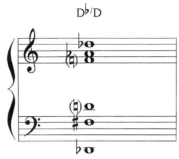

Example 20: Evans, "Proclamation": primary bitonal sonority

Examples 15 and 16 ("Where Flamingos Fly") reveal another facet of Evans's work: the use of ostinati and pedal figures to build tension. This technique is common in many of his arrangements, including "Prayer (Oh Doctor Jesus)," "Here Come de Honey Man," "The Buzzard Song," "Aos Pes Da Cruz," and "Time of the Barracudas."[39] The use of ostinati and pedal figures in jazz anticipated the development of the modal school, which was popularized by Davis's 1959 recording *Kind of Blue*. However, a year before, on the Davis-Evans collaboration *Porgy and Bess*, the use of a modal basis for improvisation was in evidence. Davis states:

> When Gil wrote the arrangement of "I Loves You, Porgy," he only wrote a scale for me to play. No chords.. . . I think a movement in jazz is beginning away from the conventional string of chords, and a return to emphasis on melodic rather than harmonic variations (Hentoff 1958).

Recorded in August 1958, this was not the first example of modality in jazz. Davis had employed a similar technique in his recording of "Milestones" in April of the same year, and as early as 1947 George Russell had written a long modal introduction to "Cubano Be, Cubano Bop" (Chambers 1983, 279–80). Nevertheless, Davis and Evans were instrumental in popularizing this new approach to jazz harmony. Periodically Evans continued his forays into modality, most notably in his original compositions "Solea" and his theme song, "La Nevada."

RHYTHM

Rhythm is at the core of the work of any jazz composer, and Evans worked with a diverse range of styles and levels of complexity, often stretching the boundaries of what musicians call "the groove." Some of his arrangements are almost static in their movement, allowing the sonorities seemingly to hover in midair ("Where Flamingos Fly," "Bilbao Song," "Sunken Treasure," "Barbara Song," "Proclamation"), whereas others swing with a high degree of intensity ("King Porter Stomp," "Struttin' with Some Barbecue," "Lester Leaps In," "Gone," "Springsville").[40] Although his proclivity for slow tempos may have been influenced by Claude Thornhill (whose theme song "Snowfall" was slow and evocative), Evans expanded this concept from that of dance music to music more orchestral in nature. In his rhythmically vigorous pieces, he frequently writes unexpected syncopations that keep his audience (and occasionally his musicians) guessing.[41] In the excerpt from Jelly Roll Morton's "King Porter Stomp" shown in Example 21, Evans uses a four-note melodic cell

(consisting of the pitches D♭, E♭, E, and F) to develop a series of rhythmic per-
mutations (Sturm 1995, 19). To build tension in "The Buzzard Song," he employs an ascending polyrhythm in the flutes and trumpets, anchored by a pad
in the French horns, trombones, and tuba (Example 22), and a rhythmic analysis of a background figure from "La Nevada" reveals how the trumpets and
trombones each play a hemiola, separated by a half beat (Example 23).[42]

Example 21: "King Porter Stomp": Evans's four-note melodic cell and rhythmic per-
mutations

Example 22: "The Buzzard Song": Evans's use of polyrhythm. *Continued on next page.*

Example 22, *continued*

Example 23: Evans, "La Nevada": rhythmic analysis

Evans was also influenced by rhythms from other cultures, most notably Spanish and South American, as evidenced by the examples from *Sketches of Spain* and *Quiet Nights*. He also incorporated rock rhythms in recordings such as *Gil Evans Plays the Music of Jimi Hendrix* and *Svengali*.

TRANSFORMING WORKS FROM THE "CLASSICAL" GENRE

Over the years, more than a few musicians from both the jazz and European art music camps have had an interest in, or fascination with, each other's styles of music. Maurice Ravel's admiration for early jazz artists such as New Orleans clarinetist Jimmy Noone (Schuller 1968, 203) no doubt imparts a certain flavor to some of his compositions, as evidenced by the distinctly "jazz-like" trombone presentation of the theme from "Bolero." Swing Era jazz pianist Art Tatum also received the admiration of classical musicians such as pianist Leopold Godowsky and composer Sergei Rachmaninov, owing in no small part to Tatum's undeniable virtuosity and pianistic aplomb (Schuller 1989, 82–83). Jazz subsequently made an impression on Aaron Copland, as reflected in his composition *Four Piano Blues*, and Igor Stravinsky, who wrote *Ebony Concerto* for the Woody Herman big band and *Scherzo à la Russe* for the Paul Whiteman Orchestra. In the 1950s and 1960s Leonard Bernstein championed the cause of jazz through his lectures and youth concerts, as well as his recording *What Is Jazz.* Bernstein's *West Side Story* also contains some of the more convincing examples of the use of jazz harmonies and Latin American rhythms in its genre. Some classical musicians, most notably André Previn, have sufficient understanding of the nature of improvisation and swing that they are able to perform effectively in both idioms.

For their part, jazz musicians have demonstrated an increasing familiarity and interest in classical music over the years. In the 1920s, Bix Beiderbecke's fascination with composers such as Ravel, Holst, Delius, and Debussy manifested itself in his use of whole-tone scales and other contemporary devices in compositions such as "In a Mist" (Schuller 1968, 192). Ellington associate Billy Strayhorn had an intense interest in European art music and focused primarily on his classical piano skills during his formative years (Hajdu 1997, 14). Many of the artists of the cool jazz movement of the 1950s, such as John Lewis, Dave Brubeck, and Gerry Mulligan, studied and consciously applied European compositional techniques to their craft, particularly in their use of improvisatory counterpoint, new instrumental timbres, extended harmonies, and forms that ventured beyond the standard 32-bar song form and 12-bar blues formats.[43] These experiments led to a movement that Gunther Schuller dubbed the "Third Stream," in which aspects of the classical and jazz traditions were merged. Works in this genre, such as John Lewis's "Three Little Feelings," J.J. Johnson's "Poem for Brass," and George Russell's "All about Rosie," are representative of this new breed of jazz composition, although it may be argued that roots of this attempt to fuse classical and jazz sensibilities go back to Paul Whiteman's 1924 premiere of Gershwin's *Rhapsody in Blue*.[44] West Coast big band leader Stan Kenton also championed the cause of twentieth-century classical techniques, which led directly to his recording of Bob Graettinger's avant-garde, four-movement composition for jazz band, *City of Glass*, as well as his sponsorship of the short-lived Los Angeles Neophonic Orchestra, an ensemble devoted to performing works that straddled the line between jazz and classical music. In addition, just as a few classical artists such as Previn were able to cross over to jazz convincingly, some jazz musicians also had sufficient experience with classical music to be active as performers in both idioms. From Swing Era clarinetist and band leader Benny Goodman (who recorded Bartók's *Contrasts* with the Hungarian composer and performed concertos with symphony orchestras) to contemporary artists such as pianist Keith Jarrett, trumpeter Wynton Marsalis, and singer-conductor Bobby McFerrin, this ability to be conversant in both genres has become increasingly common as more jazz musicians undergo traditional academic training.

The practice of "borrowing" themes from the classical repertoire was not uncommon during World War II, due in part to an ASCAP radio ban on copyrighted material, which forced big bands to "search for repertory material in the public domain" (Schuller 1989, 755). Tommy Dorsey's hit "Song of India" (taken from Rimsky-Korsakov's *Sadko* or "Song of the Indian Guest"), Freddie Martin's "Tonight We Love" (based on Tchaikovsky's *Piano Concerto in B♭ Minor*), and the pop song "I'm Always Chasing Rainbows" (from Chopin's *Fantasie Impromptu*) are among the many examples of this practice (Schuller & Williams 1983, 24). Duke Ellington also ventured into this area, imparting a uniquely African American slant to classical compositions such as his "Ebony Rhapsody" (which Schuller referred to a "jazzed-up rehash of Liszt's *Second Hungarian Rhapsody*") and his more successful collaborations with Billy Strayhorn on Grieg's *Peer Gynt Suite* and Tchaikovsky's *Nutcracker Suite* (Schuller 1989, 66). Sometimes these attempts to combine classical themes with jazz sensibilities (or vice versa) met with mixed success, often yielding trite, pretentious, or self-conscious works that occasionally find their way onto symphonic "pops" programs.

As a teenager, Evans spent considerable time in the library studying scores by Bartók, Stravinsky, Hindemith, Ravel, Debussy, Borodin, Tchaikovsky, Mussorgsky, and Rimsky-Korsakov. Of the impressionist composers, Evans stated, "That's where I learned most of my harmonic language and most of my orchestration. Actually, though, the classical composer that impressed me the most was Ernest Bloch. I like his orchestrations—his harmonic language, too" (Solomon 1961, 7). Evans had a particular fondness for the work of Spanish composers. "I've always been inclined to Spanish music. . . . the Spanish Impressionists, like de Falla" (Lees 1998).

Evans was self-taught and thus approached the European symphonic repertoire from a jazzman's perspective. He was not an academic and was not interested in producing a new hybrid form. He merely loved all kinds of music, including European art music, and treated folk songs, jazz standards, and symphonic repertoire all with the same respect and lack of pretension. Thus, his arrangements of classical compositions convey the

same personal intimacy as his other works; to the uninformed listener
they would not be readily apparent as being derived from anything but the
jazz tradition. His 1942 arrangement for the Claude Thornhill Orchestra
"Arab Dance" was based on Tchaikovsky's "Arabian Dance" ("Danse
Arabe") from *The Nutcracker Suite*. In the early 1950s he arranged
Claude Debussy's *La Plus Que Lente* for Gerry Mulligan's Sextet, and his
scores for Davis in the late 1950s included Leo Delibes's art song "Maids
of Cadiz" ("Les Filles de Cadix"), a complete rescoring of Gershwin's
opera *Porgy and Bess*, "Will o' the Wisp" (based on Manuel de Falla's
ballet *El Amor Brujo*), as well as *Concierto de Aranjuez*, a reorchestration
of the adagio section of Joaquin Rodrigo's composition for classical guitar and orchestra. Hearkening back to his youthful learning strategies,
Evans transcribed the Rodrigo work from a recording because the score
was not available to him at the time (Priestly 1978, 27). A later collaboration with Lee Konitz yielded "Prelude No. 20," which was essentially
Konitz's improvisation on Evans's harmonic reduction of the Chopin
composition (Muccioli 1997, 5–6).

THE ART OF TRANSFORMATION:
TCHAIKOVSKY'S "DANSE ARABE"

At first glance, Tchaikovsky's "Danse Arabe" from the *Nutcracker Suite*
may seem like an odd vehicle for a jazz band, but Evans's 1942 score
(coarranged with Thornhill) exemplifies many aspects of his subsequent
work. The Thornhill band was unique among dance bands, owing to its
instrumentation of seven woodwinds, two French horns, and tuba, in addition to a pared-down complement of trumpets, trombones, and rhythm
section. The Tchaikovsky score calls for three flutes, two oboes, English
horn, two clarinets, bass clarinet, two bassoons, tambourine, and strings,
adapting well to the Thornhill instrumentation and preserving many of the
tonal qualities of the score. "Danse Arabe" is also in keeping with Evans's
affinity not only for the European classical idiom, but also for music
evocative of Mediterranean countries and the Levant. It may be argued
that this piece, with its reliance on pedal figures in G minor and G major
and modal melodies, is a precursor to many of Evans's subsequent repertoire choices.
    One of the most obvious differences from the original score is the change
of meter from 3/8 to 4/4, which is more characteristic of the performance

practices of a Swing Era dance band. The ostinato figure, confined primarily to the celli and violas in the original, is variously rescored for a combination of guitar, clarinets, bass clarinets, and French horns in the Evans arrangement. He also changes the intervallic structure of the ostinato from that of parallel fifths ascending by octaves, to a modified figure, more readily played by wind instruments, in which the octave leap is merely suggested (Examples 24 and 25).[45]

Example 24: Tchaikovsky, *Nutcracker Suite*: ostinato figure in "Danse Arabe"

Example 25: "Arab Dance": Evans's ostinato figure

In Evans's version, the opening "call to prayer" figure is presented in a syncopated 4/4 manner, reharmonized, and scored variously for two French horns and trombone and for three trumpets in cup mute (Examples 26, 27, and 28). Tchaikovsky's initial melodic idea for violins is relatively unchanged in Evans's version (Examples 29 and 30). After this point, he begins to depart from the form of the original, restating the first theme in the clarinets and saxophones with increasing reliance on jazz harmonies and syncopations. The rhythm section begins to swing, using chord symbols derived from a harmonic reduction of the orchestral score (Example 31). His exploration of this theme is representative of Evans's ability to write ensemble lines of an improvisatory nature, as well as his penchant for continually rescoring reappearances of previous material (Example 32). The reappearance of the "call" is also changed into the jazz vernacular (Example 33).

Example 26: "Danse Arabe": Tchaikovsky's "call to prayer" figure

Example 27: "Arab Dance": Evans's first "call to prayer" figure

Example 28: "Arab Dance": Evans's second "call to prayer" figure

Example 29: "Danse Arabe": Tchaikovsky's opening melodic idea

Tchaikovsky expands his initial motive into a new melody for the violins and bassoons, which Evans subsequently transforms into a tutti ensemble. He extends portions of this idea and allows an improvised alto saxophone solo to ride on top of the resolution of the phrase (Examples 34, 35, and 36). At the point where Tchaikovsky returns to the initial idea and winds down by means of an echoing of the primary motive in different instruments and a modal shift from G minor to G major, Evans begins his commentary on the piece in earnest. A chromatic motive derived from the theme ascends by minor thirds in a continual rhythmic acceleration (Examples 37 and 38). The expanded

Example 30: "Arab Dance": Evans's opening melodic idea

Example 31: "Arab Dance": reappearance of the theme

Example 32: "Arab Dance": Evans's embellishment of the theme

theme is then stated in its entirety in the key of A♭ minor (Example 39). After a brief textural thinning out, the climax of the piece occurs in the key of A minor (Example 40). A return of the opening ostinato and chromatic scales in divergent motion heralds the end of Evans's rendition of Tchaikovsky's piece (Example 41).

Example 33: "Arab Dance": reappearance of the "call"

Example 34: "Danse Arabe": Tchaikovsky's expansion of the theme

Example 35: "Arab Dance": Evans's expansion of the theme

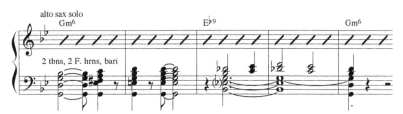

Example 36: "Arab Dance": saxophone improvisation over the theme

Example 37: "Arab Dance": Evans's chromatic treatment of the motive

Example 38: "Arab Dance": Evans's rhythmic acceleration of the motive

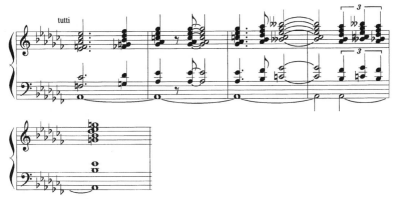

Example 39: "Arab Dance": Evans's restatement of the theme in A-flat

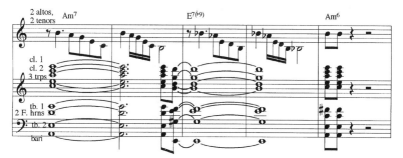

Example 40: "Arab Dance": ensemble climax

Example 41: "Arab Dance": conclusion

GERSHWIN'S "GONE, GONE, GONE"

George Gershwin's opera *Porgy and Bess* is an outstanding example of a masterwork with roots in American (or, more specifically, African American) music, expressed within the European concept of form. Gershwin stated, "The great music of the past . . . has always been built on folk music. This is the strongest source of musical fecundity. . . . Jazz I regard as an American folk music, not the only one but a very beautiful one which is in the blood and feeling of the American people" (Smith 1958).

Although all of Evans's arrangements for the Davis *Porgy and Bess* recording received a substantially new setting, "Gone, Gone, Gone" is perhaps the most remarkable example of Evans's ability to transform preexisting material into something profoundly original. Evans rescored the Gershwin spiritual for the instrumentation of jazz band and trumpet soloist but went further, creating an entirely new composition based on the seminal idea of the original. Evans retitled the new piece "Gone," commenting:

> This is my improvisation on the spiritual ["Gone, Gone, Gone"]. In the middle of it, Miles, Paul [bassist Paul Chambers], and Joe [drummer Philly Joe Jones] improvise on the improvisation (Smith 1958).

Readily apparent are the differences in tempo and mood. "Gone, Gone, Gone" is a slow lament in which the chorus (the jazz band in Evans's version) repeats a richly harmonized two-bar phrase, answered by a vocal soloist (Davis in the Evans rendition) in a call-and-response manner (Example 42).[46] Evans took the melodic contour and harmonic progression of "Gone, Gone, Gone" and introduced a sophisticated layer of syncopation, creating an up-tempo blues in which the ensemble statements are answered by Philly Joe Jones's drum breaks. Note, in Example 43, how he varies the syncopation in the third phrase.[47]

Example 42: Gershwin, "Gone, Gone, Gone": opening chorus from act 1, scene 2

Example 43: Evans, "Gone": reduction of score

THE GIL EVANS LEGACY

The legacy of Gil Evans, although not widely acknowledged by the general public, is pervasive among jazz musicians. Baritone saxophonist and arranger Gerry Mulligan commented that "not many people really heard Gil; those that did . . . were tremendously affected, and they affected others" (Hentoff 1957). Evans advanced the concept of the jazz orchestra, extending many of the innovations first introduced by Duke Ellington. Critic Max Harrison wrote that Evans's scores "surpass anything previously attempted in big band jazz and constitute the only wholly original departure in that field outside of the Ellington's work" (Hentoff 1996, 122). Evans's body of work, both as the ideal orchestrator for Davis and with his own groups, influenced multiple generations of writers, such as Bob Brookmeyer, Slide Hampton, Herbie Hancock, Maria Schneider, Jim McNeely, Kenny Werner, and Gil Goldstein.[48] Upon Evans's passing in March 1988, Davis eulogized his friend:

He never wasted a melody. He never wasted a phrase. He and Duke Ellington changed the whole sound. There's no way to describe it, because there's nobody on this earth that can do that anymore. What he did to the texture of an orchestration, what he did with pop songs was like writing an original piece. Students will discover him. They'll have to take his music apart layer by layer. That's how they'll know what kind of a genius he was (Davis 1996, 197).

Part of Evans's genius may be attributed to his constant quest for discovery and growth, and he eschewed the comfort and convenience of staying within self-imposed boundaries. His work and life may be summarized in his own words:

We're all victims of the terrible habit of convenience. When you're used to hearing a certain type of music—and it changes . . . and you don't follow it anymore—a new generation comes along and picks up on it; and then the innovator (if he's still alive and not a disaster) can get some credit. A lot of times an innovator can come and go and not have a very good life. That's convenience; the world's most prevalent addiction. We all suffer from an overuse of convenience at the expense of passion (Sidran).

NOTES

1. The first recorded example of Evans playing piano in his own ensembles occurs on his 1957 recording *Big Stuff*, rereleased on CD as *Gil Evans & Ten*. During his regular gig in the 1970s and 1980s at the New York jazz club Sweet Basil, he typically led the band from the keyboard. He occasionally played piano with the Claude Thornhill orchestra in the 1940s, and worked clubs in duo settings with Gerry Mulligan during the 1950s and Lee Konitz in the 1970s (Gitler 1989).
2. "Miles Ahead" and "Blues for Pablo" appear on the Davis recording *Miles Ahead*; "Eleven" was recorded on Evans's *Svengali,* but also appears entitled "Petit Machins" on the Davis recording *Filles de Kilimanjaro* and is miscredited exclusively to Davis's authorship. "Time of the Barracudas" was written for an unproduced play and released on *The Individualism of Gil Evans,* with Wayne Shorter as featured soloist, on *The Complete Miles Davis/Gil Evans Studio Recordings* with Davis as primary soloist, as well as on a version retitled "General Assembly" on the recording *Gil Evans* (later rereleased as *Blues in Orbit*). "La Nevada" and "Sunken Treasure" appear on Evans's *Out of the Cool*; "Variation on the Misery" appears on *Blues in Orbit*; "Proclamation" was recorded on both *Blues in Orbit* and *The Individualism of Gil Evans*;

"Bud and Bird" (actually two compositions performed sequentially) appears on the recording of the same name; "Solea" appears on *Sketches of Spain*.

3. Although Evans was not a teacher by profession or inclination, composers Maria Schneider and Gil Goldstein studied informally with him toward the end of his career.

4. Out-of-print biographies include *Svengali, or the Orchestra Called Gill* [sic] *Evans*, by Raymond Horricks, and *Las Vegas tango: Une vie de Gil Evans*, by Laurent Cugny. An analysis of Evans's compositional techniques may be found in Stephen LaJoie's 1999 dissertation, "An Analysis of Selected 1957 to 1962 Gil Evans Works Recorded by Miles Davis." Evans's work for the Claude Thornhill Orchestra is discussed in Patrick Douglas Castle's 1981 dissertation, "Aspects of Style in the Repertory of the Claude Thornhill Orchestra." A short, but intriguing, analysis of Evans's arranging techniques may be found in Clyde Cortright's article in a 1998 issue of *Down Beat*, "Gil Evans' 'My Ship' Reveals Unorthodox Arranging Techniques." Scores and parts for some of the music Evans wrote for Davis are available for rent from Classic Editions, a division of The King Brand Music Co., 250 West 49th St., NY, NY 10019. Fifteen scores not written for Davis are available in sketch format in *The Gil Evans Collection*, edited by Joe Muccioli and transcribed by Muccioli, David Berger, David Pearl, and Joey Sellers and published in 1997 by Hal Leonard Corporation.

5. *Castles Made of Sound: The Story of Gil Evans,* by Larry Hicock, was published in May 2002 by Da Capo Press. *Gil Evans—Out of the Cool: His Life and Music,* by Stephanie Stein Crease, was published in October 2001 by A Cappella Books. Steve LaJoie's book *Gil Evans & Miles Davis: Historic Collaborations* was published in 2002 by Advance Music. This appears to be an outgrowth of his 1999 dissertation, "An Analysis of Selected 1957 to 1962 Gil Evans Works Recorded by Miles Davis." Both the book and the dissertation contain transcriptions and analysis of "Blues for Pablo," "New Rhumba," "Bess, You Is My Woman Now," and "Will o' the Wisp." Hal Leonard recently published *Miles Davis: Birth of the Cool,* which contains a sketch score of Evans's arrangement of "Boplicity."

6. Gillespie's "Manteca," Monk's "'Round Midnight," Parker's "Bird Feathers," Handy's "St. Louis Blues," Armstrong's "Struttin' with Some Barbecue," and Morton's "King Porter Stomp" all may be found on Evans's recording *New Bottle, Old Wine*. Beiderbecke's "Davenport Blues," Redman's "Chant of the Weed," and Monk's "Straight No Chaser" appear on Evans's recording *Great Jazz Standards*.

7. "Saeta" is derived from an Andalusian folk melody, "Solea" is based on 12/4 flamenco rhythm, and "The Pan Piper" is inspired by a native Peruvian penny-whistle song. All three are found on *Sketches of Spain*. "Song #2," from *Quiet Nights* (later retitled "High as a Mountain," with lyrics by singer Jon Hendricks), also has its genesis in folk material.

8. "Where Flamingos Fly" is from Evans's recording *Out of the Cool*. On Ledbetter's "Ella Speed" (from Evans's *Big Stuff*, rereleased as *Gil Evans & Ten*), he approximates Ledbetter's vocal phrasing on his piano introduction. Willie Dixon's "Spoonful" is found as a bonus track on the CD rerelease of *The Individualism of Gil Evans*.

9. Evans's version of Tchaikovsky's "Arabian Dance" may be heard on his recording *Gil Evans—The Real Birth of the Cool—Transcriptions*. Chopin's *Prelude no. 20 in C minor*, op. 28, is found on the Lee Konitz recording *Heroes*. Delibes's "Maids of Cadix" is part of *Miles Ahead*, while "Will o' the Wisp" (based on de Falla's *El Amor Brujo*) and Rodrigo's *Concierto de Aranjuez* are both contained on *Sketches of Spain*.

10. Evans's transformation of Gershwin's opera *Porgy and Bess* into a setting for jazz orchestra and trumpet soloist is found on the Davis recording of the same name. "Big Stuff," from the recording of the same name (reissued as *Gil Evans & Ten*), is based on Leonard Bernstein's ballet *Fancy Free* (Gitler 1989). Weill's songs "My Ship" (from *Lady in the Dark*), "Bilbao Song" (from *Happy End*), and "Barbara Song" (from *The Threepenny Opera*) receive evocative settings from Evans on *Miles Ahead*, *Out of the Cool*, and *The Individualism of Gil Evans*, respectively.

11. Evans's arrangement of George Russell's "Stratusphunk" is found on *Out of the Cool*.

12. "My Man's Gone" and "Gone, Gone, Gone," are from Davis's *Porgy and Bess*, and "Lotus Land" is found on the Kenny Burrell recording *Guitar Forms*. "Flute Song" is from *The Individualism of Gil Evans*; the transcription from the recording is by the author and differs from the version in the Muccioli collection of sketch scores.

13. "Time of the Barracuda" is from *The Individualism of Gil Evans*; "Greensleeves" is from *Guitar Forms*.

14. "Spring Is Here" is found on *Miles Davis at Carnegie Hall*, "Las Vegas Tango" comes from *The Individualism of Gil Evans*, and "Lotus Land" is from *Guitar Forms*.

15. "Chant of the Weed" is from *Great Jazz Standards*. The excerpt from Evans's score is from a manuscript by Fred Sturm. "There's a Boat That's Leaving Soon for New York" is part of *Porgy and Bess*. The simultaneous use of three bass clarinets was demonstrated by Bill Kirchner during a talk for the BMI Jazz Composers Workshop.

16. Evans scored "Barbara Song" (from *The Individualism of Gil Evans*) for two French horns, trombone, tuba, flute, bass flute, English horn, tenor sax, harp, piano, bass, and drums—thus omitting the trumpet section altogether.

17. "The Buzzard Song" and "It Ain't Necessarily So" are from *Porgy and Bess*; "Manteca" and "Struttin' with Some Barbecue" come from *New Bottle, Old Wine*; "I Don't Wanna Be Kissed" is found on *Miles Ahead*. The excerpt from "It Ain't Necessarily So" was transcribed by the author.

18. "Moondreams" is on *Birth of the Cool*; transcription by the author.
19. "Struttin' with Some Barbecue" is from *New Bottle, Old Wine*; "The Buzzard Song" is from *Porgy and Bess*; transcription by the author.
20. The tenor violin is a lower version of the violin. "Concord," composed by John Lewis and arranged by Evans, is from *The Individualism of Gil Evans*. "Bilbao Song," composed by Kurt Weill and arranged by Evans, is from *Out of the Cool*. This excerpt transcribed by Fred Sturm.
21. Three bassists are employed on "El Toreador" (from *The Individualism of Gil Evans*).
22. "Up From the Skies," composed by Jimi Hendrix and arranged by Evans, is from T*he Music of Jimi Hendrix*; "Proclamation" and "General Assembly" come from *Blues in Orbit*.
23. This excerpt from "Bilbao Song" was transcribed by Fred Sturm.
24. "Where Flamingos Fly" and "Sunken Treasure" are from *Out of the Cool*; "Saeta" is from *Sketches of Spain;* "Prayer, Oh Doctor Jesus" is from *Porgy and Bess*. Transcription of excerpt from "Where Flamingos Fly" by the author.
25. Analysis of "Joy Spring" by the author from the recording *Great Jazz Standards*.
26. "Aos Pes Da Cruz" is from *Quiet Nights*.
27. "Moondreams" is from *Birth of the Cool*. Transcription by the author.
28. Transcription from *Porgy and Bess* by the author.
29. The quotation from "Gone" occurs 46 seconds into "There's a Boat That's Leaving Soon for New York," just after the initial statement of the bridge, and, in an altered form, at 2:43.
30. "Davenport Blues" is from *Great Jazz Standards*; "Just One of Those Things" is part of *Gil Evans & Ten*; "So Long" is from *Blues in Orbit*.
31. "Lester Leaps In" is from *New Bottle, Old Wine*; transcription by the author. For a comparison with Lester Young's improvisation on the original recording with Count Basie's Kansas City Seven, refer to the transcription of Young's solo in the author's *Creative Jazz Improvisation*.
32. "Joy Spring" is from *Great Jazz Standards*; "St. Louis Blues," "King Porter Stomp," "Bird Feathers," and "Struttin' with Some Barbecue" are from *New Bottle, Old Wine*; "Springsville" is from *Miles Ahead*.
33. "Anita's Dance" and "Makes Her Move" are from *There Comes a Time;* "Spaced" is from *Blues in Orbit*.
34. On "Time of the Barracudas" (from *The Complete Columbia Studio Recordings*), Davis's improvised solo on what eventual became known as "Hotel Me" begins 8:26 into the tune. The recreation of this solo by the trumpet section can be heard on "Hotel Me" (the version from *The Individualism of Gil Evans*) at 3:33 into the selection.
35. Saxophonist Ray Downey, describing a Gil Evans clinic at the Cornish Institute, Seattle, Oct. 1981.

36. "Where Flamingos Fly" is from *Out of the Cool*. The excerpt is from the author's analysis of the published parts.
37. This excerpt was taken from Gil Evans's unpublished scores, reduced in instrumentation for a concert with the Seattle Composers and Improvisers Orchestra, 1980.
38. "Las Vegas Tango" is found on *The Individualism of Gil Evans*; "Proclamation" is from *Blues in Orbit*.
39. "Prayer (Oh Doctor Jesus)," "Here Come de Honey Man" and "The Buzzard Song" are on *Porgy and Bess*; "Aos Pes Da Cruz" is from *Quiet Nights*; "Time of the Barracudas" was released on *The Complete Columbia Studio Recordings*.
40. "Where Flamingos Fly," "Bilbao Song," and "Sunken Treasure" are from *Out of the Cool*; "Barbara Song" and "Proclamation" are from *The Individualism of Gil Evans*; "King Porter Stomp," "Struttin' with Some Barbecue," and "Lester Leaps in" are from *New Bottle, Old Wine*; "Gone" is from *Porgy and Bess*; and "Springsville" is from *Miles Ahead*.
41. On some recordings, such as "Gone," audible rhythmic mistakes committed by his sidemen can be heard. Presumably the artistic merits of the recording overshadowed these small blemishes, warranting their inclusion on the released recording.
42. Both transcriptions by the author.
43. In particular, Brubeck studied with French composer Darius Milhaud.
44. All three compositions were released on *Outstanding Jazz Compositions of the 20th Century*, which was subsequently rereleased as *Bill, Miles, Joe, J.J., Phil & Art*.
45. Original examples taken from Peter Ilyich Tchaikovsky's *Nutcracker Suite*, op. 71, no. 42 (E.F. Kalmus Orchestra Scores). Evans's arrangement is taken from Joe Muccioli's book of sketch scores, *The Gil Evans Collection*. All examples are in concert pitch.
46. The examples are taken from the vocal score to *Porgy and Bess*.
47. The examples are derived from Gil Evans's unpublished scores, reduced in instrumentation for the Seattle Composers and Improvisers Orchestra, 1980.
48. This influence is particularly pervasive in Slide Hampton's writing for the Dexter Gordon recording, *Sophisticated Giant*, Herbie Hancock's *The Prisoner*, a great deal of Maria Schneider's work (particularly *Evanescence*, her tribute to Evans), and Gil Goldstein's scores to the Wallace Roney recording *Misterios*.

REFERENCES

Avakian, George. 1996. Liner notes for *Miles Davis/Gil Evans: The Complete Columbia Studio Recordings*. Columbia-Sony sound recording 67397.

Belden, Bob. 1996. Liner notes for *Miles Davis/Gil Evans: The Complete Colum-bia Studio Recordings*. Columbia-Sony sound recording 67397.

Castle, Patrick D. 1981. "Aspects of Style in the Repertory of the Claude Thornhill Orchestra." Ph.D. diss., University of Illinois at Champaign-Urbana.

Chambers, Jack. 1983. *Milestones 1: The Music and Times of Miles Davis to 1960*. New York: Quill & William Morrow.

Copland, Aaron. 1949. *Four Piano Blues*. London: Boosey & Hawkes.

Cortright, Clyde. 1998. "Gil Evans' 'My Ship' Reveals Unorthodox Arranging Techniques." *Down Beat* (September): 62.

Crawford, Marc. 1961. "Miles and Gil: Portrait of a Friendship." *Down Beat* (February 16): 18–19.

Davis, Miles. 1996. Liner notes for *Miles Davis/Gil Evans: The Complete Colum-bia Studio Recordings*. Columbia-Sony sound recording 67397.

Gershwin, George. 1933. The Relation of Jazz to American Music. In *American Composers on American Music*, edited by Henry Cowell. Palo Alto: Stanford University Press.

———. 1935. *Porgy and Bess*. New York: Gershwin Publishing Corporation/ Chappell & Co.

Gitler, Ira. 1989 (1957). Liner notes for *Gil Evans & Ten* (reissue of *Big Stuff*). Pres-tige sound recording OJCCD-346-2 [7120].

Hajdu, David. 1997. *Lush Life: A Biography of Billy Strayhorn*. New York: North Point Press.

Hentoff, Nat. 1957a. "Birth of the Cool." *Down Beat* (May 16): 16.

———. 1957b. Liner notes for *Miles Ahead*. Columbia sound recording CS9633.

———. 1958. Liner notes for *Porgy and Bess*. Columbia sound recording CS8085.

———. 1996. Liner notes for *Miles Davis/Gil Evans: The Complete Columbia Stu-dio Recordings*. Columbia-Sony sound recording 67397.

Kirchner, Bill. 1996. Liner notes for *Miles Davis/Gil Evans: The Complete Colum-bia Studio Recordings*. Columbia-Sony sound recording 67397.

LaJoie, Stephen. 1999. "An Analysis of Selected 1957 to 1962 Gil Evans Works Recorded by Miles Davis." Ph.D. diss., New York University.

Lees, Gene. [1964] 1988. Liner notes for *The Individualism of Gil Evans*. Verve sound recording 833 804-2.

Mandel, Howard. 1984. "Gil Evans: The Lone Arranger." *Down Beat* (April): 21.

Muccioli, Joe. 1997. *The Gil Evans Collection*. Milwaukee, WI: Hal Leonard Cor-poration.

Palmer, Robert. 1974. "Refocus on Gil Evans." *Down Beat* (May 23): 13.

Priestly, Brian. 1978. "Discourse, Part II." *Jazz Journal International* (August): 27.

Reeves, Scott. 2001. 3rd ed. *Creative Jazz Improvisation*. Upper Saddle River, NJ: Prentice Hall.

Schuller, Gunther. 1968. *Early Jazz*. New York: Oxford University Press.

———. 1989. *The Swing Era* . New York: Oxford University Press.

Schuller, Gunther & Martin Williams. 1983. *Big Band Jazz: From the Beginnings to the Fifties*. Washington D.C.: Smithsonian Collection of Recordings.

Sidran, Ben. 1986. Live radio interview show *Ben Sidran on Record*. National Public Radio.

Solomon, David. 1961. "Jazz Is Popular Music: Interview with Gil Evans." *Metro* (June): 7.

Smith, Arnold J. 1976. "Gil Evans: 21st Century Synthesized Man." *Down Beat* (May 20): 15.

Smith, Charles Edward. 1958. Liner notes for *Porgy and Bess*. Columbia sound recording CS 8085.

Stein, Stephanie. 1986. "Gil Evans: 1912–88." *Down Beat* (June): 12.

Sturm, Fred. 1995. *Changes over Time: The Evolution of Jazz Arranging*. Rottenburg, Germany: Advance Music.

Tchaikovsky, Peter Ilyich. 1892. *Nutcracker Suite*, op. 71, no. 42. New York: E. F. Kalmus Orchestra Scores.

DISCOGRAPHY

Bernstein, Leonard. 1957. *What Is Jazz*. Columbia Special Products 42A 02053.

Burrell, Kenny. 1965. *Guitar Forms*. Verve sound recording V68612.

Davis, Miles. [1949–1950] 1971. *The Complete Birth of the Cool*. Capitol/EMI sound recording 7 92862.

———. 1957. *Miles Ahead*. Columbia sound recording CL 1041.

———. 1958. *Porgy and Bess*. Columbia sound recording CS 8085.

———. 1959. *Sketches of Spain*. Columbia sound recording CS 8280.

———. 1961. *Miles Davis at Carnegie Hall*. Columbia sound recording CS 8612.

———. 1964. *Quiet Nights*. Columbia sound recording CS 8906.

Davis, Miles, and Gil Evans. 1996. *The Complete Columbia Studio Recordings*. Columbia/Sony sound recording 67397.

Evans, Gil. [1957] 1989. *Gil Evans & Ten [Big Stuff]*. Prestige sound recording OJCCD-346-2 [7120].

———. [1958] 1988. *New Bottle, Old Wine*. EMI-Manhattan Records CDP 746855 2 [Pacific Jazz sound recording WP 1246].

———. [1959] 1997. *Great Jazz Standards*. Capitol/Pacific Jazz sound recording CDP 7 46856 2.

———. [1961] 1996. *Out of the Cool*. MCI/Impulse sound recording IMPD-186 [Impulse AS 4].

———. [1964] 1988. *The Individualism of Gil Evans*. Verve sound recording 833 804-2 [V6 8555].

———. [1969] rerelease date unknown. *Blues in Orbit [Gil Evans]*. Enja sound recording 3069   [Ampex sound recording 10102].

———. 1973. *Svengali*. Atlantic sound recording SD 1643.

———. 1974. *Plays the Music of Jimi Hendrix*. RCA sound recording CPL1-0677.

———. 1976 . *There Comes A Time*. RCA sound recording APL1-1057.

————. 1983. *Priestess*. Antilles sound recording ANCD 8717.

————. 2000. *Gil Evans—The Real Birth of the Cool—Transcriptions*. The Jazz Factory sound recording JFCD 22803.

Johnson, J.J.; Lewis, John; Russell, George. [1957] 1981. "Poem for Brass," "Three Little Feelings," "All About Rosie." *Bill, Miles, Joe, J.J., Phil & Art [Outstanding Jazz Compositions of the 20th Century]*. Columbia sound recording PC 370122.

Kenton, Stan. [1953] 1995. *City of Glass*. Capitol sound recording 7243 8 32084 2 5.

Konitz, Lee. 1986. *Heroes*. Verve sound recording 511 621.

DJANGO REINHARDT'S
"I'LL SEE YOU IN MY DREAMS"

Ben Givan

A jazz improvisation is like a palimpsest in sound. Beneath the music that reaches our ears lies a theme that simultaneously inspires and constrains the performer. From time to time traces may appear on the music's surface that, like ghostly pentimentos, provide us with clues to the improviser's underlying conception of the theme. As the soloist weaves melodic lines that unfold dynamically in time, we may glimpse signs of the static, cyclical form that is his "model," or "referent."[1] An awareness of the omnipresent model is a sine qua non of competent performance—and a vital, if not essential, element of informed listening—in most jazz styles that emerged between 1920 and 1950.

My subject in this article is one of the most famous improvised guitar solos by the Belgian-born Manouche Gypsy Django Reinhardt (1910–53). He recorded "I'll See You In My Dreams,"[2] a 1924 composition by the Chicago bandleader Isham Jones, on June 30, 1939, just weeks before the outbreak of World War II truncated the most productive years of his recording career with the Quintet of the Hot Club of France. The disc, which features Reinhardt accompanied only by guitarist Pierre Ferret and bassist Emmanuel Soudieux, finds him at the peak of his creative powers and exemplifies many of the hallmarks of his mature style prior to his encounter with bebop and adoption of the electric guitar during the postwar period.

Reinhardt's recordings with the Quintet are widely esteemed as the apotheosis of Swing Era European jazz, but they differ markedly from contemporaneous American forms in several respects. Most notably, they employ an all-string instrumentation, and favor a two-in-a-bar rhythmic feel that had become *passé* in American jazz ever since masters of the string bass, such as Pops Foster and Walter Page, transformed the accompanying role originally assigned to the tuba. But perhaps a more significant stylistic feature of the Quintet's music is the near absence of any musical interaction among the performers. During the Swing Era, under the guiding influence of Louis Armstrong, jazz became a soloist's art for the first time, and there was less emphasis on the heterophonic interplay characteristic of earlier New Orleans jazz.[3] It was not until the advent of bebop, and especially its stylistic successors, that musical interaction experienced a renaissance. Yet even in music of the Swing Era, we are accustomed to hearing accompanimental drum fills, piano figurations, and so forth, which can often function as structural markers, communicating information about the underlying theme for the benefit of both the soloist and listeners.[4] In the case of the Quintet of the Hot Club of France, Reinhardt's accompanists—perhaps intimidated by their leader's extraordinary virtuosity and forthright refusal to regard them as his equals in the ensemble[5]—play an unusually subservient role.[6] They maintain the rhythmic pulse and articulate the music's harmonic form, but for the most part all remaining responsibility for providing clues to the improvisational model rests entirely with the soloist himself. This is music that may appear to run contrary to the spirit of democratic participation commonly celebrated as central to the jazz aesthetic. But it serves as a reminder that, as Ralph Ellison wrote, jazz embodies an inherent contradiction—while on the one hand it prizes the individual's identity "as a member of the collectivity and as a link in the chain of tradition," on the other, it is equally "an art of individual assertion within and against the group."[7]

A soloist's adherence to a given harmonic formal structure is often expressed by his selection of melodic pitches drawn from the underlying harmonies; the most basic use of this procedure being the straightforward arpeggiation of triads that André Hodeir disparaged as the "do-mi-sol-do" technique.[8] However the following analysis deals primarily with rhythmic and motivic devices, as well as medium-range linear progressions, that Reinhardt uses to provide supplementary clues to his orientation within the form. I also consider the guitarist's use of paraphrases of the original melody as an alternative means of signifying formal location. The paper concludes by addressing several features of the solo that are suggestive of techniques of "thematic" improvisation.

Isham Jones's "I'll See You In My Dreams" is a theme with no real history as a favored vehicle for jazz improvisation. The original sheet music is reproduced in Example 1. The song's chorus conforms to a common archetype of the Tin Pan Alley literature: it is a thirty-two-bar form divisible into four eight-bar phrases arranged in the form ABAC. Each eight-bar phrase consists of two balanced, four-bar subphrases, and almost all of the note values are either whole or half notes (or two whole notes tied together).[9] The only points of rhythmic variety (comparatively speaking) are m. 11 and m. 15 of the chorus, where quarter notes are used to set the lyrics "out of my arms" and "thrill of your charms." This song is thus characterized by extreme rhythmic regularity, and a phrase periodicity that Reinhardt's rendition replicates by its customary

Lyrics by
GUS KAHN

Music by
ISHAM JONES

Example 1: "I'll See You in My Dreams"; original sheet music: *I'll See You in My Dreams*, by Gus Kahn and Isham Jones, © 1924 (Renewed) EMI Feist Catalog Inc. Rights for Extended Renewal Term in U.S. controlled by Gilbert Keyes Music and Bantam Music Publishing Company. All Rights outside the U.S. controlled by EMI Feist Catalog Inc. All Rights Reserved. Used by Permission. Warner Bros. Publications U.S. Inc., Miami, FL 33014. *Continued on next page.*

Example 1, *continued*

cyclic repetitions of the entire form. Example 2 shows a transcription of Reinhardt's solo, juxtaposed with the melody as published.[10] The harmonies heard
on the recording are simpler than those in the sheet music (for instance,
the chromatic G♯-diminished-seventh and E-major harmonies in m. 6 are
omitted).

Example 2: Reinhardt, guitar solo on "I'll See You in My Dreams"; original melody. *Continued on next four pages.*

In his first chorus, Reinhardt gives an exposition of the preexisting theme and subjects it to a considerable degree of transformation and embellishment. I draw special attention to one such embellishment: the chromatic turn figure about the pitch D that prefixes the second eight-bar section of the chorus (m. 1_8).[11] This ornamental figure is, by means of

Example 2, *continued on next three pages*

consistent usage, established as an important structural marker facilitating the listener's means of temporal orientation. The turn figure first recurs at the equivalent point in the second half of the opening chorus (m. 1_{24}). It reappears at approximately its original location during the second chorus (m. 2_8) (transposed an octave higher) and at m. 3_9 of the penulti-

Example 2, *continued on next two pages*

mate chorus (again, at the higher octave). It also occurs midway through the second half of the penultimate chorus (m. 3_{24}). (Every occurrence is circled in Example 2.) In each case the turn figure appears in a slightly different guise; it is never replicated verbatim. The figure is absent from the equivalent formal locations at mm. 4_8, 2_{24}, and 4_{24}. However, during

Example 2, *concluded on next page*

the second half of every chorus the sectional boundary at m. 25 is always, without exception, marked by the prominent appearance of the
pitch E♭ on the downbeat. This is, of course, a pitch drawn directly from
the original melody itself, and it acts as a particularly effective structural
marker because it is already a "marked" note in the published score owing to its location near the apex of the song's pitch ambitus, and because

Example 2, *concluded*

of its chromatic status—it lies outside of the diatonic F-major scale (the song's home key) and foreshadows a momentary tonicization of D minor in m. 28.

In the two choruses when the pitch E♭ on the downbeat of m. 25 is not prefixed by the chromatic turn figure (i.e. m. 2_{25} and m. 4_{25}), this formal juncture is instead preceded by a tritone-spanning melodic descent, as shown in Figure 1. (The stemmed pitches in Figure 1 all receive dynamic accents, in addition to being associated by virtue of their similar register.) These descents also manifest two different rhythmic techniques that consistently function as structural markers during this solo: repeated notes (or short motives), and consecutive three-beat-long motives. In Figure 1a the downbeat of m. 2_{25} is preceded by three entire measures filled with eighth-note reiterations of the pitch E♮. And in Figure 1b the descent is characterized by a series of three-beat-long motives that contravene the underlying duple meter (the polymetric effect is particularly pronounced because these measures are preceded by a passage dominated by strict repetitions of two-bar motives [mm. 4_9–4_{20}]).

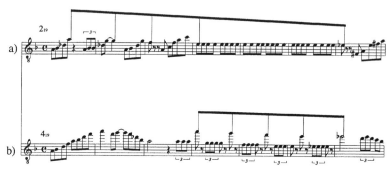

Figure 1: Tritone-spanning melodic descents

Both of these rhythmic techniques create a temporary sensation of comparative instability that is resolved by their cessation on the downbeat of a formally significant measure (i.e., a measure that begins an eight-bar formal unit, or phrase). The first—the rhythmically undifferentiated reiteration of a single pitch—heightens the listener's sense of expectation. Leonard B. Meyer writes that "a figure which is repeated over and over again arouses a strong expectation of change because continuation is inhibited and because the figure is not allowed to reach completion."[12] A repeated pattern thereby intensifies the music's forward-directed impetus because the listener's expectation of change militates against any sense of stasis. Consequently, the successive repetition of a given pitch, or small fragmentary motive, not only can endow its point of cessation with added emphasis, but may also prevent the improvised melody from reinforcing a point of harmonic or melodic closure in the original theme. Steve Larson has used the general term "cadence avoidance" to describe any melodic gesture that transcends an underlying point of harmonic closure (his definition is not restricted to repetitive patterns of the sort considered here).[13] Another repetitive figure of this sort occurs between mm. 2_{29} and 2_{32}, acting to "keep the ball rolling," so to speak, as the song form comes to an end. This particular figure also attenuates the underlying stable tonic harmony by outlining a (dissonant) diminished triad between the tritone D–A♭.[14]

The D–A♭ tritone is itself made the basis of a "cadence avoidance" at the equivalent point during the previous chorus (mm. 1_{28}–1_{32});[15] here, as the exposition of the theme draws to a close, the "cadence avoidance" represents the furthest departure yet from the original melody, and heralds the first improvised chorus. By choosing not to play the melody's final phrase, Reinhardt signals that this is not in any sense an ending, but the beginning of a foray into uncharted musical territory. In addition, this passage involves repeated three-beat motives (specifically at mm. 1_{30}–1_{32}), which is the second of our two structure-marking (and instability-producing) rhythmic techniques (see Figure 1b).[16]

A series of three-beat patterns also occurs at mm. 2_2–2_4, contributing to the sense of arrival on the tonic harmony at m. 2_5.[17] This "sense of arrival" may be represented graphically. Figure 2 utilizes the "branch" notation invented by Lerdahl and Jackendoff to propose a time-span reduction of mm. 2_1–2_8.[18] Figure 2a is a reading of the four pairs of measures within the written melody's first eight bars; these are grouped into two trochaic pairs of pairs. The strongest structural downbeat within this passage is at m. 5 (where the tonic harmony arrives). Figure 2b displays the opening eight measures of Reinhardt's first improvised chorus. Here the primary downbeat is preceded by a series of five ascending gestures that may be described as a "fragmented upbeat chain." These reiterated gestures heighten the listener's sense of anacrusis, as well as an expectation of the coming downbeat at m. 2_5, endowing the passage with an increased sense of dynamic, forward-directed momentum.[19] Another instance of the same procedure occurs fleetingly at the equivalent point in the second half of the same chorus (mm. 2_{19}–2_{20}).

If Reinhardt were to signal each and every eight- (or even four-) bar unit of the song form with some type of structural marker, the cumulative effect would probably be quite dull. Such is the extreme periodicity of most themes favored by jazz musicians that, providing a sufficient number of structural landmarks are articulated from time to time, the listener is able to maintain his or her sense of temporal orientation (with reference to the music's regular pulse) and thus follow the underlying form without any need

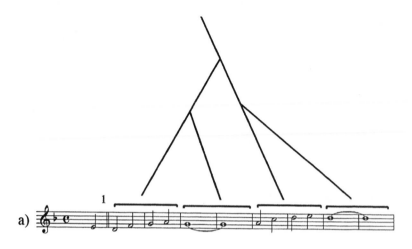

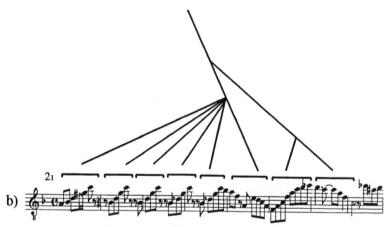

Figure 2: Branch notation indicating rhythmic hierarchy in "I'll See You in My Dreams" (a) and in Reinhardt's improvisation (b)

for constant explicit cues.[20] The performer is then free to seek greater variety by, from time to time, deemphasizing, or even explicitly contravening or obscuring, points of formal import. I will draw attention to just two such passages from the present performance: the midpoint of the second chorus and the beginning of the final chorus. Clearly the real potential of the improviser's theme lies not only in the possibility that it may be explicitly concretized from time to time, but in that, so long as its fixed constraints are firmly established in the mind of the performer (and, secondarily, the listener), a considerable degree of creative freedom is available, such that his continual adherence to the theme, or "model," may at times be entirely inexplicit.

In the passage between mm. 2_{11} and 2_{20} Reinhardt develops a motive that is, in most of its variants, characterized by the interval of an ascending minor seventh. The listener's attention is primarily absorbed by the linear, processual aspects of the ongoing motivic development, and we are not provided with any clues reminding us that meanwhile we are traversing the midpoint of the binary song form (m. 2_{17}). Intimations of formal location are also withheld as Reinhardt begins the final chorus (m. 4_1). This juncture arrives in the midst of a flamboyant passage of quarter-note triplets, one of Reinhardt's stylistic trademarks (the faster the tempo, the more he was prone to use them). These are the solo's climactic moments, and this is also a passage in which it is most difficult for the listener to maintain her or his temporal orientation—for instance, Reinhardt creates a brief polymetric effect in mm. 4_2–4_3 with a sequence of four-note-long motives based on quarter-note triplets, and these two measures themselves straddle the theme's underlying two-bar groupings, briefly creating a hypermetrical syncopation. Rhythmic stability is quickly reestablished by the series of extremely regular two-bar phrases (mm. 4_9–4_{20}) noted earlier.

So far I have focused exclusively on Reinhardt's various means of signaling, and on occasion obscuring, aspects of the regular periodic phrase structure of Jones's theme. But this is only one aspect of the improviser's underlying model that may "show through" to the musical surface from time to time. Another way in which the performer may indicate "where we are" in the form is by explicitly referencing the original melody. Hodeir has, in an influential formulation, labeled jazz improvisations that simply embellish or slightly modify the preexistent melody, preserving its recognizable features, as "paraphrase improvisation."[21] Many jazz musicians speak of keeping the original melody in mind as a continual, conscious source of reference throughout their improvised solos.[22] Reinhardt, like many other musicians of the Swing Era, often returned briefly to the original melody between creative excursions that ventured further afield. In "I'll See You In My Dreams," such melodic references range from the wholly explicit to the fairly subtle.

The most extended and most literal paraphrase of the original melody takes place between mm. 3_{25} and 3_{31}. During these measures Jones's melody, while fully recognizable, is subjected to considerable embellishment, and it undergoes a register transfer to a higher octave at m. 3_{27} (Reinhardt has already hinted at the latter procedure during his exposition of the theme [m. 1_{21}]). As the penultimate chorus concludes, this paraphrase of the melody's final phrase is elided into the previously mentioned flamboyant passage of quarter-note triplets. Thus, the paraphrase prepares the listener for the forthcoming excursion by providing an explicit reminder of our formal location, ensuring that we are "on track."

The solo contains a number of less explicit melodic paraphrases, many of them appearing like faint traces, seamlessly interwoven into larger melodic gestures. Some are used consistently, such as the rhythmic diminution of the theme's basic melodic contour that immediately precedes the extended melodic paraphrase at the close of the third chorus, described above (mm. 3_{22}–3_{23}, in which a single lower-neighbor prefix ($C\natural$) is interpolated before the phrase's final note). I mention this separately from the succeeding paraphrase because the same figure, preceded by a descending and then ascending arpeggiation of an F-major triad, also occurs at the equivalent point during the first half of the third chorus (mm. 3_6–3_7)—though in this instance it is shifted a single beat earlier—and also, in a still different variant, a whole chorus beforehand, in mm. 2_6–2_7. All three occurrences are shown in Figure 3.

Figure 3: Recurrent material in Reinhardt's solo

In some cases it may not be possible to distinguish with certainty between paraphrase techniques, in which melodic pitches are invoked at their original formal location, and procedures of "thematic" improvisation, whereby motives drawn from the composed melody are developed independently of their original location.[23] Recall that the two position-signifying linear progressions through the interval of a tritone, displayed in Figure 1, both begin their descents with the pitch A, followed by G. Together, these two pitches constitute a "signature" dyad of Jones's melody. The note A is heard as an upper-neighbor to G in mm. 2–3 of the song—these pitches act as the major seventh and added sixth of the underlying subdominant harmony.[24] The same two pitches recur at the end of the first half of the song, where they constitute the sixth and fifth of the dominant harmony (thus the melody arrives on scale-degree 2 midway through the piece, in the manner of a Schenkerian "interruption form"). And this neighbor-note motive is also manifested over a four-measure span, between the note A in m. 12 and the note G in m. 16. However, the pervasiveness of this dyad throughout the original melody can make the distinction between paraphrase and thematic improvisation problematic with respect to Reinhardt's solo. In terms of melodic paraphrase, one could perhaps posit the A–G dyad that appears in m. 3_{16} as a diminution of the same dyad found in that approximate location (strictly speaking, a measure earlier) in the published melody; similarly the A–G–F descending trichord that occurs at the beginning of m. 2_{27} could be classified as a diminution of the same melodic pattern in mm. 28–29 of the original theme. But such a determination would need to be predicated on the artist's intent, and knowledge of this is unavailable to us.[25]

Elsewhere, Reinhardt makes the signature A–G dyad the object of thematic development that clearly goes beyond paraphrase techniques. The dyad appears under inversion—thus spanning the interval of a minor seventh—in m. 2_{16}, whereupon it is highlighted as the uppermost pitches of the pair of ascending gestures in mm. 2_{17}–2_{18} (which, after being repeated [mm. 2_{19}–2_{20}], initiate one of our descents to the structural-marker pitch E♭). Similarly, the A–G dyad pervades the measures preceding the next descent to E♭; these pitches appear at the apex of the ascending gesture that occurs in mm. 4_{17}–4_{18} (and is immediately repeated in mm. 4_{19}–4_{20}). In fact, from a (modified) Schenkerian perspective, the pitch A is prolonged for the entire span of m. 4_6 through m. 4_{27}, and highlighted by its prominent registral placement (mm. 4_6–4_{14}) and insistent repetition (mm. 4_{15}–4_{16}) (shown in Figure 4). How much significance one wishes to ascribe to these phenomena ultimately depends upon whether one favors a performer-oriented perspective or an external, listener-oriented standpoint.

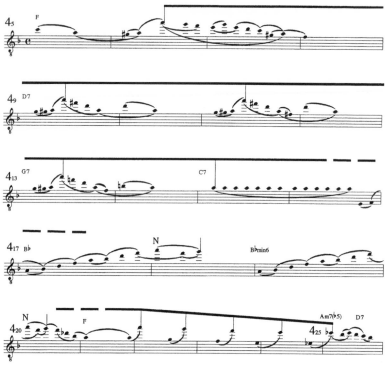

Figure 4: Prolongational voice leading in mm. 46–425

Whether by happenstance or conscious design, Reinhardt frequently shows a tendency to emphasize specific pitch classes in a consistent manner. For instance, his a cappella introduction begins with a harmonization of the published melody's opening, but after just four chords it deviates from the tune as written by introducing the pitches C and B♭ in the upper voice (mm. I_3–I_4).[26] These same pitches are then interpolated in the equivalent position when the real thematic exposition begins (m. 1_3) (and the upward leap to a pitch lying a perfect fourth above the final note of the first four-bar subphrase is of course replicated in m. 1_6, with the interpolation of the pitch G♮, likewise not part of the written melody). The notes B♭ and C form the boundary pitches of the repeated motive with which Reinhardt begins the first improvised chorus (mm. 2_1–2_4), and the identical pitches, with C acting as an upper-neighbor note to B♭, are also very prominent at the beginning of the next chorus (mm. 3_1–3_3).

The subject of "thematic improvisation" in jazz has been critiqued by advocates of a culturally grounded, rather than a formalist, interpretive perspective.[27] Without entering into a detailed discussion of this issue, I would simply submit that the notion of "coherence" (whose ideological heritage is the European idea of the artwork as an autonomous, integrated whole), which is embedded in the concept of thematic improvisation, is not so strongly privileged by the analysis of structural markers, which has been this article's principal focus. Instead, structural markers and other position-signifying events are primarily associated with cognitive aspects of the improvisational process and the listening experience.

I mentioned at the outset that an awareness of the model (theme) is essential for competent performance, and perhaps for informed listening also.[28] Since the musical model is a temporal phenomenon, an awareness of it must involve some means of calibrating one's inner, experiential time sense with the "real" clock time in which the music takes place.[29] This psychological process is facilitated by structural markers and other position-signifying musical devices. The importance of these is suggested by a telling remark of Dizzy Gillespie's, noted by Scott DeVeaux, to the effect that, when playing the blues "you forget about changes . . . but every now and then you put a little lick in there to let 'em know, 'Here's where I'm at, really.'"[30] Thus the metaphor of jazz as a palimpsest: in the ongoing stream of real-time creation, many musical events may communicate information regarding the theme that pervades the performer's inner consciousness. Position-signifying events need not create any semblance of large-scale coherence; they may simply be functional devices that assist listeners (and collaborating musicians) in temporally orienting themselves with respect to the improvisational model. And even if this function is not strictly necessary—experienced players and listeners may well be able to adhere to a conceptual model with only the aid of an articulated pulse, or by recognizing the implicit harmonies being outlined by a single-line melody—their role can be confirmatory.[31] In Reinhardt's "I'll See You In My Dreams," the simple presence of a recognizable bass line and audible harmonic accompaniment also helps us find our place in the form, but, as I have suggested, the guitarist's accompanists' failure to provide additional structural markers means that he, as soloist, assumes a greater share of this role.

The foregoing analysis has been highly reductive; by focusing on manifestations of the static, constant, improviser's model I have overlooked substantial stretches of the solo. Neglected passages include mm. 3_{10}–3_{20}, as well as the remarkable descending sequence that traverses the midpoint of the second full chorus (mm. 2_{11}–2_{20}). In the latter passage, as mentioned

earlier, Reinhardt privileges matters of linear succession over strict obser-
vance of the theme's harmonic structure (thus the appearance of the pitches
B♭ and A♭ over a C7 chord in m. 2_{15}); this serves as a salutary reminder that
what we hear on the recording is the result of a dynamic process. And, in
concluding, this raises an important point: certain specific musical events
do not necessarily have preestablished functions as signifiers of formal location. Rather, these functions may accrue by means of consistent usage
during the course of a performance. In the improvisation considered here,
such musical devices have been shown to include (1) specific pitches or
motives that recur in the same locations during successive reiterations of
the song form; (2) repeated notes, consecutive three-beat motives, and linear melodic descents preceding an important structural moment; and (3)
paraphrases of the original melody.[32]

Django Reinhardt never recorded another rendition of "I'll See You In
My Dreams." We will never know for certain if his performance of 1939
was at all preconceived, or whether its conception was entirely extempora-
neous.[33] But in the years since, it has been elevated to canonic status by the
music community. The musician's biographer, François Billard, writes that
"this improvisation has been copied a thousand times by young Manouche
guitarists. Today it has become a great classic, a sort of 'must,' that one
plays, or rather *interprets*, without changing a note."[34] It is a performance
from which we can learn as much about our own ways of listening as about
the creative process of Reinhardt himself.

NOTES

1. The term "model" is used by Bruno Nettl ("Thoughts on Improvisation: A
   Comparative Approach," *The Musical Quarterly* 60/1 [1974]: 1–19); "referent" is the name preferred by Jeff Pressing ("Cognitive Processes in Improvisation," in *Cognitive Processes in the Perception of Art*, ed. W. Ray Crozier
   and Antony J. Chapman [Amsterdam: Elsevier, 1984], 345–66).
2. Matrix number: OPG 1721-1; original 78 rpm catalogue number: Swing 211.
   This recording is currently available on numerous compact disc compila-
   tions, including *The Best of Django Reinhardt* (Blue Note CDP 7243 8 37138
   2 0); *Parisian Swing* (Avid AMSC 648); *Django Reinhardt Vol. 5: The Solo
   Sessions* (Jazz Archives [No. 80] 158202); and *The Complete Django Reinhardt and Quintet of the Hot Club of France Swing/HMV Sessions
   1936–1948* (Mosaic MD6-190).
3. It should, however, be emphasized that, rather than being based purely on
   "collective improvisation," the heterophony of New Orleans jazz included

significant rehearsed, pre-composed, and even written elements (see, for in-
stance, Lawrence Gushee, "King Oliver's Creole Jazz Band," in *The Art of
Jazz: Essays in the Nature and Development of Jazz*, ed. Martin Williams
[New York: Da Capo, 1971 (1959)], 46; discussed in Mark Tucker, "Musi-
cology and the New Jazz Studies," *Journal of the American Musicological
Society* 51/1 [1998]: 145–46).

4. See, for instance, Paul Berliner, *Thinking in Jazz: The Infinite Art of Improvisation* (Chicago: University of Chicago Press, 1994), 298–99, and passim.

5. On Reinhardt's views towards his colleagues see Charles Delaunay, *Django
Reinhardt*, trans. Michael James (New York: Da Capo, 1981 [1961]), 19.

6. Ben Ratliff writes, "Except for [Reinhardt's] violin playing foil, Stephane
Grappelli, . . . the all-string group Hot Club of France [*sic*] wasn't much of
a band, just a background" (*The New York Times*, Sunday, December 12,
1999, AR44, AR48).

7. Ralph Ellison, "The Charlie Christian Story," in *Shadow and Act*; reprinted
in *The Collected Essays of Ralph Ellison*, ed. John F. Callahan (New York:
Modern Library, 1995), 267.

8. André Hodeir, *Jazz: Its Evolution and Essence*, trans. David Noakes (New
York: Grove Press, 1956), 145–48.

9. Alec Wilder describes this song as "perhaps the best example in all of popular music of minimal notes" (*American Popular Song: The Great Innovators,
1900–1950* [New York: Oxford University Press, 1972], 403).

10. Note the clef—the music sounds an octave lower than written.

11. Measures have been numbered with a standard arabic numeral for each successive chorus and a subscript indicating the measure number within that
chorus. For instance, "measure 2_{17}" refers to the seventeenth measure of the
second chorus.

12. Leonard B. Meyer, *Emotion and Meaning in Music* (Chicago: University of
Chicago Press, 1956), 135–36. Meyer cites a famous instance of such repetition from the first movement of Beethoven's Symphony no. 6. Repetition
may, however, elicit other responses in different contexts. Richmond Browne
hypothesizes that "if the [jazz] player starts a repetitive pattern, the listener's
attention drops away as soon as he has successfully predicted that it is going
to continue. Then, if the thing keeps going, the attention curve comes back
up, and the listener becomes interested in just how long the pattern *is* going
to continue" (personal communication quoted in Jerry Coker, *Improvising
Jazz* [New York: Fireside, 1987 {1964}]).

13. Steve Larson, "Dave McKenna's Performance of 'Have You Met Miss
Jones?,'" *American Music* 11 (1993): 293–94.

14. Repetitive figures such as these may also serve a more purely utilitarian
function in terms of the improviser's creative process—they allow him a few
extra moments in which to gather inspiration.

15. This is a favorite formula of Reinhardt's that most often occurs either at the
end or beginning of a chorus (or, less often, any eight-measure formal unit).

Compare, for instance, the beginning of his solo on "Sweet Georgia Brown" (January 31, 1938; mx. DTB 3524-1).

16. The cadence avoidance in mm. 4_{15}–4_{16}—the reiterated As—constitutes a rhythmic diminution of this device because every third eighth note (rather than quarter note) is accented, thus obfuscating the beat rather than the meter (this is another of Reinhardt's favorite formulas).

17. One of the few noteworthy aspects of the song's harmonic structure is that it begins on the subdominant harmony, delaying the arrival of the tonic harmony for the first four measures. Hence m. 5 is a fairly important structural moment, even though it only represents the start of a four-measure subphrase, rather than a full eight-measure phrase.

18. Lerdahl and Jackendoff, *A Generative Theory of Tonal Music* (Cambridge, MA: MIT Press, 1983). My loose appropriation of Lerdahl and Jackendoff's work bowdlerizes their notation by omitting the dots and brackets they place beneath the score to indicate hierarchical levels of rhythmic emphasis and phrase groupings, and I have also, in Figure 2b, flouted their "well-formedness rules." Simply put, Lerdahl and Jackendoff's notation indicates hierarchical relationships between musical events in which events of lower status "branch out" from events of greater emphasis. Thus, when one is dealing with rhythm, as in Figure 2, a set of events subsumed beneath a given branch is understood to have a comparatively weaker rhythmic emphasis than the events that are subsumed beneath a (longer) branch to which the first (shorter) branch is attached.

19. This sort of procedure can be found elsewhere within the African-American musical tradition: Aretha Franklin uses it with powerful dramatic affect in her well-known 1972 recording of "Amazing Grace" (Atlantic 2-906-2), where the anacrustic lyric may be repeated several times, in *tempo rubato*, as the congregation's response rises with their growing anticipation of the next downbeat.

20. The number of structural markers that may be "sufficient" depends on the listener's level of competence; of course the frequency of such structural markers varies from one performer to another, and between different styles of jazz.

21. Hodeir distinguishes paraphrase improvisation from "chorus phrase" improvisation, which is based solely on a theme's harmonies (*Jazz: Its Evolution and Essence*, 144).

22. For instance, Milt Jackson states, "I keep the melody in mind. I always remember the melody and then I have something to fall back on when I get lost" (quoted in Whitney Balliett, *American Musicians II: Seventy-Two Portraits in Jazz* [New York: Oxford University Press, 1996], 308).

23. The classic article establishing the term "thematic improvisation" is Gunther Schuller, "Sonny Rollins and the Challenge of Thematic Improvisation," *The Jazz Review* 1/1 (November 1958): 6–11, 21, reprinted in *Musings: The Musical World of Gunther Schuller* (New York: Oxford University Press, 1986), 86–97.

24. Allen Forte describes the use, under these circumstances, of the *chord of the added sixth* (such as in mm. 2–3, where it is decorated by the major seventh as upper neighbor) as the "assimilation" of added decorative notes "that are *melodic* in origin and result from the voice-leading strands that are unfolding dynamically in the music" (*The American Popular Ballad of the Golden Era, 1924–1950* [Princeton, NJ: Princeton University Press, 1995], 8). Thus, a reading of the linear voice-leading structure of the song's opening measures might identify an ascending melodic progression from the pitch F (m. 1) through G (mm. 2–4; the added sixth) to A (m. 5).

25. This issue is addressed in Henry Martin, *Charlie Parker and Thematic Improvisation* (Lanham, MD: Scarecrow Press, 1996), 35–37.

26. The pitch class B♭ is particularly marked because it is the only member of the diatonic scale of F major, the song's key, which never occurs in the melody as written.

27. A very brief summary of the major issues can be found in Brian Harker, "'Telling a Story': Louis Armstrong and Coherence in Early Jazz," *Current Musicology* 63 (1999): 46–47.

28. Thomas Brothers argues that an awareness of the underlying cyclical structure is indeed "essential to the appreciation of jazz solos" ("Solo and Cycle in African-American jazz," *Musical Quarterly* 78/3 [1994]: 488–89). I would agree that it is especially germane to the experience of listening to jazz, but I would not rule out the possibility that individual listeners may find other ways to appreciate the music even without this knowledge.

29. The problems that arise when a performer loses his sense of orientation within the underlying form are discussed in a detailed analysis of "Bassment Blues" in Ingrid Monson, *Saying Something: Jazz Improvisation and Interaction* (Chicago: University of Chicago Press, 1996), 133–91.

30. Dizzy Gillespie with Al Fraser, *To Be or Not . . . to Bop: Memoirs* (Garden City, NY: Doubleday, 1979), 371, quoted in Scott DeVeaux, *The Birth of Bebop: A Social and Musical History* (Berkeley: University of California Press, 1997), 343.

31. For another perspective on this issue, see the discussion of jazz improvisers' use of "functionally redundant coded communication" in David T. Bastien and Todd J. Hostager, "Jazz as Social Structure, Process, and Outcome," in *Jazz in Mind*, ed. Reginald T. Buckner and Steven Weiland (Detroit: Wayne State University Press, 1991), 154.

32. Nonetheless, it could be argued that paraphrases of the underlying melody do indeed possess preestablished functions as signifiers of formal location, so long as the melody has already been played at the outset (or is already familiar to listeners and fellow performers).

33. On the evidence of those of Reinhardt's recordings that have been issued along with alternate takes, he sometimes relied on preconceived strategies (compare the two takes of "I've Got My Love to Keep Me Warm" [September 1, 1938;

mx. DR 2903-1 and DR 2903-2]). On other occasions, consecutive takes show no indication of any consistent preparation (for example the two widely divergent takes of "Baby Won't You Please Come Home" [November 19, 1937; mx. OLA 1980-1 and OLA 1980-2]).

34. François Billard, *Django Reinhardt: Un géant sur son nuage* (Paris: Lieu Commun, 1993), 148–49: "L'improvisation de ce morceau a été recopiée mille fois par les jeunes guitaristes manouches. Elle est devenue aujourd'hui un grand classique, une sorte de *must* que l'on rejoue, ou plutôt que l'on <interprète>, sans en changer une note."

WHEN BACKWARD COMES OUT AHEAD: LUCKY THOMPSON'S PHRASING AND IMPROVISATION

Tad Shull

INTRODUCTION:
PLAYING BACKWARD, MOVING FORWARD

"That backward style." That is how musicians often refer to Eli "Lucky" Thompson's playing. His phrasing is the opposite of what one might expect, they say. His accents fall in the "wrong" places, on the "wrong" beats, in the "wrong" order. As they speak, their tone mixes awe with irony. Irony, that is, because his style seems to counter the hip way of phrasing they worked so hard to cultivate. And awe, because he pulls it off.

Thompson, an eccentric even to admirers, a marginal figure in histories of jazz, is a master of the tenor and soprano saxophones. (Though still alive at this writing, Thompson has unfortunately not been active for almost 30 years.) His career bridged the worlds of the canonical Charlie Parker and John Coltrane, and he often stood at the cutting edge with both. Thompson's distinctive rhythmic approach actually grew from and advanced a significant jazz tradition. Bringing that context back in will help make sense of his "backward" style and show how forward looking it really was. Focusing in particular on his deft use of phrasing tools such as accents, articulation, and timing can yield some valuable insights on the role they play in jazz improvisation.

To understand how and why Thompson's unexpected phrasing works, it is essential to grasp what might have been expected in the first place. The best way to do that is to view his art in the context of the polyrhythmic ensemble performance.[1] Jazz derives essential rhythmic material by exploiting intricate variations on, or subdivisions of, an underlying basic beat stated or implied by the rhythm section (generally in 4/4 time until the innovations of the 1960s). Notes falling on an unstressed metric beat, or on a subdivision of the metric beat—the so-called weak beats—receive accents, challenging the expectations of the listener and other performers. The soloist also derives material for rhythmic variation by establishing, and then often shifting, a pattern of accents. The very terms "swing" and "bebop" connote this supple and evolving use of irregular accents.

Thompson helped introduce a new level of complexity, and new possibilities for creative tension and release, to the polyrhythmic mix. He builds his phrases with straight eighth notes (eighth notes of equal value or emphasis), contrasting them with the standard jazz triplet (an eighth-note triplet with the first two notes tied together). That practice adds an additional layer of polyrhythmic subdivision to the patterns typically stated or implied by the rhythm sections. Since it implies a basic subdivision into duple time, the straight eighth-note feel not only rests on top of, but pulls against, the jazz triplet implied by the drummer's ride cymbal figure (and against expectations that soloists might be expected to employ jazz triplets as their basic rhythmic unit). The resulting tension and uncertainty gives the soloist plenty of room for "playful ambiguity," as Paul Berliner points out in his discussion of jazz phrasing.[2] Thompson exploits the opportunity by placing emphasis on what were once strong beats (for instance, the first beat of four eighth notes) rather than weak beats without sounding blandly obvious—contributing to the counterintuitive style musicians refer to.

Thompson's use of the straight eighth-note feel is not unique. Many of his contemporaries used it.[3] What makes Thompson special is that his approach to it is dynamic: it is a central part of his expressive technique. He tends to shift from jazz triplets to straight eighths within a single phrase, gradually accenting eighth notes more forcefully and more evenly, creating a subtle sense of pushing ahead of the beat. Thompson builds tension in this way toward the middle or the end of a phrase, and over the course of a whole solo, which may also enhance the "backward" sense his phrasing creates. I shall designate this subtle push ahead into the straight eighth-note feel, and the increase in rhythmic tension that it creates, as a "time crescendo" (the corresponding relaxation of tension would be a "time decrescendo").

To explore why Thompson's phrasing is effective, I shall begin by examining the backdrop for his rhythmic dynamics. I shall survey the layers of pulse or basic rhythmic figures used by rhythm sections that accompanied him, providing him a backdrop against which to generate his own style of accents. This survey will help explain the dynamics of the straight eighth-note feel: how it evolved as a natural extension of existing patterns of polyrhythms and accents, and where its provocative tension comes from. I shall then examine how Thompson implies the straight eighth-note feel and builds time crescendos through patterns of accents in typical rhythmic and melodic motifs. Finally, I shall analyze how he structures an entire solo by developing these key motifs into larger phrases and complementing the underlying harmonic structure of the song.

Thompson's other remarkable qualities—his melodic subtlety and flexibility, and his unusual choice of scalar and chromatic passing notes—are evident in the selection I have transcribed, "Mr. E-Z," from his *Accent on Tenor* of 1954.[4] Within the scope of this article, however, I shall be able to deal with them only insofar as they relate directly to his phrasing and articulation. My conclusion will suggest the applications of the insights gained from Thompson's work in further studies of rhythmic dynamics in jazz improvisation. Before the analysis of his work, let us turn to a brief summary of Thompson's unusual career.

BIOGRAPHICAL NOTE:
A BRILLIANT AND OBSCURE CAREER

Thompson remains an invisible man—often present, yet never truly seen. He has rarely received extended discussion in histories of jazz or been mentioned in lists of great or influential horn players.[5] The caption to Thompson's picture in *The Pictorial History of Jazz* comments cryptically that his sound was "not exactly in the Hawkins or the Young 'school' of tenor sax," leaving readers to wonder what it was he really did sound like.[6] Even those who would gain directly from Thompson's music do not seem to really know him. The cover of a recent Thompson CD titled *Good Luck in Paris 1956* presents us with a photograph of Don Byas.[7] Why is it so hard to fix Lucky Thompson in our view?

Thompson was indeed hard to pin down stylistically, even physically. Born on June 16, 1924, he had a career that spanned from the end of the Swing Era to hard bop and electric music (i.e., from 1942 to 1974) and jumped between many cities. Though his approach to the saxophone became a little more understated over the years, he kept the resonant tone and richly modulated phrasing (particularly on ballads) of idols who led the 52nd Street small bands during Thompson's formative years: Coleman Hawkins, Don Byas, and Ben Webster. Yet Thompson was closer in age and social milieu to Parker and Dizzy Gillespie and had the technical facility and harmonic sophistication to fit well in their combos. Toward the 1960s, Thompson made a conscious effort to absorb the music of Coltrane, particularly his "Giant Steps" period—an effort that showed in his compositions, in his ability to negotiate the frequent modulations and complex chord substitutions of that style, and in his use of intervals of a 4th or 5th as basic melodic units.

Coupled with his high artistic reach was Thompson's refusal to make concessions to entertainment. A former owner of the Half Note, Sonny Cantorini, remembered back-to-back engagements with Thompson and Sonny Stitt.[8] He said that the latter (no slouch as a musician) was a far greater crowd pleaser, with his one-note choruses and endless turnaround tag lines. Thompson's playing combines full tone and technical facility, swing's romanticism and bebop's melodic density, the sensual and the cerebral. It is a strong mix, and perhaps not to every listener's taste.

Thompson was known to be as uncompromising professionally as he was artistically. He clearly maintained the respect of leading musicians. He made important recordings with Parker, Benny Carter, and Dinah Washington in the 1940s, with Miles Davis, Stan Kenton, Milt Jackson, and Oscar Pettiford in the 50s, and later with Hank Jones, Tommy Flanagan, Cedar Walton, and Billy Higgins (the latter were all sidemen on his few but superb recording dates) during the 1960s. But Thompson also made important enemies on the business side of the music industry through a tendency to speak the unvarnished truth. He never chose to stay in one place for long, moving between his native Detroit to New York, Los Angeles, and Paris a number of times, and then finally to Georgia and Seattle during his inactive period. Further signs of professional restlessness and stubborn independence were Thompson's venture into music publishing during the early 1950s (he hoped to give a boost to compositions he thought were being outflanked by commercial hacks) and study of classical composition at the Paris Conservatory in 1956 (he felt tired of purveying what he saw as mere entertainment and wanted to push his technical mastery even further). Profoundly discouraged with the music business, he retired from it in 1974.

Thompson left a legacy of fine recordings, but no "school." That is perhaps one reason he seldom appears in overviews of jazz history. His style cannot be readily codified, elevated into a method, and taught later, as Parker's arpeggios or Coltrane's modal substitutions have been (Thompson did share Parker's and Coltrane's intense study and practice habits). Like Sonny Rollins, Thompson worked intuitively and spontaneously, using characteristic motifs but no elaborately worked out patterns or choruses. To say that an artist tends to be idiosyncratic, however, does not mean he is not susceptible to analysis. His distinctive approach to rhythm, and to working with the rhythm section, makes a tantalizing target.

BACKGROUND TO THOMPSON'S STYLE: DIGGING THE POLYRHYTHMIC LAYERS

As jazz grew, each cohort of musicians found new ways to subdivide the basic beat and new opportunities to create surprising yet compelling accents.

As each rhythmic innovation became hip, it gained the aura of inevitability, rhythm sections and soloists made it standard practice, and, in turn, the expectations of the listening and performing community were set. As each innovation thus became convention, the next generation sought new rhythmic challenges, expanding the polyrhythmic strata still further. By the time Thompson made his first important recordings, immediately after World War II, soloists, rhythm sections, and listeners had internalized this complex rhythmic culture and understood it tacitly in any given performance.

To fully understand the rhythmic possibilities Thompson made use of, then, it will be helpful to separate the layers of this polyrhythmic structure and then reconstruct them schematically. I shall analyze the divisions and subdivisions of the basic pulse that would be stated or implied by Thompson's accompaniment and that the soloist would be expected to follow and build upon. Then it will be possible to explain why soloists like Thompson began to use the straight eighth-note feel, and how its peculiar energy and tension are derived. This highly simplified schematic account fast-forwards through a great deal of jazz history and corresponding rhythmic subtlety to get to the key point. Nevertheless each layer, however simple, will be a vital reference point for tracking Thompson's rhythmic dynamics.

Let us begin in 4/4. When listening to or counting four beats to a measure alone, with no accents or subdivisions, the ear will tend to hear 1 and 3 as strong beats (Example 1). Accents are shown in brackets, because this emphasis is perceived rather than played. It is a habit of Western listeners to group in twos, or to perceive what comes first as having the greatest emphasis, and therefore they tend to perceive 1 and 3 as strong beats. It will be important to bear this perception in mind, however, during the investigation of Thompson's use of straight eighth notes later in this article.

Example 1

If the basic pulse is 4/4, with 1 and 3 felt as strong beats, then the upbeats, beats 2 and 4, would be perceived as weak. Accenting them would create the desired element of rhythmic surprise. Example 2 shows these accents added to the 4/4 pulse. The accents could be created by simply adding a new layer of notes played on 2 and 4, by playing louder on 2 and 4, or both. Example 2, then, could represent the drummer's bass drum on the lower line and cymbal or snare on the higher line, but these accents could also be implied in a single line through dynamics. I shall refer to accents created by increased volume as "dynamic accents" throughout: this is the main type of accent Thompson uses, except where noted.[9]

Example 2

The soloist, adding his or her own layer to the rhythm section's, can accent not only beats 2 and 4 but the eighth-note upbeats of any beat in the measure in various combinations. They could also tie weak beats together with strong beats, creating syncopation. Despite the introduction of accents on 2 and 4, note that an underlying feeling of a strong four-beat pulse remains (as Example 2 indicates). Otherwise simply accenting the upbeats would create a jerky "oom-pah" feel, and even ragtime music avoided it. At this basic level, then, the superimposed rhythmic currents provide enough material to suggest the coordinated motion of dance—to swing.

The next rhythmic layer to take into account subdivides the basic 4/4 pulse further into units of three (Example 3). This is the jazz triplet: eighth-note triplets with the first two tied together and the last remaining as a separately articulated beat. The jazz triplet was a standard part of the basic pulse that rhythm sections used to accompany soloists by the end of the Swing Era, and the basis for the eighth-note phrases soloists used. At this point it is possible to speak of polyrhythms—that is, subdivisions of the basic pulse into different multiples, such as 2 and 3.

Example 3

A particularly common rhythm section figure was based on a quarter note alternating with a jazz triplet (Example 4), which drummers used to accompany soloists. Note that the two more basic layers are still stated or implied: the basic 4/4 pulse is sounded in the quarter notes played on each beat (and are also generally stated by the bass and guitar). In addition, the drummer places a dynamic accent on the second and fourth quarter notes of the figure, as shown in Example 4. Count Basie's drummer Jo Jones built his signature beat on this figure, playing it on his hi-hat cymbal continuously as he accompanied soloists. As bebop emerged, the figure became an accepted practice and thus the expected baseline for the soloist.

Example 4

THOMPSON'S FEELING:
THE STRAIGHT EIGHTH-NOTE SERIES

That expectation, in turn, creates a new opportunity for polyrhythmic innovation that is essential for understanding Thompson's contribution to jazz phrasing. Why not begin to accent the last eighth note of the jazz triplet figure, as in Example 5? The last eighth note would be the weak beat in this series. The quarter notes are stronger, because of the underlying pulse in four beats. The second and fourth beats are the strongest, owing to the drummer's dynamic accents on them. Accenting the last eighth note in the eighth-note triplet would therefore counter the listener's expectations at this level. This shift in accent, however, nearly undermines the jazz triplet feel itself.

Example 5

Accenting the last eighth note in the jazz triplet figure, through extra volume and percussive attack, tends to push it slightly ahead of the beat (or the listener perceives it that way by virtue of its extra emphasis). It should therefore be thought of as a combination of durational accent and dynamic accent: the single eighth-note triplet becomes longer as well as louder. Note, however, that this change in duration makes the notes more even (it is still an accent because it counters expectations of the jazz triplet feel). The more this eighth note is pushed ahead, the closer it seems to revert to a simple series of eighth notes—the most basic and obvious subdivision of the original underlying 4/4 time (Example 6). The shift in emphasis is subtle: there is actually only a sixth of a beat of difference between Example 5 and Example 6 (i.e., the second straight eighth note of any two in a series is only a sixth of a beat ahead of the last eighth note in the jazz triplet figure). This push ahead was precisely what the first bebop drummers like Kenny Clarke and Max Roach began to suggest in their rides (now on a suspended cymbal, rather than the hi-hat Jones used). Younger drummers such as Connie Kay and Billy Higgins (both protégés of Clarke's) incorporated a more even eighth-note feel into their trademark ride cymbal sound, so that it was close to Example 7. Bebop saxophonists like Dexter Gordon and Thompson were also using it by the late 1940s.

Example 6

Example 7

In the context of the standard jazz triplet feel in the rhythm section, the soloist's use of the straight eighth-note feel has a special tension and uncertainty. As noted above, the straight eighth-note feel originates when the soloist emphasizes the upbeat, or every second note in a series of eight eighth notes, thus stressing a weak beat. Yet as the eighth notes become more equal, it is harder for the listener to tell which ones are weak beats or strong beats in the first place. In fact, it becomes harder and harder to tell where any phrase falls with regard to the underlying beat and to stay oriented to that basic pulse.

Say for example that the soloist starts a phrase on a weak beat. That weak beat may be perceived as a strong beat within the context of the phrase. The listener will follow the soloist and tend to hear the even eighth notes in this phrase in groups of four starting at that point. Recall from the discussion of Example 1 that, in a series of eighth notes of equal duration in 4/4 time, there is a natural tendency for the listener to hear the main emphasis falling on the first beat of any series (or on every other eighth note beginning with the first) and to group the notes into divisions of two and four. This choice of starting points would affect the harmonic and melodic structure, of course. What might have been a leading tone, falling on an upbeat, and anticipating a strong chord note on the next downbeat, might now be perceived as receiving the most emphasis, creating a sense of instability in the phrase that would not be there otherwise.

Examples 8 and 9 show highly simplified and schematic versions of such phrases. Actual jazz phrases would be far more irregular in length and placement. In these hypothetical examples a pattern is created that, once set in motion, will never resolve itself with the underlying bar divisions in 4/4. Overlapping groups of four started on different beats will never mesh again (for example if the patterns in Examples 8 and 9 were extended indefinitely). A series of straight eighth notes started on a weak beat is unlike a hemiola, in which groups of three superimposed on a 4/4 meter will eventually resolve back to the downbeat of the measure after four measures. Resolution comes only when the soloist simply ends the phrase and allows the underlying pulse, or ride, to become established again.[10]

Example 8

Example 9

Since the soloist is pushing ahead of, and against, the standard jazz triplet feel of the drummer's ride, it is harder to use that as a reference. Seasoned listeners retain a sense of grounding in the basic time. But as they follow the soloist along with it, they have fewer cues to signal what beat a phrase begins and ends on or where the soloist is in the measure at any given point—at least maintaining their orientation takes more concentration. The listeners are challenged, in other words, to follow the soloist away from familiar signposts and are rewarded when the tension is resolved.

On the other hand, there is little danger, given the polyrhythmic context, that a series of straight eighth notes will convey a sterile uniformity or a mechanical lock into duple time. Recall that the rhythm section is implying not only a steady four but a steady two—enough to break up the uniformity of the eighth-note series in itself—not to mention triple time as well in the drummer's ride cymbal. (Another factor that prevents any stasis or mechanical quality is that Thompson allows his phrases to breathe by moving in and out of straight eighths, as I shall try to demonstrate later in the article.) The subtle destabilization of the listener's expectations and corresponding possibility of a rebalance of the interlocking metric divisions are keys to Thompson's unusual mode of placing accents. They make it possible for him to accent beats that might be expected to be strong, and still to maintain the sense of dynamism and forward motion to swing. Let us turn from analytical sketches to Thompson's actual practices.

THOMPSON'S RHYTHMIC DYNAMICS: THE TIME CRESCENDO

The smallest, most basic rhythmic unit Thompson uses is shown in Example 10 with his characteristic accents indicated. He tends to place a strong dynamic accent on the first and third eighth notes of a four-note series. But he also clips the second and fourth eighth notes, making these too stand out. Though clipped, the second and fourth eighth notes occupy more space than the expected single eighth-note triplet, and so they qualify as a durational accent. This jagged phrasing creates the perception that no eighth note has more emphasis than any other and that they are all even in duration—i.e., straight. Thompson may also place dynamic accents on any two consecutive eighth notes in a series, to merely imply the straight eighth-note feel within a shorter sequence of notes.

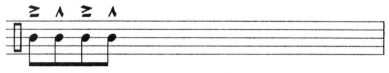

Example 10

Example 11 shows how this unit typically fits into a larger phrase. Thompson tends to move toward straight eighths in the second half of a bar of eighth notes. He often accents the fourth eighth note as strongly as the fifth, anticipating the straight eighth-note feel in the second half of the phrase. In addition, he introduces the straight eighth-note feel in tandem with a slight increase in volume and in pitch (i.e., in the general pitch direction of the phrase, since individual pitches may vary).

Example 11

Again, I shall refer to this characteristic increase in intensity as a "time crescendo." Because "crescendo" literally means "growing," the term is apt here: tension grows as Thompson multiplies accents and pushes the time feel ahead. The term "crescendo" also holds in its standard musical sense, because in Thompson's hands the surge of dynamic accents is often accompanied by an increase in overall volume in that part of the phrase. In phrases where Thompson uses the time crescendo, the most intense elements—harmonic and melodic as well as rhythmic—occur around the middle or toward the end of the phrase. This practice requires more skill of the performer, and more concentration of the listener, than placing the elements of most intense interest at the very beginning or very end of a phrase. His phrases tend toward an arched shape, with the greatest intensity and highest pitch near the middle of the phrase (one more factor in the perception that Thompson's phrases are "backward"). Thompson will also use the time crescendo in the second bar rather than the first, or introduce it in a four-bar phrase and then intensify it in a second four-bar phrase. In fact, he uses it more and more frequently over the course of a solo. The effect of this controlled use of the time crescendo is to lend a sense of rising energy and forward motion to the solo as a whole, and it becomes a crucial element in its structure.

One of Thompson's typical phrases with a time crescendo can be heard on a 1949 recording with Parker of the latter's "Cheryl" (Example 12).[11] The phrase exemplifies Thompson's "backward" phrasing, with its surprising accents and harmonic elements that enhance their effect. Thompson plays it on the first bar of the second chorus of a 12-bar blues. The eighth notes are straight, and are more heavily accented toward the end of the

Example 12: Excerpt from Lucky Thompson's "Cheryl" solo (3rd chorus, 1st 2 bars)

phrase — a time crescendo. The general pitch direction is upward, intensifying the arc of the crescendo. Thompson also uses pitch to intensify the sense of irregular and unstable accents.

The phrase outlines a D-major 7 arpeggio in its first half, then implies a D-flat 7 to resolve back to D major in the next bar. Passing tones, which conventionally would anticipate chord tones that fall on strong beats, occur here on strong beats, whereas the chord tones appear on weak beats. The passing tones also become harmonically more and more tense or remote from the tonic chord as the phrase progresses. After stating the leading tone, C♯, on beat 1, the downbeat of the measure, Thompson follows with the tonic on a weak beat, the upbeat of beat 1. The major third and fifth occur on relatively weak beats: that is, on beat 2 and the upbeat of beat 2. The leading tone, C♯, appears again as the major seventh of the chord on beat 3, one of the strongest beats in the measure, with the ninth of the chord falling on the next eighth note. Then, forming a rather tense interval relative to the D-major arpeggio, a C♮ falls on beat 4. (Although the C♮ is the minor seventh of the tonic chord, D, it functions as the thirteenth of the resolving minor second chord, E flat). The phrase culminates in a minor second on the final eighth note, completing the minor second chord resolution to the tonic D-natural in the next measure. Distinctive as it is, Thompson uses this exact figure in other solos, a fact that suggests the figure is central to his approach and had become second nature.[12]

Thompson does not use time crescendo figures such as the one in Example 12 immediately or constantly in any given solo. He holds the latent possibilities for creative tension in reserve to build interest and structure the solo. For example, in one of his longest and best-known recorded solos, on "Walkin'" with Miles Davis (1954), he does not introduce the straight eighth-note feel until the sixth bar of the second chorus of this 12-bar blues (Example 13).[13] Accent marks indicate the time crescendo. Thompson has used jazz triplets or 16th notes up to this point in the solo. The phrase with the time crescendo is also novel in that it is the first stock blues phrase after almost wholly diatonic or chromatic melodic material earlier; he returns to the latter in bar 8. Only four eighth

Example 13: Excerpt from Lucky Thompson's "Walkin'" solo (2nd chorus)

notes long, the phrase in bar 6 foreshadows the extensive use of the straight eighth feel coupled with blues clichés later on, beginning in the fifth chorus.

Parker, possessed of an impeccable sense of time, does not use timing in the same way as Thompson. Parker accents unexpected beats, of course. But he does not push groups of notes or phrases ahead nor pile up consecutive accents to intensify phrases, as Thompson's time crescendos do. Example 14 is a chorus from the same recording of "Cheryl" as the one excerpted in Example 12. Parker's accents vary practically from beat to beat, not across whole phrases. Parker consistently uses the jazz triplet figure, not the straight eighth-note feel Thompson achieves by steadily accenting consecutive beats. Parker tends to combine dynamic accents with contour accents: that is, he places the strongest attack on the highest pitch in that portion of the phrase.[14] That practice stands in contrast to Thompson's tendency to accent both passing tones and chord tones on consecutive weak and strong beats. Parker's pitches also tend to rise and fall steeply before and after his accents, creating fluid, waved contours that contrast with the more regularly arched shape and steadily rising intensity of Thompson's phrases. Moreover, Parker generally places a dynamic accent on the weak eighth notes in each bar: the upbeat of beats 1, 2, or 3, or the slightly stronger beats 2 or 4. (As the example indicates, Parker does alternate these with accents on strong beats, such as 1 or 3, to create further interest and variation.) Thompson's rhythmic materials, therefore, are quite distinct from those of the phenomenally influential Parker. Let us examine how Thompson develops them in the course of an entire solo.

Example 14: Excerpt from Lucky Thompson's "Cheryl" solo (1st chorus)

"MR. E-Z": ANALYSIS OF A THOMPSON SOLO

I have deliberately chosen a solo of modest scope, played over a simple set of chord changes at a moderate tempo, in order to focus on the subtle dynamics of Thompson's phrasing. The chord sequence is a variation on "Mean to Me," a familiar 32-bar, AABA-form standard tune. Its medium tempo makes it relatively easy to hear both the underlying beat of the rhythm section and the expressive variations and accents Thompson supplies. Thompson phrases mostly in eighth notes on this recording, not in the intricate, double-time passages or broken, heterogeneous melodic units he often used in other solos. Perhaps the title, "Mr. E-Z," reflects a conscious intent on the part of the tune's composer, clarinetist Jimmy Hamilton, to convey relaxation and directness.

Thompson's comfort with this rhythm section, which includes pianist Billy Taylor, bassist Wendell Marshall, guitarist Sonny Gross, and drummer Osie Johnson, belies his Swing Era roots. The rhythm section supplies a straightforward, unornamented pulse. Johnson uses a crisp, straight ride beat with standard jazz triplets, an ideal foil for Thompson's dynamic rhythmic approach. Brackets below the notes in the transcription highlight time crescendos. I have left out individual accents for reasons of space, but they follow the patterns outlined above for typical Thompson time crescendos. Their contours resemble those in the example from "Cheryl" discussed above: rising in pitch and attack toward the middle or end of a short phrase. Thompson introduces the time crescendo right away, but sparingly. The latent energy of the straight eighth-note feel is suggested but kept tightly controlled.

Example 15: Lucky Thompson's "Mr. E-Z" solo

The phrase structure in the initial 16 bars is very regular, further enhancing the effect of a calm, controlled exposition. In fact, the symmetry of Thompson's phrases in this section is quite elegant (a fact as clear to the eye regarding the transcription as it is to the ear). The phrases are two or four bars long. Their beginnings and endings conform to or complement the eight-bar divisions of the AABA chord structure. Thompson uses the time crescendo at a regular rate, though increasing it steadily: twice in the first A section of the chord progression, in bars 2 and 6, then four times in the next A section, in bars 10, 11, 13, and 16 (bar 10 is actually a special case, of which more shortly).

Thompson also builds symmetry by using the time crescendo in the same place in each of the phrases. In the first A section, he does so in the second measure of both of his four-bar phrases (i.e., bars 2 and 6). Note that the symmetry of the two phrases is enhanced by their complementary length and structure: the first rises in pitch, the second falls about the same distance, then ends only two beats later than the first, in effect answering it. Thompson leaves a measure of rest at the end of each of these phrases, furthering the highly economical tone at this point.

In the next A section, the tension rises slightly. Thompson begins to use the time crescendo more often, now once every two bars, and with more variation in each phrase.. The figures in bars 9 and 10 are quite similar. Thompson is answering himself again, though at a more frequent rate. The figure in bar 10 contains one extra note (leaving aside the grace note in bar 9). Otherwise it is a simple transposition up one chord tone within the diatonic scale. But in the "answer," he places a strong accent on the sole extra note, which falls on the upbeat of beat 2, and also accents the next eighth note. The second phrase thus expands the first slightly, by turning what was a grace note and a tied-over eighth into two strongly accented eighth notes and subtly implying the feeling of straight eighths—a time crescendo. Within this one short passage Thompson builds tension toward the later parts of the phrase, furnishing a compact example of his typical "backward" phrasing.

In the second eight-bar segment of the solo, the sense of symmetry starts to break down just as the number of time crescendos increases. The phrases in bars 13 and 14 also mirror the ones in bars 11 and 12 very closely. But the fulcrum of the symmetry is the bar line between bars 12 and 13, thus extending beyond the regular four-bar boundaries Thompson has stayed within so far. The length of the phrases has shifted from four, to one, to two bars in the course of the solo, leaving room for one unmatched phrase at the end, in bar 16 (with a pickup in bar 15). Strong symmetry, then, begins to give way to suggestive uncertainty and irregularity.

In the first part of the B, or release, section, there are two more time crescendos, also in the second bar of each of two two-bar phrases; that is, in bars 18 and 20. Note the striking use of unusual passing notes in these same bars.[15] Then something still more unexpected occurs. Time crescendos have been occurring roughly every two bars in this section and the last. But near the end of the release section in bar 22, Thompson uses a falling phrase that contrasts with the subtle push and upward arc of all of the time crescendos earlier. (It actually resembles one of Parker's phrases that tend to fall after the highest accented note.) In addition, Thompson actually lets the last three notes of the phrase fall behind the beat—a time decrescendo. The first of the laid-back notes also happens to fall on a tense chord tone: a C$\sharp$, which is an augmented 9th above the B-flat dominant 7 chord currently sounding (although it is the third of the next chord, an A dominant 7). Thompson thus suspends the expectation of rising pitch and rising rhythmic intensity he himself has created within the framework of the solo.

He makes this shift at what is arguably the most dramatic part of the underlying chord progression of the original tune itself. This is the point of the strongest feeling of harmonic cadence, where the release, or B section, of the AABA form, itself a device of contrast, begins to direct the ear back to the initial and familiar eight-bar chord sequence.[16] In bars 23 and 24, Thompson builds the drive to the cadence back to the tonic chord of the last A section further through both harmonic and rhythmic means. Bars 23 and 24 contain a phrase that arpeggiates the resolution to C major in descending chromatic chords.[17] Thompson also resumes the forward rhythmic motion with a time crescendo at this point: he places strong, even accents on the seventh and eighth eighth notes of bar 23 and on the first two eighth notes of bar 24.

After this climax, the final A section brings the denouement. The latent energy, having now been released, is rushing to spend itself. There are more time crescendos than in any other eight-bar section: in bars 25, 26, 28, 29, 31, and 32. The phrases in which they occur are now more complex, with 16th notes and 16th-note triplets added to the typical eighth notes, often toward the top of the arc of the time crescendo. The harmonic invention and use of technical facility have also become more intense, with chromatic arpeggios (bars 25, 26, 29, and 30), unusual passing tones (bars 27, 31, and 32), abrupt phrase endings (bar 27) and rapid, nearly ghosted passages (bars 25 and 26). The last phrase, in bars 31 and 32, contains Thompson's manner of controlling rhythmic tension and release in microcosm. It contains a typical time crescendo: arching upward, with tenser chromatics toward the top. The phrase comes to rest suddenly, and in perfect accord with the underlying harmony, on a figure outlining a descending C-major arpeggio, in bar 33, which begins the next chorus.

LOOKING FORWARD

Further work on phrasing and improvisation could make a more systematic comparison of Thompson's phrasing with that of other saxophonists, which was only implicit here. There is also ample room for study of the elements of phrasing and rhythmic dynamics of other saxophonists and other soloists on their own terms. I have tried to suggest the basic tools for such analysis. My approach has been to consider phrasing in a dynamic way, focusing on how it varies to help structure the motivic development of the whole solo and contributes to the artist's total range of expressive tools. I have also paid close attention to the rhythmic context in which the soloist performs — looking at attack and duration in reference to other musical elements — to the contributions of other musicians, and to expectations of group interaction surrounding any given performance.

In each study, the chief aims would be to look first for elements of rhythmic continuity and then identify the possibilities for expression and creativity in the ways the soloist complements or contrasts them. Critical factors are the basic time feel and rhythmic expectations the soloist establishes at the outset, the rhythmic pulse and accents supplied by the rhythm section, and the possibilities for tension in the interaction between them. After noting how the soloist uses these basic rhythmic materials, it will be possible to ask how he or she structures the solo as a whole, with reference to other musical elements that form that structure.

This approach could be applied in studies of rhythmic dynamics at different tempos. At the slowest tempos, there is far more freedom in articulation, and so it is difficult to measure or notate all of the rich elements the soloist might use. A fruitful compromise would be to start with slower medium tempos, in which the soloist's basic beat is clear but there is sufficient space on any given note for dynamic articulation. Saxophonists rooted in rhythm and blues, such as Arnett Cobb or Gene Ammons, are natural specialists in this area. Beboppers like Rollins or Hank Mobley also have a great deal to say at this tempo: they express themselves with timing without double-timing. On fast tempos, the challenge is that variations in attack and duration must give way to legato phrases of a generally consistent eighth-note feeling. Subtle shadings of timing are harder to detect, although series of notes may be played ahead or behind the beat. Players that retain a richly articulated phrasing at fast tempos, such as Cannonball Adderley and Johnny Griffin, would make a productive starting point. Soloists on other instruments with a robust approach to phrasing and time would provide equally fertile material (regardless of tempo): pianists Bud Powell and Tommy Flanagan, vibraphonist Milt Jackson, or trumpeters Kenny Dorham and Miles Davis, for example.

There are other significant areas of phrasing and rhythmic dynamics beyond articulation alone, and hence opportunities for more work examining their role in jazz improvisation. I have concentrated on the rhythmic subdivisions and accents within a phrase. Other work would study the rhythmic structure of whole phrases and their development throughout a given solo (I touched on the length, placement, and relationship of certain phrases Thompson's "Mr. E-Z" solo developed, though only in the context of the focus on accents and articulation). This rhythmic phrase building is a critical ordering principle in jazz solos, ignorance of which is one factor leaving new listeners with the impression that jazz is deliberately chaotic.

The approach I am suggesting would start by viewing a definite series of notes, most commonly eighth notes in mainstream jazz, as a key unit of thematic development of a solo. It would then examine each phrase's length, general pitch direction, and placement in the song form or chord structure, and then compare and contrast the phrases to discern what patterns are established over the course of the solo. As in the present study, harmony and basic rhythmic configurations would be relevant, but only insofar as they related to phrase building. This approach would in effect look at a horn or piano solo as a drum solo for the sake of a focus on the rhythmic aspects of melody (drummers can imply pitch variation through timbral effects available in their kit). Thomson would have much to offer the study of jazz improvisation in this realm as well.

Thompson the historic figure is as surprising and thought provoking as Thompson the saxophonist. A musician this hard to classify, straddling so much of jazz history, is bound to tell us something about that history. Thompson dipped into the same pool as Parker (the small bands of 52nd Street) and played with the same rhythm sections. Yet he came up with distinct rhythmic material. With lingering Swing Era influences, he was as advanced as Coltrane or Rollins in certain ways and fit easily with rhythm section players who backed them. Such artists call into question views of jazz that see it evolving in a linear fashion. In the latter view, the introduction of greater rhythmic and harmonic complexity or freedom, and the technical facility needed to handle them, allow the ascent toward some wholly new plateau of sophistication and modernity. If one takes that linear view of progress, one would naturally arrive at the conclusion, all too current, that there is nothing new to be done in jazz, because every creative freedom and technical advancement has itself already been tried. Individualists like Thompson, who stake out separate but equally valid currents alongside the canonical ones, remind us that techniques are simply tools, vast in their range and heterogeneity, and that their use is a matter of artistic choice and specific milieu, not historic inevitability. Thompson is alive, and the possibilities his music and his mastery pose are alive.

NOTES

1. Major recent works on the theory and practice of jazz improvisation emphasize the importance of the context of the solo performance—both the rhythmic foundation of the ensemble and the tacit expectations of listening community—as a framework or reference point for analyzing the possibilities for rhythmic variation and accents available to the jazz soloist. See Paul Berliner, *Thinking in Jazz* (Chicago: University of Chicago Press, 1994), 146–159; and Ingrid Monson, *Saying Something* (Chicago: University of Chicago Press, 1996), 26–72. Keith Waters, "Blurring the Barline: Metric Displacement in the Piano Solos of Herbie Hancock," *Annual Review of Jazz Studies* 8 (1996): 19–37, analyzes the range of rhythmic techniques soloists use in varying the underlying formal structure of the composition, and it includes a discussion of accents and their relationship to the meter or pulse.

2. Berliner, 148.

3. Dexter Gordon, another important early bebop tenor saxophonist, is a prime example. Gordon's fundamental eighth-note feel is quite even, but he uses it to build a hypnotic groove, and does not shift in and out of it the way Thompson does. Gordon also deliberately lets his eighth notes fall behind the beat. For an example, refer to "Three O'Clock in the Morning" on *Go* (Blue Note 84112). Sonny Rollins moves in and out of jazz triplets, straight eighth notes, and other rhythmic patterns with great facility. But, once again, the straight eighth-note feel is not his central thematic element. An example is "The Most Beautiful Girl in the World" on *Tenor Madness* (Prestige 7657). Coltrane sometimes used the straight eighth-note feel in his early period when not double-timing, for example on "You Say You Care," *Soultrane* (Prestige 7142), particularly the initial a cappella solo break. Soloists on other instruments used the straight eighth-note feel: for example, Clifford Brown uses it consistently throughout "Brownie Speaks," *The Clifford Brown Memorial Album* (Blue Note 1526).

4. Urania UJLP1206 (LP); Saga XIC4001 (CD). The transcription is the first whole chorus Thompson takes on this recording, though he exchanges 16 bars in a section that actually precedes his first full solo.

5. Biographical information here is drawn from Lars Bjorn and Jim Gallert, *Before Motown: A History of Jazz in Detroit, 1920–60* (Ann Arbor: University of Michigan Press, 2001); Scott Yanow, *Bebop* (San Francisco: Miller Freeman, 2000); Christopher Kuhl, "A Visit with Lucky Thompson," *New Arts Review* (December 1981): 13–16; Mark Gardner, "Lucky Thompson in the Sixties," *Coda* 9.1 (1969): 3–8; and private conversations with Benny Carter, Paul Jeffrey, Jamil Nasser, Randy Sandke, and Kenny Washington. Despite a mercurial career, Thompson made hundreds of recordings. See Yanow for a selected discography.

6. Orrin Keepnews and Bill Grauer, Jr., *A Pictorial History of Jazz: People and Places from New Orleans to Modern Jazz* (New York: Crown, 1966, 2nd

ed.), 244. Thompson, by his own account, was steeped in both of these masters' playing; so was Sonny Rollins, who sounded completely different. A thorough discussion of saxophonists who may have influenced Thompson deserves more extended treatment than is possible here. An extended comparison with selected contemporaries such as Rollins or Coltrane could also be fruitful.

7. EMI France, Jazz Time Collection 827217-2.

8. Recollection of a private conversation, 1993.

9. See Waters, p. 21, for a discussion of differing ways of implying accents. Along with the dynamic accent (created through variation in volume), he discusses the durational accent (a note that sounds or is played longer than others around it, also known as an agogic accent); the contour accent (pitches at the upper or lower end of a melodic phrase); and pattern-beginning accents (the beginning note of a repeated motif tends to imply or receive an accent).

10. See Waters, p. 22, for a discussion of grouping and meter.

11. Charlie Parker, *Live Broadcasts from the Royal Roost*, LP Savoy ZDS-4413/CD Nippon Columbia Savoy Box Set, disc 8.

12. For example, on "Translation" from *Tricrotism* (Impulse GRD 135).

13. Miles Davis, *Walkin'* (Prestige 7076).

14. See discussion of Waters in note 9.

15. Thompson's distinctive harmonic modulations and passing notes in this phrase should not go without a remark. The phrase in bar 18 outlines an E flat 7 #11, which resolves to D minor in bar 19. Then an F diminished with a major 7th resolves to the same D-minor chord in bar 21. As if that were not enough, the G# in the F-diminished chord would be expected to resolve to the A in the D-minor triad. Yet it is followed by a G♮, which with the preceding two notes outlines an E minor. The latter chord is comprehensible only as part of D Dorian mode, and its insertion creates a folkloric, modal segue, as opposed to a classically tonal resolution, to the D-minor key.

16. On bar 27 of the standard "Mean to Me," the C-minor concert gives way almost directly to the C-major concert—a use of mode mixture that is relatively rare in Tin Pan Alley tunes. Some of the resulting surprise in the original song is actually diluted here by the substitute changes. Hamilton uses an A flat 7 descending chromatically to F 7 in the corresponding passage.

17. This phrase is a favorite device of Thompson's, as well as of Hawkins, Byas, and Eddie "Lockjaw" Davis. Although the harmonic background is simply an ascending or descending chromatic series, Thompson picks only certain notes out of each succeeding chromatic chord, thus creating a rapid alternation of tense, wide intervals, with a hocketlike timbral effect, because the notes tend to fall in different registers of the saxophone.

AFTER THE MELODY:
PAUL BLEY AND JAZZ PIANO AFTER
ORNETTE COLEMAN

Norman Meehan

Born in Canada in 1932, Paul Bley began his musical studies at an early age and attended both the McGill and Quebec Conservatories. He moved to New York in 1950 to study composition at Juilliard School of Music and pursue his burgeoning career as a jazz pianist. After gigging, recording, and finally graduating in New York, he found his way to California, where he formed a quartet. In 1958, while leading his band at the Hillcrest Club in Los Angeles with Charlie Haden, Billy Higgins, and Dave Pike, Bley heard Ornette Coleman and Don Cherry play when they sat in with the group. His response was to fire Pike (vibraphone) and hire Coleman and Cherry. As a consequence of this decision, the Hillcrest Club engagement became "the beginning of avant-garde jazz in America" (Gioia 1992, 331). Bley was hugely influenced by his exposure to Coleman's unique approach to jazz improvisation, and it was this approach that predicated much of the music Bley subsequently made. He went on to perform and record with many other notable musicians, including Charles Mingus, George Russell, Albert Ayler, and John Gilmore. In 1961 he worked with bassist Steve Swallow in a trio led by Jimmy Giuffre. Giuffre's music, based on a contrapuntal conception and concerned primarily with the horizontal (linear) aspects of the music (to the extent that vertical considerations were at best secondary), proved a significant influence in Bley's career. During 1962 and 1963 Bley spent 12 months in the band of saxophonist Sonny Rollins. Although it is almost certain Bley learned many lessons during his tenure with Rollins, his style was well formed by the time of that engagement, and his mature work could reasonably be said to have begun around that time.

This article examines examples of the music that Bley has recorded from 1963 onward and considers the following questions: In Bley's improvisations, what constitutes the melodic vocabulary, in what ways is that vocabulary organized, and to what extent does it reflect the "jazz language"? Further, in what ways does Bley create coherence and continuity in his solos?

Although it is difficult to trace "influence" in an individual musician's style, the article draws parallels between Bley's mature style and that of the musician who seems to have been most significant in his development: Ornette Coleman. To this end, consideration is given to the aspects of Bley's playing that reflect Coleman's music, and examples of the most cogent aspects of any identifiable influence are documented.

As a pianist, Bley belongs to a tradition of performance altogether different from that of Coleman, a saxophonist. This difference not only has implications for how their respective recordings actually sound (they sound very different) but also determines many of the sources each draws upon when playing. The honks, squeals, and glissando effects that are ubiquitous in Coleman's playing are not available to pianists, just as polyphony or the playing of chords is not possible on a saxophone (beyond a few multiphonic effects that can approximate some chord sounds). In addition, there are distinct stylistic differences between these musicians; Coleman's recordings are often scattered and frenetic and can feel "emotionally charged," whereas Bley's recordings are generally spare and often feel more tranquil and "considered." Although it would be of great interest to examine the ways in which their respective recordings reflect the nature and limitations of the instrument on which each performs, or to consider the different aesthetic values that inform their individual styles, this article focuses instead on the musical materials that are common to both players. It is in this area that the greatest similarities between their improvisations are evident.

Some definitions are in order at this point. "Melodic vocabulary" will mean the organization of the pitch and rhythmic content of the improvised lines. At times "melodic vocabulary" will focus on the specific pitches contained in a phrase, and at times on the contour or motivic content of a phrase. The "jazz language" refers to the pitch content, rhythmic organization, phrasing, and articulation of melodies that together form the common musical vocabulary of performers in the jazz tradition. Direct reference is made to some musicians in the text along with examples of their art as it is relevant to Bley's music. It is not clear that Bley drew his inspiration from particular artists, but the text does identify some individuals whose music is representative of the milieu in which Bley is a practitioner.

METHODOLOGY

In selecting a method for the examination of Bley's music, one has to identify his music's principal components.

Commentators agree that the music Bley makes can be categorized as jazz, and Bley himself is unequivocal in describing it as such.[1] He states,

"All along I have accepted or discarded things on one critique—their va-
lidity as jazz" (Heckman 1964). He is quick also to acknowledge the cen-
trality of improvisation to that conception:

> There are differences between classical and jazz, and I love the differences be-
> cause they are exact opposites, polar opposites of each other. . . . The jazz
> world likes mistakes because you can hear the process and you can hear the
> musicians correcting. In the classical world there is a willingness to rehearse
> pieces until they are perfect. 'How do you get to Carnegie Hall? Practice!'
> That's not the way you get a jazz reputation. The more daring you are as an
> improviser, as a jazz musician, the more engaged the listener is. So it's a dif-
> ferent aesthetic. The whole idea of getting it right the first time is a "jazz aes-
> thetic."[2]

In addition to its place within the jazz tradition, Bley's music also
strongly reflects the influence of Coleman. Bley himself acknowledges this
debt and has said, "I like to think that I am an Ornette Coleman disciple,
having been there so early and being one of the early people to be at the piano chair in that environment."[3]

A third consideration in selecting analytical tools for the examination of
Bley's music is his thorough grounding in the traditions of Western art music during his studies at the Quebec and McGill conservatories and his composition studies with Henry Brant at Juilliard between 1950 and 1954.

In light of these disparate influences, the analytical tools chosen for this
article reflect, to some extent, the multifaceted nature of Bley's music.
These tools include: examination of thematic development, a technique
primarily associated with the analysis of compositions although also used
to examine improvised jazz performances;[4] consideration of motifs and
concatenations of motifs, a technique used in the examination of Coleman's
music;[5] and consideration of the ways Bley's performances reflect his roots
in the jazz milieu.

For this study a number of solos on "standard" tunes, with recognizable
melodies and chord progressions, were transcribed. The performances were
drawn from a 30-year period and are found on several commercially available recordings made between 1963 and 1993. Although there is evidence
of development in Bley's playing over that time, the similarities over that
period are striking, and the solos considered for this study are to some extent representative.[6]

Bley is particularly faithful to the essential metrical framework of the
pieces examined (32 measures or 36 measures). Consistent with his ap-
prenticeship under Coleman, however, Bley adopts a fairly free approach to

these pieces. He often pays little regard to the accepted chord changes of the tunes and instead allows his melodic line to determine its own path through the performances. In addition, Bley often disregards the melody of the tunes and begins with his own new melody. In conversation he has noted:

> My feeling these days is that if you can tell what song we are playing, we are not doing our job properly, even if you were a pianist sitting beside my left hand and were listening to a piece you have played for years. If at the end of the performance you say, "What was that piece?" then I have succeeded in really reworking the piece. I don't want to play every section as it was written; I am trying to change as much as possible. It's recomposition, essentially.[7]

Transcription and analysis of recordings Bley made prior to his experiences with Coleman reveal an altogether different pianist, one rooted in the conventions of bebop and playing improvised lines consonant with, or complementary to, the chord progressions.[8] Bley's solos from 1958 onwards exhibit a number of traits found in Coleman's improvisations, and so it is useful to begin by considering Coleman's melodic conception.

ORNETTE COLEMAN

Coleman's arrival on the jazz scene, and particularly his tenure at The Five Spot in 1959, was surrounded by controversy. Reactions ranged from adulation to disgust, and musicians as well as critics joined the debate. Criticism of Coleman sprang largely from his rejection of predetermined harmonic frameworks as a formative element in jazz performance and the basis for improvisation. In addition, an apparently lackluster technique and the use of tones outside the equally tempered scale added fuel to his detractors' accusations. Roy Eldridge stated, "He's putting everybody on. They start with a nice leadoff figure, but then they go off into outer space. They disregard the chords and they play odd numbers of bars. I can't follow them" (Hentoff 1976, 218). For his devotees however, Coleman's music heralded a new approach to jazz performance and the solution to a longstanding impasse in the evolution of jazz. Bley explained:

> You see, Ornette solved, in a single swoop, a problem that had been accumulating for ten years. . . . There was nothing left to play on songs . . . [they] had been worn out as a basis to play on. So what Ornette did was to say that after

the tune is over you only have to play on one of the centres of the tune. . . .
And by ignoring the deadlines at the end of the chorus lines, it opened up the
player to be able to breathe when he wanted, to think what he wanted to think,
and to pay as little or as much attention to the chord progression as he chose
(Klee and Smith 1974, 13).

Coleman's approach to improvisation during the late 1950s exhibited
several traits that were later to become defining characteristics. These signature features are found on his first two recordings for Contemporary and
his early recordings for Atlantic and were in evidence when Bley played
with him in 1958 (documented on *The Fabulous Paul Bley Quintet*, America AM 6120). The first, and perhaps most significant, of these distinguish-
ing features is the predominantly modal orientation (to the point of nursery
rhyme simplicity) of his playing, with the important caveat that the tonal
center of the improvisations shifted at the improviser's will. This shifting
contravened the "rule" of jazz improvising that declared that the harmony
of the tune should determine the direction of the solos. It also forced Bley
to reconsider his hypothesis regarding the possible origin of ideas leading
to a new direction for jazz:

We really thought that composition would point the way, because our jazz
experience—regardless of how any of us felt about the song form—had
taught us that the direction of the improvisation is described by the nature of
the written material. Suddenly it was clear that the improvisation could be
directed not by the nature of the composition, but by the nature of what the
premise is to improvise on (Bley and Lee 1999, 67).

Coleman's solos exhibited great melodic impetus, but the most startling
feature was the way in which that impetus determined shifts in tonality.
Ekkehardt Jost (1974) identified in Coleman's playing a new type of motivic improvisation, which he described as "motivic chain association."[9].
With this term Jost described the way in which Coleman developed themes
during his solos that were independent of the melody of the piece (and any
chord progression) and allowed their continuing evolution to direct his solos. Coleman's solo on "Chronology"(Figure 1) reveals this type of playing.[10] In this example, the melodic cells that form chains of associated motifs are bracketed to demonstrate this characteristic. Although motivic
development had been evident in the playing of Sonny Rollins some years
earlier, [11] Coleman was the first to allow the motifs forming the improvised
melodic line to stray from the chord progression of the tune and shape the
harmonic structure of the material.

Figure 1: Ornette Coleman solo: "Chronology"

Charlie Haden described this approach as "a constant modulation that was taken from the direction of the composition, and from the direction inside the musician, and from listening to each other" (Litweiler 1992, 148), although Jimmy Garrison's explanation is perhaps more helpful:

> I really had to study his theory, which is too long to go into here: but an integral part of it is that you take a note like C: C can be the tonic of C; it can be

the major third of A♭; it can be the fifth of F; it can be the ninth of B♭. Knowing that any note can be part of a whole spectrum of notes, you train yourself to think in that manner and as a result you come up with melodies you didn't know existed (Wilson 1999, 39).

With the introduction of this technique, Coleman signaled one of his major innovations—the primacy of melodic continuity over adherence to predetermined harmonic structures. This melodic conception of sequentially associated motifs can be identified throughout both Coleman's and Bley's solos, creating such a similarity between their work that critic Stanley Crouch observed, "Paul Bley is to Ornette Coleman what Bud Powell was to Charlie Parker" (quoted in Davis 2000).

PAUL BLEY

Harmonic Mobility

By 1958 Coleman had articulated his desire to move away from fixed chord changes and toward a spontaneously and collectively determined music. In the liner notes to his first album, *Something Else* (Contemporary, 1958, COP 024 [C3551]), he reports to Nat Hentoff, "I would prefer it if musicians would play my tunes with different changes as they take a new chorus so there'd be all the more variety in the performance."[12] Bley elaborated upon this point, noting:

> The idea is that you are going from point "A" to point "B," and it's totally up to you what you want to do in that interval, so long as you leave point "A" and you arrive at point "B." I call that "harmonic improvising." Improvising doesn't need to be confined to melodic and rhythmic improvising; why not include harmonic improvising? And if an idea occurs in an improvising context, it shouldn't happen again—it should only happen at that one point. That way it keeps its freshness and its surprise. You haven't reharmonized the piece; you have just improvised a harmonic innovation in a piece. That keeps it in the spirit of improvisation.[13]

This music, above all, celebrates the supremacy of the melodic line over the harmony. In his biography, Bley confessed to "never having been a lover of chords," adding, "I always thought that a chord was a vertical melody played simultaneously—if a chord couldn't be stripped down and each note made to line up to make a meaningful melody, it wasn't a good chord" (Bley and Lee 1999, 71). This statement perhaps reveals why he was so willing to embrace Coleman's approach and allow the improvised line such a defining role in his music.

This approach to improvising is perhaps the most striking feature of Bley's solos. Listeners accustomed to hearing more conventionally resolved harmonies are confused and sometimes shocked by the divergence that exists in this music between the harmonic progression (chord changes) and the improvised line. Henry Martin (1996) has observed, "Bop tunes will usually maintain harmonic and formal clarity in order to provide a solid large-scale basis for improvisation" (13), yet it is this very formative element that Bley (and Coleman before him) abandoned in their improvising. This type of playing, where the new melodies shift in and out of a number of clearly discernible tonal centers without settling into bitonality or polytonality (music simultaneously in two or more keys) could be described as "pantonal."[14] In Bley's solos this pantonality assumes several forms. The most common approach is to play a phrase in a tonality completely unrelated to the underlying chords. A very clear example of this approach is found in "All The Things You Are" (1963), measures 77–84, where a long phrase in D major is superimposed over essentially unrelated chords (see pp. 107–111). Bley sometimes begins lines that are consonant with the changes but continue in that tonality while the changes move on through their progression. The example in Figure 2 shows a long phrase (heard as a blues gesture) in F that remains in that tonality even after the chords have moved to a new tonal center (A♭). On occasion, Bley plays lines that anticipate approaching chords. Such lines begin "outside" of the chord changes but are resolved consonantly when the chords "catch up" with his line.

Figure 2: Harmonic mobility in "Long Ago and Far Away" (1993), mm. 133–39

Motivic Improvisation

Examination of Bley's solos reveals many instances of melodic motifs adjacent to identical, similar, or related melodic motifs. These concatenations, examples of motivic chain association, are present in a variety of forms and provide valu-

Melodic Device	Description
MCA pitch	adjacent motifs with similar pitch material (including transposition of ideas)
MCA contour	adjacent motifs with similar melodic contours
MCA rhythm	adjacent motifs with similar rhythmic content
MCA variation: initial	adjacent phrases that begin in a similar manner but then diverge
MCA variation: terminal	adjacent phrases that begin differently but converge to end in a similar manner
Repetition	adjacent motifs that are identical
Step Progression	fragmented melodic lines contained within a longer phrase

Figure 3: Melodic motif examples (note: MCA = motivic chain association)

able insights into understanding Bley's music. Categorized by Michael Cogswell (1995) in his article discussing Coleman, they are listed in Figure 3.

The categories MCA pitch, contour, and rhythm are not mutually exclusive; clearly chains that share pitch content will also have the same contour. In many cases the chains are combinations of two or all three categories.

Step Progressions are examples of audible, if sometimes fragmented, melodic lines contained within longer melodic phrases. Generally these embedded lines follow a scale upwards or downwards, and the pitches are emphasized by their placement in the local melodic contour or by being accented. Figure 4 shows a step progression from Bley's solo on "All the Things You Are" (1993). Pitches that make up the embedded line are linked with slurs.

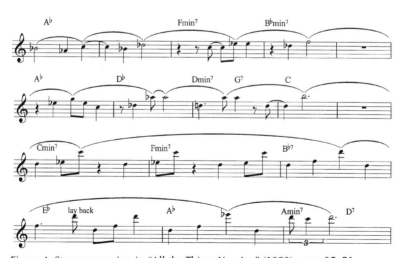

Figure 4: Step progression in "All the Things You Are" (1993), mm. 35–51

All of the devices listed in Figure 3 were used repeatedly throughout the sample considered and create melodic cohesion throughout the solos. The aesthetic imperatives that are in play with each performance determine the degree to which particular devices are used. For example, in the mid-1980s Bley had only recently returned to playing standards,[15] and the novelty of that return, coupled with the more "romantic" tenor found in his approach at that time, meant that overall the solos from that period were less chromatic and more tonally resolved than those recorded 20 years earlier or 10 years later. A contrasting approach is evident in the earlier solos (from the early 1960s) when Bley was a recent convert to the free jazz movement and chromatic content was present to a greater degree. All of the transcriptions, however, revealed these melodic devices in use, and in performance they flow seamlessly into one another. Analysis of Coleman's improvised solos has led researchers to comment on a similar continuity, one observing that "almost without exception, every motive is related to the preceding as well as to the succeeding motive" (Cogswell, 1995, 115). The same can certainly be said of these solos by Bley, and it is melodic continuity that distinguishes his improvised performances from those of many others at the "freer" end of the jazz spectrum. To a very large extent the coherence of these solos is attributable to the way chains of related melodic material form a more or less continuous thread through each performance. Considering the degree to which Bley played ideas tonally "at odds" with the chord changes, such melodic coherence is surprising. For example, in the 1963 recording of "All the Things You Are," 58 of the 109 measures transcribed are dissonant with the chord progression; in a 1993 recording of "Long Ago and Far Away," 86 of the 242 measures transcribed are dissonant with the changes.[16]

Clearly each chain of associated motifs flows together to create melodic continuity. In addition, Bley frequently segues smoothly from one chain of ideas to the next, using melodic elision to do so. Very clear examples of this are evident in all of the solos considered, and obvious instances in "All the Things You Are" (1963) are found in measures 12–13, 25–27, 34–35, 37–39, 44–45, 53–55, 65–68, and 100–102.

A particularly musical example of such melodic elision is found at the beginning of this solo, where Bley's first phrase duplicates and then develops the phrase Coleman Hawkins had played to end his solo. This kind of communication between the musicians is common in Bley's work and reflects both his musicianship and the communal values in his art:[17]

There's no need to bring your own set of inspiration to the bandstand if you are playing with geniuses. It's already going to be inspired; you just have to listen. To be able to pick up on somebody else's idea and further elaborate it is an added finesse. If I play what the other musicians played and add to it, continuing the ideas, that's an extra skill. I am not just bringing my own particular universe to [a] recording; I am taking [a] universe and adding to it, instructing it. I can play [their] ideas and squeeze them together more or stretch them out more. I can continue the process.[18]

In most cases the melodic chains indicated employ very similar rhythms, and so the transcription refers primarily to the pitch or contour relationships. In a few cases the MCA rhythm category is identified in conjunction with pitch or contour constructions. In these cases the pitch or contour is somewhat ambiguous, and the rhythmic similarities (or differences) between the fragments contributes to the unity of the passage. A good example of rhythm contributing to unity between adjacent passages is found in Figure 5. In this example Bley plays four rhythmically identical figures consecutively, but the melodic fragment is reversed (retrograde) partway through the phrase. The retrograde phrase creates a discontinuous melodic contour but does not compromise the unity of the phrase. Rhythm is also used to great dramatic effect when phrases with similar pitch and rhythmic content are displaced with respect to the beat, as shown in Figure 6. On occasion, displacement combined

Figure 5: Rhythmic unity in "All the Things You Are" (1993), mm. 128–31

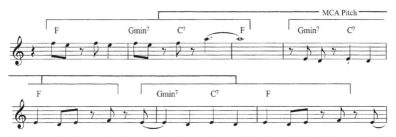

Figure 6: Rhythmic displacement in "Long Ago and Far Away" (1985), mm. 49–55

with variance of the pulse is used to such good effect that very similar motifs become (superficially, at least) almost unrecognizable, while still conveying a *sense* of thematic unity. Rhythmic variance (diminution and elongation, for example) is also used to introduce subtle differences between similar motifs.

Step Progressions appear a number of times throughout the sample, most commonly moving in a scalar manner. The whole-tone scale forms the template of the step progression in measures 37–40 of "All the Things You Are" (1963), whereas diatonic compliance with the major scale (E♭) is the organizing principle of the step progression shown in Figure 7. Some of these embedded progressions hover in a local and harmonically ambiguous area; others are organized chromatically. One progression of particular interest is that found during "All the Things You Are" (1963) in measures 55–60, where the entire line is a sequence of principally triadic structures whose roots move through a modified E Mixolydian scale. The harmonically disorienting effect of the major, minor, and suspended triads is offset by the tonality implied by the root progression—E Mixolydian—the scale generated by the chord that would normally appear at the end of the bridge (measure 59).

Figure 7: Step progression in "All the Things You Are" (1993), mm. 1–16

Freedom within the Jazz Ensemble

The harmonic mobility Bley was employing, along with the rhythmic freedom and nuance he brought to the music (by playing well behind the beat or pushing and pulling the phrases in the time, for example), required the bassists and drummers he worked with to engage in the same kind of musical dialogue that Coleman's ensemble had pioneered in the 1950s.

Because the soloist now determined the harmonic and rhythmic direction of a piece, it became imperative that the other musicians hear that new (and evolving) direction and respond to it. It became necessary for bassists (and any other players who accompanied harmonically) to follow the direction of the soloists, responding to their lead. That response could be to accommodate or contrast a harmonic change implied by the soloist or to initiate a new harmonic direction of their own. The point of the music making had become interaction among the players and collective responsibility for the direction of the performance. This was a move away from the primacy of the soloist, a stylistic trait of bebop and postbebop jazz. As a consequence, bassists (and any chordal instrument players) had to engage with the music rather more actively than they had previously.[19]

This change liberated these instruments from their more traditionally accepted roles and allowed the introduction of great variety in the accompaniment they provided. This emancipation of the traditional hierarchies in the jazz ensemble can be heard to good effect on the recordings considered in this study, where Bley, bassists Peacock, Lundegaard, and Johnson, and drummers Motian, Higgins, and Naussbaum weave in and around one another's lines, troubling the underlying pulse of the tunes and generally exhibiting a very robust harmonic conception. The debt to Coleman is clear, and the group interplay of these recordings is strongly reminiscent of Coleman's quartet recordings for the Atlantic label.[20]

Although this approach to melodic improvising and interaction within the jazz ensemble was an advance on previous models, the pitch material both Bley and Coleman used to create their phrases was quite conservative and closely related to the melodic language of jazz at the time.

Continuity with the Jazz Tradition

Despite Bley's move away from the dominant paradigm of jazz improvisation, a move that correlates to Coleman's radical advances, he, like Coleman, did not abandon the jazz vocabulary. Both musicians play phrases that are clearly located within the jazz tradition, employing blues phrases, harmonic devices common to jazz (flatted 3rds and 5ths against dominant chords, common substitutions), and phrasing and articulation consistent with that of the Louis Armstrong–Lester Young–Charlie Parker continuum.[21] Bley's playing exhibits continued use of many of the devices (common among jazz musicians) that he himself employed during the 1950s before his exposure to Coleman. Examples of blues phrases, bebop lines, sequences, enclosure phrases, chord spelling, and common substitutions can be found to varying degrees throughout the solos considered. Their collective effect is to help the music retain its "jazz identity," and coupled with Bley's secure swing feel and phrasing, they locate this music very firmly in the jazz tradition. Bley himself has said, "[W]e were actively trying to figure out what we could play that would take us into new territory, yet still make us feel like jazz musicians. . . . these were the criteria, all based on a traditional jazz aesthetic" (Bley and Lee 1999, 87). Consequently, the chains of associated ideas played by both Bley and Coleman often resemble the lines played by jazz musicians working closer to the tradition.

Examples of simple diatonic passages that include chord spelling and scalelike lines are very common in the sample examined, and Figure 8 reveals both in a single passage.

Figure 8: Scalar lines and some chord spelling in "Long Ago and Far Away" (1993), mm. 51–61

Bley also regularly employs blues phrases, and his fondness for both the sound of the blues and the blues form itself is evident from his earliest recordings.[22] In the solos considered, blues fragments appear frequently, and an excellent example is shown in Figure 9. This phrase would sound equally appropriate in a Parker or Young blues improvisation.

Figure 9: Blues phrase in "Long Ago and Far Away" (1993), mm. 95–100

Bley also made use of the whole-tone scale, another staple of the jazz vocabulary. Among jazz improvisers the champion of this hexatonic scale was Thelonious Monk, who made frequent use of it both in his compositions and in his improvised solos. Improvisers generally employ this sound against augmented triads and seventh chords, but Bley is more catholic in his choice of contexts for the scale. A clear example is shown in Figure 10. Another example of the whole-tone scale in Bley's playing can be found in "All the Things You Are" (1963), measures 37–38.

Figure 10: Whole-tone scale in "All the Things You Are" (1993), mm. 60–63

Enclosure phrases, sometimes referred to as those embellished by upper and lower neighbor tones, have been a part of the jazz argot since Armstrong began recording. Many jazz improvisers have used this type of melodic embellishment during the past 70 years, and one of the performers most proficient in their use was hard bop trumpeter Clifford Brown. Bley's use of an enclosure phrase in Figure 11 is typical of his use of this particular melodic embellishment.

Figure 11: Enclosure phrase in "Long Ago and Far Away" (1993), mm. 45–48

Bley's use of altered dominant sounds, such as flatted 9th tones against dominant seventh chords, or the Superlocrian scale for more dissonant effect, also reveals his jazz heritage.[23] In many places the use of chromatic passing tones gives his lines a jazz flavor, and in places the Superlocrian scale is used in its entirety. Figure 12 contains a clear example.

Figure 12: Superlocrian phrase in "All the Things You Are" (1993), mm. 89–91

Bley also makes regular use of the diminished scale, both to create a diminished tonic sound and to suggest an altered dominant (flatted 9th) tonality.

These passages are often brief, comprising four or five notes, but in places, such as in Figure 13, they extend over a number of measures.

Figure 13: Diminished phrase in "All the Things You Are" (1993), mm. 122–28

Considering Bley's determination to make music that was part of the jazz tradition, it is not surprising that he puts many of these devices together to create lines that sound entirely consistent with the style of jazz he played during his formative years. These lines infuse Bley's solos with a character

Figure 14: Jazz phrase in "Long Ago and Far Away" (1993), mm. 70–75

redolent of bebop and hard bop jazz playing. The phrase in Figure 14 includes arpeggios, scalar lines, enclosures, and "bluesy" acciaccaturas and unmistakably belongs within the jazz idiom.

Clearly Bley's choice of pitch material was largely located within the jazz tradition, and by drawing upon the conventions established by Armstrong, Young, Parker, and Dizzy Gillespie he created music strongly reminiscent of their styles. It is the *way* he utilized that material relative to the harmonic framework of the tunes that marked his improvising as distinct from those earlier styles. This melodic concept, drawing on ideas that were related to Coleman's shift away from the hegemony of fixed harmony and tonality,[24] heralded Bley's move beyond tonal music.

Beyond Tonal Music

An important idea found in Coleman's music is that of "erasure phrases." Bley described these as being, "where there were some phrases that were tonal and well-tempered, and some phrases that were deliberately not tonal and well-tempered" (Bley and Lee 1999, 67). Examples of these passages are found in many of Coleman's solos; and the performances, such as "Focus on Sanity" and "Bird Food," contain excellent examples.[25] Bley elaborated upon this idea:

> An "erasure phrase" is meant to do nothing else except erase from your memory what you just heard . . . clean the blackboard, so to speak, before you write the next music. It's not there to tell you anything; it is there to make you forget. It's there to cleanse the palette.[26]

It was not possible for Bley, as a pianist, to reproduce Coleman's erasure phrases, employing as they did unequal temperament and microtonality, yet he still managed to produce their *effect* in his solos from the early 1960s onwards.[27] During "All the Things You Are" (1963) Bley repeatedly follows passages that are largely tonal with phrases of densely packed notes that do not register any particular tonal center, phrases that are more like "sound gestures" than coherent melodies. These lines obscure the tonality and sometimes unsettle the time and so have an effect on the listener much like that created by Coleman when he played his nontempered erasure phrases. They are effective to that end for several reasons. First, all these passages are played quickly, and this rapid execution serves to intensify their disorienting affect. Second, the subdivisions in use are almost always varied subtly over the course of the phrase, and whereas they might appear in a score as triplets or sixteenth notes, they often "fall between the cracks" of these subdivisions. Bley observed:

> [Jazz playing is about] being able to go from any of the ways to play time at any moment to a different way, informing each part of the music with something different, [something] opposite. You need to be able to have that kind of control. I should, hopefully, be able to play so slowly that listeners are sure that I am not even playing time, when in fact I am playing an exaggerated form of "behind the time." I could also play an exaggerated form of "ahead of the time" or right on the time. I can change that in a phrase: the first part of the phrase could be this aesthetic, followed by the second part of the phrase, which is another aesthetic.[28]

Third, erasure phrases frequently contain pantonal (and at times atonal) material.[29] The effect of these various tonalities being juxtaposed in such a short period of time is harmonically disorienting and enhances the climate of uncertainty these passages generate. Measures 50–53 of "All the Things You Are" (1963) contain an erasure phrase moving through a variety of tonal centers largely at odds with the changes of the tune. In performance the effect is startling; erasure phrases create a sharp demarcation between the phrases that precede them and those that follow. Although this device was drawn from Coleman's music rather than from twentieth-century concert music, it is not the only idea Bley utilizes from Coleman's approach that has corollaries in Western art music of the last century.[30]

Nonequivalence of Pitch Classes

Cogswell (1995) identifies alternation of register as an effective tool in Coleman's solos, concluding that its use "displays an inspired balance between continuity and contrast" (134). In Bley's performances such movements across registers not only balance continuity and contrast, but also denote nonequivalence of pitch classes.

> If you are sitting at a keyboard, you find a universe below middle C and a universe above middle C, and as Ornette [Coleman] said, they should have picked 88 different names for the notes on the piano, because they are not really related. The fact that they give them the same names gives you a false way of viewing them. They are sound sources that are unlike each other; every note is different from every other note.[31]

A good example of such nonequivalence is shown in Figure 15. In this passage Bley plays a small blues phrase in several registers at such speed that the harmonics of the notes register very clearly even though the sustain pedal is not in use. The passage illustrates that the small fragments *sound* different in each register, partly because their fundamental pitches are different and partly because the *harmonic color* of each phrase is altered by its register on the piano. Although the pitch classes contained within these fragments are more or less identical, they demonstrate a lack of total equivalence in the sound of each fragment. This lack of equivalence will obviously have an effect on how such phrases register with the listener. Similar examples appear in many of Bley's solos.[32]

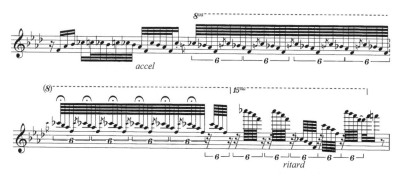

Figure 15: Nonequivalence of pitch classes in "Willow Weep for Me" (1987)

Thematic Unity

Bley views improvisation and composition as the same activity. To him, a jazz musician is a "composer in real-time," and he rejects the more traditional model of composers, noting:

> This whole ethos of composers locking themselves up to produce a master-piece is an old model, a prerecording model. It's not the model for the present. Nobody comes to your house and composes for you to make music.[33]

In light of this view, and considering Bley's training in composition at Juilliard in the 1950s, it is not surprising to find techniques commonly employed by composers in the classical arena present in Bley's improvised music. A notable example is in the area of thematic development and recapitulation. Just as these devices are effective in unifying scored compositions, they serve to create threads of thematic unity throughout Bley's performances. Although Gregory Smith (1982) regards with suspicion the possibility that this kind of thematic unity can be routinely, spontaneously improvised, other writers are more comfortable with the idea. Gunther Schuller's advocacy of this view was declared in his article "Sonny Rollins and Thematic Improvisation" (1960). Martin's (1996) study of Parker's improvisations also uses this type of analysis, and Jeff Pressing (1983) defends its use with his set theory representation of improvisation, stating that "[d]ecision making in the [next moment] may in principle extend well back before [the present moment], depending upon the degree of pre-selection used by the performer, and will also extend slightly into the future . . ." (153). Whatever the arguments, however, there do appear to be clear examples of thematic development and unity in Bley's improvisations. In most cases the themes developed are melodic in nature, but timbral and rhythmic ideas are also developed in this manner during his solos.

Examples of melodic material being developed are found in all Bley's solos considered for this study, and it is particularly noticeable at a local level, where motivic chain association is in play. Such examples of local thematic development lend his improvisations coherence and a "story-telling" quality. In places, a single motif is developed over extended periods, creating considerable coherence. For example, in Figure 16 a single motif is reworked and developed over almost an entire chorus. More rare, but of great interest, are the instances where Bley revisits a motif that has been developed earlier in a performance. In "All the Things You

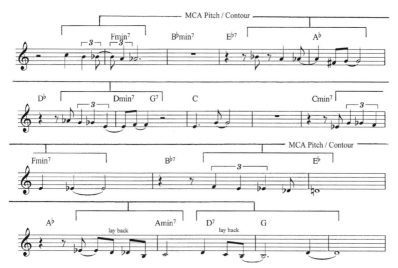

Figure 16: Single motif developed in "All the Things You Are" (1993), mm. 1–16.

Are" (1963), Bley plays a small melodic cell in measure 62 that is repeated and developed until measure 66. After a short break, the motif reappears in measure 69 before the flow of the improvisation moves elsewhere. During the last few measures of the solo, however (measures 106–108), the motif makes a striking reappearance, subtly altered and transposed down a third. The effect of reintroducing this motif to end the solo creates a sense of closure and completeness that allows the music to settle at that point in the performance. Similar examples exist in many of Bley's performances, and such instances of thematic recurrence are examples of compositional thinking during improvised performance, a hallmark of Bley's music.[34]

Along with this kind of thematic elaboration, another device Bley employs, and one he shares with Sonny Rollins, is the use of fragments of the melody to reorient the solo to the song form. This device enhances the melodic contour of the solos and increases their coherence. Examples of passages that refer to the melody of the tune are marked on the transcription and occur in all but one of the performances. Taken together, these various approaches lend great variety and interest to Bley's improvisations.

CONCLUSION

After his exposure to Coleman, Bley abandoned the dominant paradigm of the time, which mandated that improvised lines spring from the functional harmony of the tune. Instead he looked to Coleman's example as a means of generating melodic material for his solos. Generally, Bley's solos are characterized by a mixture of passages that observe the harmonic framework of the tune, passages that are consistent only with their own harmonic and melodic verities, and passages of indeterminate tonality.

Several characteristics of Coleman's music are reproduced in these lines. First, they stray from the chord progression of the tune, although at times they relocate themselves within the chord changes.

Second, the "flow" of these solos, evidenced by the way ideas throughout the solos follow on from one another throughout the performances, reflect the motivic chain association that Jost (1974) identified in Coleman's music. More than a succession of phrases that may or may or not coincide with the chord changes, Bley's solos are coherent musical statements by virtue of the sure way in which he develops melodic ideas and motifs in a logical, "storytelling" manner and moves artfully from one set of ideas to the next.

Third, Bley employs erasure phrases to "cleanse the palette" between distinct musical passages, in addition to playing lines that suggest the nonequivalence of pitch classes in his music.

Finally, by employing a more democratic conception with regard to the roles of the instruments within the piano trio, an approach that mirrored Coleman's concept of ensemble jazz performance, he freed the instruments from their defined responsibilities in the context of the piano trio.

By embracing a freer harmonic concept, Bley made harmony a by-product of his improvised melodic lines (and not vice versa, as was the case in many earlier jazz styles). Though his lines retained essential elements of the jazz language, they were filtered through his understanding of the advances made by Coleman. As a consequence, familiar materials appeared in unfamiliar contexts.

Although there have been subtle changes in Bley's approach to improvising since his first jazz recordings after working with Coleman, the essential elements of his style have been present from that time. By building upon the ideas of Coleman, Bley pioneered a new approach to jazz piano that still holds promise 40 years after it was first advanced.

> Bley has the wonderful ability to allow his music to move where it will. The effect is one of total freshness, of music that has never been heard before and never will be heard again (Balleras 1985).

Figure 17: "All the Things You Are" (1963). *Continued on next four pages.*

Figure 17, *continued on next three pages*

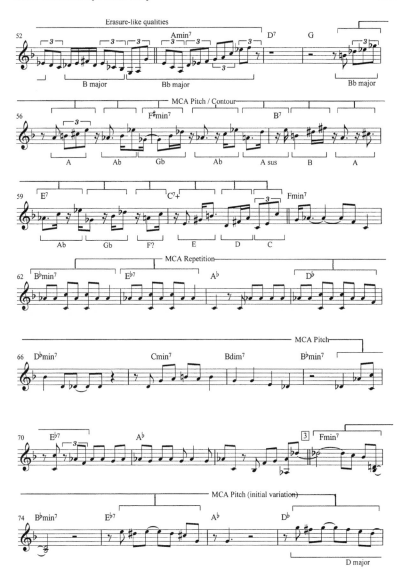

Figure 17, *continued on next two pages*

Figure 17, *concluded on next page*

Figure 17, *concluded*

NOTES

1. Bley has claimed that to find out what to play, it is necessary to first identify everything that has been played before and then to do something different. This approach is evidence of a "modernist" aesthetic and differs from the approach of many in the jazz tradition (bebop or hard bop musicians, for example), who prefer to elaborate on the conventions of established styles. Bley, however, has tempered his own modernist tendencies with a desire to remain faithful to the jazz tradition and so has created a kind of dialectic with his music: "Could you go to a place that had relevance to the history of jazz? You could always sit and rumble around on an instrument but would it mean something to a perspective based on, say, [New Orleans trumpeter] King Oliver?" (Smith 1979). Further, Bley has said: "I'm trying to preserve the jazz element in quite random material . . . . I'm trying to find out what the jazz element is" (Lyons 1989, 164).

2. Paul Bley, interviews by author, tape recordings, Boston, Mass., and Cherry Valley, N.Y., February through August 2001.

3. Ibid.

4. For example, Schuller (1960), Martin (1996).

5. See Jost (1974), Cogswell (1995), and Wilson (1999).

6. "Representative," in the case of Paul Bley, is somewhat elusive, though there are aspects of his musical style that single him out from other jazz pianists. *The Penguin Guide to Jazz on CD* (Cook and Morton 2000) states, "There is probably no other pianist currently active with a stylistic signature as distinctively inscribed as Paul Bley's—which is ironic, for he is a tireless experimenter with an inbuilt resistance to stopping long in any one place." The solos considered in this study are representative in as much as they reveal the way he introduces sudden harmonic shifts, utilizes a subtly varied pulse, and plays strongly melodic lines. They are not representative of his electronic music, his more contrapuntal work (for example, with Giuffre), his extensive solo catalog, and his completely freely improvised music. Those areas do, however, exhibit the three traits mentioned above.

 7. Bley, interview.

 8. For a more detailed examination of this earlier style, see the author's article "Paul Bley: Building on the Innovations of Ornette Coleman" (Meehan 2001).

 9. This idea, advanced by Jost (1974, 50) in his chapter on Coleman, provides one of the clearest explanations of what makes Coleman's music so melodic, coherent, and attractive.

10. Coleman, Ornette. *Beauty Is a Rare Thing.* Atlantic Recording Corporation R2 71410, 1959–1961.

11. See Schuller (1960) and Wilson (2001).

12. Bley's approach differs from that of Coleman in that Coleman generally makes "no attempt to follow [the] form in the improvisation" (Porter 1994–95), although Eric Charry suggests that the group does in fact adhere to these frameworks (1997–98). Observation supports Bley's claim that he closely adheres to the metrical framework of the tunes he uses as the basis for his improvisations. On this point he is emphatic, stating, "If you hummed the melody of the song over the entire performance you would be at the right point of the song at all times. That's the bottom line" (Bley, interview).

13. Bley, interview.

14. "Pantonality" is a term coined by Rudolph Réti in *Tonality, Atonality, Pantonality* (1958). First evident in the music of Wagner and Debussy, this notion of "movable tonics" has been applied to the music of Bartók, Stravinsky, and Hindemith among others in the twentieth century.

15. Bley, interview. This claim is substantiated by examination of his recordings over the course of his career. During the 1960s he predominantly played free music and compositions by Carla Bley and Annette Peacock, whereas during the 1970s he explored similar music but often did so using electronic instruments. The 1980s and 1990s have seen the inclusion of more of the standard jazz repertoire in his concerts and recordings along with the material he had investigated during the previous 20 years.

16. From the album *If We May,* Steeplechase SCCD 31344.

17. Another outstanding example of Bley's musicianship operating as a concomitant to musical communication within the ensemble is found in the first measures of "All The Things You Are" (1985), when Jesper Lundgaard (bassist) mistakenly plays a measure of 3/4, an error Bley immediately accommodates in his improvised phrase without any loss of coherence.

18. Bley, interview.

19. It is interesting to compare the early recordings of Bley considered in this article with those pianist Bill Evans made the same year with the same standard trio alignment. Evans's *Trio 64* (Verve [1963]), with bassist Gary Peacock and drummer Paul Motian, reveals a pianist somewhat at odds with his freewheeling rhythm section and performing with notable conservatism both rhythmically and harmonically. The authors of *The Penguin Guide to Jazz on CD* observe: "It's hard . . . listening to [Bley's] *Footloose* [Savoy {1962},

with bassist Steve Swallow and drummer Pete La Roca {Peter Sims}] after nearly twenty years, to understand why there was so very much excitement about Bill Evans when Bley was producing far more interesting and challenging piano trio music, sometimes only a couple of blocks away" (Cook and Morton 2000, 120).

20. Between 1959 and 1961 Coleman recorded nine albums for the Atlantic label, often using Don Cherry on trumpet, Charlie Haden on bass, and either Billy Higgins or Ed Blackwell on drums. These quartet recordings represent a high-water mark among free-jazz recordings.

21. Tenor saxophone player James Clay noted that Coleman could sound exactly like Parker (Litweiler 1992, 54). Bley toured with both Young and Parker and when asked, in 1955, to identify his main musical influence, replied, "Louis Armstrong" (Fulford 1994).

22. The blues also plays a significant role in the music Coleman has made, and his affinity for both the form and the feeling of the blues led avant-garde saxophonist Archie Shepp to describe him as "the blues man." His use of the blues tradition is explored in Lewis Porter's article "The 'Blues Connotation' in Ornette Coleman's Music — And Some General Thoughts on the Relation of Blues to Jazz" (1994–95).

23. The Superlocrian scale has been commonly used in jazz performance since the 1940s and is generally played against dominant chords resolving to their tonic chord (i.e., G7 to C major). It is the seventh mode of the melodic minor ascending scale; C Superlocrian is enharmonically equivalent to D♭ melodic minor ascending. It is also known as the "diminished whole-tone scale," the "altered scale," and in some circles the "Pomeranian scale."

24. Cogswell (1995) commented, "Although his motivic vocabulary comes directly from the vocabulary of swing, bebop, and rhythm & blues, Coleman strings these traditional motives together into novel metrical and melodic patterns. His innovation lies not in the creation of a new vocabulary, but in his redefinition of musical grammar and syntax" (109).

25. Coleman, Ornette. *Beauty Is a Rare Thing*. Atlantic Recording Corporation, 1959–1961.

26. Bley, interview.

27. Bley has said, "[Coleman] could play A440, A444 or A436 or any A you wanted. Unfortunately I didn't have the flexibility that he had when it came to hitting A" (Smith 1979, 4). Perhaps this limitation of the acoustic piano was one of the reasons Bley was drawn to electronic music and synthesizers.

28. Bley, interview.

29. "Atonal" in this case refers to passages that have no fixed tonal center, but that are not necessarily serial in nature. In fact, there do not appear to be any strictly serial passages in the music under consideration.

30. It could be said these ideas are related to Bartók's use of polymodal chromaticism and the atonal music of the Viennese school.

31. Bley, interview.

32. Roger Dean's (1992) study of improvised music discusses the chords Bley plays and contrasts his use of clusters with the motivic use of widely spaced intervals, noting that they "create a harmonic openness beyond the simpler implications of the pitches themselves when reduced to the closest spacing" (110). Dean identifies this as an awareness of "a lack of total equivalence of pitch sets" (110) and relates it to some of the timbral devices Bley uses.

33. Bley, interview.

34. Many of Bley's solo recordings contain excellent examples of this kind of musical thinking. "Never Again," from the album *Sweet Time,* is a particularly cogent example.

A NOTE ABOUT TRANSCRIPTIONS

Schuller has said that "notated musical examples are of course no substitute for the music itself" and that in jazz music "the written score is both impossible and—if scores existed—irrelevant" (1968, x). These comments notwithstanding, for this study of Bley's music, transcriptions of his improvised performances were made. Although transcriptions are an extremely useful tool in studying the pitch material in jazz piano performances, they are of questionable value in monitoring rhythms in the idiom. Traditional notation is too limited to reflect the complexity of what is played in this genre (or any genre in which the *performance*, rather than the *score*, is considered the final artifact), and at best we can produce a very rough sketch of the rhythms employed by the improvising musicians. In places where the feel is markedly ahead of, or behind, the beat a note appears above the staff to that effect. It is strongly recommended that any transcription be studied along with its recording. All care has been taken to ensure that the examples are as accurate as possible. Generally the tonality of the passages has been marked beneath the staff, but in places where Bley's lines are consonant with the chord changes tonality has *not* been specified. In places where Bley plays notes from a tonality other than the changes, but a tonality that is unsurprising in a jazz context (i.e., D Superlocrian against an Am7 chord and the subsequent D7 chord), this divergence is usually noted in brackets.

SOLOS TRANSCRIBED

Ornette Coleman:	"Chronology" (excerpt)	1959
Paul Bley:	"All the Things You Are"	1963
	"All the Things You Are"	1985
	"All the Things You Are"	1993
	"Long Ago and Far Away"	1963

"Long Ago and Far Away"	1985
"Long Ago and Far Away"	1993
"Willow Weep for Me'	1987

SELECTED DISCOGRAPHY

Paul Bley
The Fabulous Paul Bley Quintet. America AM 6120 [1958].
Paul Bley with Gary Peacock. ECM 1003 [1963].
My Standard. Steeplechase SCCD31214 [1985].
Live Again. Steeplechase SCCD31230 [1987].
If We May. Steeplechase SCCD31344 [1993].
Ornette Coleman
Beauty Is a Rare Thing. Rhino/Atlantic Jazz Gallery R2 71410
    [1959–1961].
Sonny Rollins
Sonny Meets Hawk. RCA Victor LSP2712 [1963].

REFERENCES

Balleras, Jon. "Paul Bley: No False Moves." *Down Beat* 52, no. 11 (November 1985): 42–43.
Bley, Paul, and David Lee. *Stopping Time*. Montreal: Véhicule Press, 1999.
Charry, Eric. "Freedom and Form in Ornette Coleman's Early Atlantic Recordings." *Annual Review of Jazz Studies* 9 (1997–98): 261–94.
Cogswell, Michael. "Melodic Organization in Two Solos by Ornette Coleman." *Annual Review of Jazz Studies* 7 (1995): 101–144.
Cook, Richard, and Andrew Morton. *The Penguin Guide to Jazz on CD*. London: Penguin, 2000.
Davis, Francis. "Out Front When Jazz Freed Itself." *New York Times,* February 13, 2000, Arts & Leisure section, 29–30.
Dean, Roger. *New Structures in Jazz and Improvised Music Since 1960*. Milton Keynes: Open University Press, 1992.
Fulford, Bob. "Paul Bley—Jazz Is Just About Ready for Another Revolution." *Down Beat* 61, no. 7 (July 1994) 31. First published in *Down Beat* 22, no.14 (July 1955): 13.
Gioia, Ted. *West Coast Jazz*. New York: Oxford University Press, 1992.
Heckman, Don. "Paul Bley." *Down Beat* 31, no. 7 (March 12, 1964): 16–17.
Hentoff, Nat. Liner notes to *Something Else*. Los Angeles: Contemporary Records COP 024 [C3551], 1958.
Hentoff, Nat. *Jazz Is*. London: W.H. Allen, 1976.

Jost, Ekkehardt. *Free Jazz*. New York: Da Capo Press, 1974.

Klee, Joe, and Will Smith. "Paul Bley." *Down Beat* 41, no. 1 (January 17, 1974): 12–13.

Litweiler, John. *Ornette Coleman: A Harmolodic Life*. New York: William Morrow, 1992

Lyons, Len. *The Great Jazz Pianists*. New York: Da Capo Press, 1989.

Martin, Henry. *Charlie Parker and Thematic Improvisation*. Lanham, Maryland: Scarecrow Press, 1996.

Meehan, Norman. "Paul Bley: Building on the Innovations of Ornette Coleman." *Jazz Research Proceedings Yearbook* 29 (2001): 67–73.

Pressing, Jeff. "Pitch Class Set Structures in Contemporary Jazz." *Jazzforschung / Jazz Research* 14 (1983): 133–171.

Porter, Lewis. "The 'Blues Connotation' in Ornette Coleman's Music—And Some General Thoughts on the Relation of Blues to Jazz." *Annual Review of Jazz Studies* 7 (1994—1995): 75–95.

Réti, Rudolph. *Tonality, Atonality, Pantonality*. London: Barrie and Rockliff, 1958.

Schuller, Gunther. "Sonny Rollins and Thematic Improvising." In *Jazz Panorama*, edited by Martin Williams. New York: Collier Books, 1960. First published in *Jazz Review* 1, no. 1 (1958): 6–11, 21.

Schuller, Gunther. *Early Jazz*. New York, Oxford University Press, 1968.

Smith, Bill. "Paul Bley Interview." *Coda Magazine* no. 166 (April 1979): 2–8.

Smith, Gregory. "Homer, Gregory, and Bill Evans? The Theory of Formulaic Composition in the Context of Jazz Piano Improvisation." Ph.D. diss., Harvard University, 1982.

Wilson, Peter Niklas. *Ornette Coleman: His Life and Music*. Berkeley, Ca.: Berkeley Hills Books, 1999.

Wilson, Peter Niklas. *Sonny Rollins: The Definitive Musical Guide*. Berkeley, Ca.: Berkeley Hills Books, 2001.

A PHOTO GALLERY:
THE INSTITUTE OF JAZZ STUDIES
CELEBRATES ITS FIRST FIFTY YEARS

In 1952, the pioneering jazz scholar Marshall Stearns, a professor of English at Hunter College, decided to incorporate his world-famous collection of recordings, books, periodicals, sheet music, photographs, clipping files, and memorabilia as the Institute of Jazz Studies. There was, Stearns noted, no place where interested students, scholars, and collectors could do research on jazz; and so he made his collection, housed in his spacious apartment in New York's Greenwich Village, available by appointment. Assisted by volunteers and an impressive advisory board, he began to solicit musicians, record producers, and journalists for donations of materials. As the collection expanded and acceptance of jazz within the academy began to grow, Stearns began the search for an institution of higher learning that would house the Institute. His conditions for this generous donation were summed up by three words: acquisition, access, and autonomy. In short, the receiving institution had to ensure that the collection would continue to grow, that the materials would be made accessible to a wide range of users, and that not only would the Institute retain a degree of autonomy within the university but the collection would not be subsumed within general institutional holdings.

Thanks to the efforts of several knowledgeable jazz enthusiasts on its faculty and a keen interest in American popular culture on the part of its president, Mason Gross, in 1966 Stearns chose Rutgers as the permanent home for the Institute. Unfortunately, Stearns died in December of that year before the transfer could take place.

Originally located in the basement of the John Cotton Dana Library, the Institute moved in 1974 to larger quarters in Bradley Hall. In 1984, IJS became part of the Rutgers University Libraries and formally affiliated with the Dana Library. This action paved the way for additional staff support, substantial growth in collections, and a new emphasis on cataloging and documentation. In 1994, the Institute moved back to Dana into a state-of-the-art facility on the newly added fourth floor.

The Institute has continued its many activities, such as publishing *Annual Review of Jazz Studies* (since 1973) and producing the weekly radio program *Jazz from the Archives* (WBGO-FM, Newark, since 1979) and has added new programs, such as the monthly Jazz Research Roundtable. It also serves as a key resource for the Rutgers-Newark Master's Program in Jazz History and Research, the first of its kind, now in its seventh year. In October 2002, the Institute of Jazz Studies celebrated its fiftieth anniversary with a gala at the Newark Club.

Note: All photos on pp. 123–133 are courtesy of Ed Berger.

Sheldon Harris, the Institute's first curator, outside Marshall Stearns's apartment at 108 Waverly Place, 1965.

Sheldon Harris (left) and Stearns inside the Institute, late 1950s.

Top: Early IJS-sponsored symposium and Newport, ca. 1955: musicians Bob Wilber (far left), Bill Britto and John Glasel, and panelists Richard Waterman, Marshall Stearns, Father Norman O'Connor, Dr. Norman Margolies, Eric Larrabee, and Henry Cowell. Photo courtesy Bob Parent.
Bottom: Stearns and Thelonious Monk

Stearns and Quincy Jones in Greece, U.S. State Department–sponsored tour with Dizzy Gillespie, 1956.

Top: Collection Specialist John Clement in IJS stacks, Bradley Hall, 1989.
Bottom: Reception celebrating acquisition of world-renowned Harold Flakser jazz periodicals collection, 1986. L-R: Milt Gabler, Dan Morgenstern, Flakser, Charles Nanry, William Weinberg, David Cayer, Caroline Coughlin. Nanry, Weinberg, and Cayer were instrumental in establishing IJS at Rutgers.

Bradley Hall celebration with participants of NEA-sponsored Jazz Oral History Project, which was transferred to IJS in 1979. Top, L-R: Ron Welburn, project co-ordinator; Sonny Greer; Snub Mosley; and Eddie Durham. Bottom: Larry Ridley and Doc Cheatham view videotaped interview.

Top: Benny Carter conducts a workshop with Rutgers Jazz Ensemble members, New Brunswick, 1986. Participants include Robin Carter (far left), Jeff Rupert (far right), Harry Allen (second from right), and Joey Cavaseno (third from right).
Bottom: Milt Hinton and Professor Lewis Porter at IJS-sponsored summer institute for high school teachers, 1988.

Some of the many notable instruments donated to IJS through the years. Top: Dan Morgenstern receives horns belonging to Rahsaan Roland Kirk from wife Edith and son Rory. Bottom: Catherine (Mrs. Cootie) Williams holds her late husband's trumpet.

In 1983, IJS cofounded the American Jazz Hall of Fame in collaboration with the New Jersey Jazz Society. Dan Morgenstern inducts Roy Eldridge in 1984.

Top: Vincent Pelote prepares for the move from Bradley Hall to the new facility in Dana Library, 1994.
Bottom: IJS reopens in new quarters, 1994.

Wynton Marsalis tries out Red Nichols's vintage cornet during visit to IJS in 1997 while David Cayer looks on.

Since 1995, the IJS monthly Jazz Research Roundtables have served as a forum for scholars, musicians, and students engaged in all facets of the music. Top: Stanley Crouch, 1997. Bottom: Vincent Pelote (left) hosts guitar legends Lawrence Lucie (center) and Remo Palmier in 1998.

More roundtables. Top: Kenny Washington, 2003. Bottom: Grachan Moncur III, 2000.

In 1999, IJS received one of its most extensive and important collections—that of Mary Lou Williams. In November 2002, IJS sponsored a conference on her life and music. Top: Panelists Father Peter O'Brien, Becca Pulliam, and Dan Morgenstern. Bottom: Isotope, an ensemble comprised primarily of Rutgers-Newark students, performs Williams's music. Left to right: Edgar Jordan (flugelhorn), Corey Rawls (drums), Joe Peterson (bass), Rashida Phillips (vocals), Jeff Lovell (piano).

In July 2003, IJS received another invaluable collection—that of New Jersey native James P. Johnson. Looking over the newly arrived materials are Dan Morgenstern, archivist Annie Kuebler, and Barry Glover, Johnson's grandson and director of the James P. Johnson Foundation.

Current views of IJS facility in Dana Library. Exhibit cases were installed in the IJS reading room in 2001 through the generosity of Stanley Roth. Saxophones on display are those of Ben Webster (left) and Lester Young. Photos courtesy Robert E. Nahory.

THE GOUGE

Dick Spottswood

The practice of recycling good melodies is as old as music itself. Classical composers have always viewed folk and popular tunes as fair game for inclusion in extended formal works, and dance melodies have moved easily from one nationality to another. The ancient and well-known southern fiddle tune "Flop Eared Mule" exists in Swedish, Lithuanian, Ukrainian, Irish, Italian, and Polish versions. The popular Yiddish dance tune "Ma Yofus" has been widely appropriated by non-Jewish musicians throughout eastern Europe.

An Old World melody, "Tiger Rag," was played and danced as a quadrille in New Orleans, according to Jelly Roll Morton. Following an influential 1918 recording by the Original Dixieland Jazz Band, the Tiger reappeared in numerous disguises. Other New Orleans pieces, notably "Gate Mouth," "My Bucket's Got a Hole in It," and "I Wish I Could Shimmy Like My Sister Kate," are folk-derived themes that have been recycled with new titles.

Other forms of borrowing occurred when appealing solos, arrangements, or other creations appeared on records and got the attention of musicians who creatively appropriated what they liked, often putting it into new settings. A well-known instance is the extended cornet chorus created by Joe Oliver for "Dipper Mouth Blues" on two 1923 recordings. The tune was renamed "Sugar Foot Stomp" and given new arrangements over the years, but never without someone replicating—and honoring—Oliver's signature solo.

A remarkable three-stanza trombone solo was inserted by Charlie Green into a Fletcher Henderson record in 1924. Subsequent recordings reveal that Green's solo reverberated throughout the jazz world, even if his contribution was rarely, if ever, overtly acknowledged. Though not a structured blues, Green's solo, like Oliver's, was extended and very bluesy, and it was the highlight of an otherwise unremarkable record called "The Gouge of Armour Avenue."

The tune was a 1924 composition by W.C. Handy, who also issued it through his New York publishing firm. Handy had successfully introduced the blues through his 1910s successes, "Beale Street Blues," "Joe Turner Blues," "Memphis Blues," "Yellow Dog Blues," and "St. Louis Blues." The 1920s were less receptive to Handy's efforts, even though by then he had become a household name. He seems to have felt he'd captured some hip local jargon in his 1924 songs "The Chicago Gouge" and "The Gouge of Armour Avenue." The sheet music cover of the first claims that it's "a mirror life reflection of Chicago's South Side, more dignified than the blues"—a startling assertion from a man who had taken blues to the bank. A special GOUGE logo was designed for the bottom of each cover, suggesting that Handy felt he was onto something.

Was Handy exploring a new career track to avoid becoming stale? The cover statement ignored his past successes, extolling him instead as "the originator and creator of the gouge—the advanced rhythm in syncopation." A clumsy lyric described Handy's epiphany:

> I took my pencil out in all scrouge
> And named that music Gouge
> Just for the landlords Chicago's Gouge
> And for the swell broads, they really Gouge
>   The Chicago Gouge

Another one summarized its inspiration:

> I gouged the beauty from the Blues
> Poured in some boiling Jazz
> Stirred in a little spirits not the kind the spiritual has
> I gouged the lock on ragtime melody, with a minor key
> Stole some pickled beats from Charleston Pat in one flat
>   The Chicago Gouge

A second offering, "The Gouge of Armour Avenue," concerned a quarreling couple whose female half is finally soothed when her partner teaches her to dance the scrouge. The verb *scrouge* appears in the *Oxford English Dictionary*, defined thus: "to incommode by passing against (a person); to encroach on (a person's) space in sitting or standing; to crowd." Was Handy thinking of crowded South Side tenements? An oppressively intimate dance? I can speculate no further. At any rate, neither *gouge* nor *scrouge* found a place in the public vocabulary, and neither song became a Handy classic.[1]

Both were first recorded on a Paramount coupling by vaudeville blues singer Faye Barnes (a.k.a. Maggie Jones) in June 1924, with a small group from Henderson's orchestra that included trombonist Ted Nixon and arranger Don Redman on clarinet. In July, the Henderson band moved from the Club Alabam on 44th Street to the prestigious Roseland Ballroom at 51st and Broadway. At the same time, Nixon was replaced by Charlie Green.

Green was born in Omaha around 1900. His early résumé included performing with carnival and marching bands and work with trumpeter Red Perkins's band in Omaha. Green was a solid, assertive blues player, who became Henderson's first soloist of stature and New York's second major jazz trombonist, after Miff Mole. On July 31, 1924, the band recorded a dance arrangement of "The Gouge of Armour Avenue" for Vocalion, with a lengthy feature spot for the band's new star.

The performance opens with a major-key ensemble verse and chorus, and modulates to a minor-key ostinato vamp, played by piano, banjo, and guïro (or another form of scraper), over which Green plays a bold, bluesy cadenza. Two relatively sedate choruses by cornetist Howard Scott follow; a brief reprise of Handy's tune concludes the record.

Comparing the Green and Scott solo parts is instructive. Scott's competent, self-effacing playing served the arrangement well, maintaining the unthreatening Henderson style of the time. Green's growling, charging solo was filled with blues energy, pointing the way to where the band—and jazz at large—would inevitably go, as northern sophistication was supplemented with southern testosterone. To Walter Allen, Green's contribution was "surely one of the earliest HOT [Allen's emphasis] trombone solos of lasting merit to be recorded."[2] Compared to his contemporaries, Green has received comparatively little attention from jazz historians. I'm unaware of any others who've paid tribute to his "Gouge" solo in print.

Ragtime pianists aside, I think a case can be made that, following Sidney Bechet, Green was the second important hot soloist in New York. He was a primary and pioneering force in moving jazz from its earlier grounding in ragtime, military music, dixieland, and conventional dance formulas towards a hotter, freer, blues-based music. Henderson records of the 1924–26 period show the progression, and the subsequent contributions of soloists like Coleman Hawkins, Buster Bailey, and Louis Armstrong, who joined Green as additional catalysts.

Though Green's "Gouge" solo was revolutionary, it wasn't without precedent. Five years earlier, one of the first Ted Lewis Columbia records was "O" or "Oh!" from December 9, 1919. The record included part of a second piece called "The Vamp," played in a minor key that contrasted with "O." Recorded medleys were a frequent practice from 1917 to 1921, the result of an arrangement between record companies and music publishers that allowed an extra tune to be included on a dance record without payment of additional royalties. In addition to being a creative form of song plugging, the device allowed record companies to acquire extra royalty-free titles for their catalogs.

"The Vamp" was a feature for Lewis's trombonist Harry Raderman, an extended cadenza performed over a minor-key ostinato figure. Raderman was a busy musician, both as a Lewis sideman and as leader on informal dance band record dates in the early 1920s. He was born into a musical Ukrainian Jewish family in 1885 and absorbed the music traditions of eastern Europe before sailing to New York in 1898. In music, a vamp is a repeated figure that precedes a melody or, in this case, serves as its rhythmic foundation. Raderman's Old World roots provided a familiar context for the device, investing it with an oriental flavor.

The original vamp was silent film star Theda Bara, who had been cast as a seductive, posturing vampire in several hit films, including *Cleopatra* (1917) and *Salomé* (1918). Bara became emblematic of the new post-Victorian sexuality, and her films created a vogue for exotic oriental fashions. "Vamping" became the word for aggressive female sexual behavior, witness Perry Bradford's song "Lucy Long" from 1925:

> Rides a taxi 'round the town
> Vamps the meter upside down
> Don't pay the butcher one red cent
> Vamps the landlord for her rent

In Ottoman Turkish music, an extended solo or collective cadenza performed over a rhythmic ostinato is called *chifte telli*; the ostinato is also called "vamp." Americans associated the music with Theda Bara's predecessor Little Egypt, who created a sensation when she brought belly dancing to the World's Fair in Chicago in 1893. Turkish music was influential with Greeks, Armenians, and Jews, who incorporated Turkish elements into their own traditions. Even the *son* in Cuba features a Turkish-like cadenza called *montuno*.

"Dardanella," "Palesteena," "China Boy," "San," "Chinatown, My Chinatown," "Japanese Sandman," "Nagasaki," and a host of other postwar songs were inspired by oriental themes. U.S. participation in the war heightened Americans' awareness of the rest of the world, and songs like these remained popular through the 1920s. Examples of orientalia from the jazz catalogs include "Shanghai Shuffle" (Henderson), "Oriental Strut" and "Cornet Chop Suey" (Armstrong), and "Shanghai Honeymoon" and "Oriental Man" (State Street Ramblers).

Harry Raderman's "Vamp" encored on later Ted Lewis records in other melodic contexts. Otherwise, it had no musical descendants. Charlie Green's "Gouge" solo, on the other hand, bred children for more than a generation. Almost immediately, others incorporated it into new contexts. The tune never acquired a name and so has been hard to spot, even though it appears on dozens of subsequent recordings, beginning with one made in the autumn of 1924, not long after "Gouge" was released. Here is a sequence of early covers, or instances of extended solo cadenzas played over rhythmic vamps:

KANSAS CITY FIVE, Get Yourself a Monkey Man and Make Him Strut His Stuff (Pathé, October 1924) features a rudimentary echo of "Gouge" by trombonist Jake Frazier.

FLETCHER HENDERSON AND HIS ORCHESTRA, Play Me Slow (Columbia, January 23, 1925). A Green encore in the form of a two-chorus blues solo, inserted into the middle of a pop tune. It suggests that Henderson considered Green's device appropriate in multiple contexts.

JULIA MOODY, Midnight Dan (Columbia, September 18, 1925) features a long cadenza by cornetist Robert (Bobby) Stark, the first known recorded solo by the later Henderson and Chick Webb trumpeter.

LOUIS ARMSTRONG AND HIS HOT FIVE, Yes! I'm in the Barrel (OKeh, November 12, 1925)

LOUIS ARMSTRONG AND HIS HOT FIVE, You're Next (OKeh, February 26, 1926). Armstrong's tenure with Henderson's orchestra began a couple of months after Green joined, and their southern styles were important to the musical changes Henderson was introducing. Armstrong had appropriated the Joe Oliver solo in the band's popular record of "Sugar Foot Stomp." These records, made soon after Armstrong's return to Chicago, show that he was enamored of the Green cadenza as well.

"Yes! I'm in the Barrel" begins with a repeated three-note figure from the piano and banjo. Armstrong joins at the fourth bar, with a short introductory cadenza played on muted cornet. "You're Next" commences with a lavish, tongue-in-cheek (we trust) piano introduction. Then Armstrong joins, contributing a variation on "Gouge" that becomes another influential solo, as well as a reference point for Jack Teagarden's "Makin' Friends" a couple of years later.

LOUIS ARMSTRONG AND HIS HOT FIVE, The King of the Zulu's [*sic*] (OKeh, June 23, 1926) shows that Armstrong wasn't through with "The Gouge." Kid Ory's trombone offers a two-chorus reprise of the original Green solo, played over the three-note vamp that premiered in "Yes! I'm in the Barrel." A curious comic exchange follows between Armstrong, Lil Armstrong, and actor Clarence Babcock. Though the King of the Zulus is a traditional New Orleans Mardi Gras figure, Babcock represents him instead as a semicoherent Jamaican with an appetite for chittlins. In retrospect the skit seems pointless and misdirected, and it's probably the reason that historians have tended to ignore the record.

Things get back on track with two trumpet (not cornet, I think) choruses that build on both Ory and Green. Armstrong lovingly takes the "Gouge" solo apart, reconstructs it, and forms something new and compelling in the process. The result is a startling composition of incendiary beauty. Armstrong's playing in these few moments takes a leap forward, adding rare introspection to his customary virtuosity. Johnny St. Cyr follows with a quiet variation on solo banjo, yielding to a final dramatic ensemble chorus that becomes an emotional *cri de coeur* with few rivals in recorded jazz.

"The King of the Zulus" didn't displace "The Gouge of Armour Avenue," but the Armstrong solo choruses became a second compelling model. The record stayed in print for several years and was reissued in 1935. As we listen to subsequent jazz tunes with minor-key solo passages, with and without rhythmic vamps, it often isn't difficult to detect traces of "King of the Zulus." Armstrong rerecorded it for Decca on January 25, 1957, as part of Decca's *Musical Autobiography* project, eight years after serving as King of the Zulus himself, in the 1949 Mardi Gras parade.

ETHEL WATERS AND HER JAZZ BAND, Ev'rybody Mess Aroun' (Columbia, July 29, 1926) features a "Gouge"-like cadenza by trumpeter Thornton Brown, later a bandleader in Detroit through the 1930s and 1940s.

DIXIE WASHBOARD BAND, King of the Zulus (Columbia, October 22, 1926)

NEW ORLEANS BLUE FIVE, The King of the Zulus (Victor, November 2, 1926), dixieland-like clones of the Armstrong record. Each includes the Jamaica-chittlins dialogue, but not the musical insights, of the master's version.

LLOYD SCOTT AND HIS ORCHESTRA, Symphonic Scronch (Victor, January 10, 1927). Jazz critic André Hodeir published a 1957 book, *Jazz: Its Evolution and Essence*, in which he trashed a good deal of pre–Swing Era jazz. An exception to his bias was a rhapsodic appraisal of 17-year-old Dicky Wells's trombone solo on this, his first record. Hodeir was unaware that it was a straightforward clone of Charlie Green's "Gouge" solo, including the vamp.

JOHN WILLIAMS' SYNCO JAZZERS, Pewee Blues (Gennett, ca. March 7, 1927). The leader was married to his 16-year-old pianist, Mary Lou Williams, whose talent exceeded his. Nevertheless, this record features his alto sax and a reasonable reprise of "The Gouge."

CLARENCE WILLIAMS AND HIS ORCHESTRA, New Down Home Blues (QRS, ca. August 1928). Trombonist Ed Cuffee contributes a short "Gouge" near the end of this revival of the 1921 Ethel Waters hit.

EDDIE CONDON AND HIS FOOTWARMERS, Makin' Friends (OKeh, October 30, 1928), a feature for Teagarden who, like Green, brought a healthy dose of southwestern blues to New York jazz. His playing here combines elements of "Yes! I'm in the Barrel" with "The Gouge." The arrangement moves from major to minor when Teagarden solos.

GOODY AND HIS GOOD TIMERS, Digga Digga Do (Pathé, ca. November 16, 1928). Teagarden offers a reprise of "Makin' Friends" at the end. He'll do it again, to conclude Red Nichols's "Sweet Georgia Brown" in 1930. It seems to have been a popular feature.

THE RHYTHM ACES, Jazz Battle (Brunswick, January 29, 1929) features the feisty 20-year-old Jabbo Smith. His two-chorus solo near the end borrows portions of "King of the Zulus." Many thought of Smith as the only 1920s horn player whose technique rivaled Armstrong's. This remarkable and provocative performance is a memorable tribute, and it's one of the first occasions that an Armstrong solo is paraphrased at length.

KENTUCKY GRASSHOPPERS, Makin' Friends (Banner and other labels, April 4, 1929). The strongest version and a landmark Teagarden performance.

EDDIE LANG AND HIS ORCHESTRA, Hot Heels (OKeh, May 22, 1929). This Jack Pettis–Al Goering tune had been recorded twice by Jack

Pettis and his Pets a year earlier, once for Vocalion and again (as the Cotton Pickers) for the Cameo labels. Here the tune serves mostly as a framework for an extended cadenza. Tommy Dorsey plays trombone in the opening ensemble, switching to trumpet as the band sets up a minor vamp. He plays an extended, mostly free form, solo, followed by brother Jimmy's clarinet and the leader's guitar, as each works to keep the improvisation going. Neither Tommy nor the others specifically quote "Gouge" or "Zulus," though by this time it's clear that the cadenza and minor vamp device has become familiar to jazz players. If it served no other purpose, it could at least dress up an ordinary melody by allowing a soloist to depart from it.

TINY PARHAM AND HIS MUSICIANS, Sud Buster's Dream (Victor, October 25, 1929). Without the usual vamp, a melody resembling "King of the Zulus" shifts to the relative major at the bridge to give the melody more conventional contours. "Blue Drag" (1932) would perpetuate it and present it as a more finished piece. This record was a follow-up to Parham's "Washboard Wiggles" from a few months earlier. The percussionist Ernie Marrero is featured on two virtuoso washboard choruses, though the title reminds us of the instrument's original purpose.

RED NICHOLS AND HIS FIVE PENNIES, Sweet Georgia Brown (Brunswick, July 2, 1930). Teagarden's trombone coda-cadenza resembles the one that concluded "Digga Digga Do" in 1928.

THE HARLEM FOOTWARMERS, Rockin' in Rhythm (OKeh, November 8, 1930)

THE JUNGLE BAND, Rockin' in Rhythm (Brunswick, January 14, 1931)

DUKE ELLINGTON AND HIS ORCHESTRA, Rockin' in Rhythm (Victor, January 16, 1931). This tune morphed into a piece called "Kinda Dukish" in the 1960s, when Duke added a piano solo as a prelude. Barney Bigard's original clarinet solo played to a minor vamp was retained in later arrangements.

BALTIMORE BELL HOPS, Comin' and Goin' (Columbia, March 19, 1931). Fletcher Henderson's band, led by his brother Horace, whose composition and arrangement this is. Trombonist Benny Morton pays a brief homage to the band's early star, Charlie Green, as the tune begins.

RED PERKINS AND HIS DIXIE RAMBLERS, Minor Blues (Champion, May 6, 1931). This comes from the only record session by the Omaha, Nebraska, band whose roster had included Charlie Green a decade earlier. Trombonist Andre Oglesby reproduces the "Gouge" solo as the music begins. Jesse Simmons's alto sax takes up the theme later on. It's hard to judge how important this recording is, though we can infer that the Green cadenza was featured by the Dixie Ramblers during his pre-1924 tenure and perpetuated by other Perkins sidemen thereafter. That's a large assumption, and one that may not be possible to prove or disprove. But if it were the case, it would have been an early instance of the blues riff structures that characterized southwestern jazz in the 1920s and 1930s.

EARL HINES AND HIS ORCHESTRA, Blue Drag (Brunswick, July 14, 1932)

WASHBOARD RHYTHM KINGS, Blue Drag (Vocalion, December 14, 1932). This tune by Joseph Myrow was covered several times by jazz groups in London and Paris in the 1930s, as well as by the Original Yellow Jackets of Hot Springs, Arkansas, in 1937. Like "Sud Buster's Dream," its melody derives from "King of the Zulus," though it omits the vamp and adds a bridge. The result hints at "Bei Mir Bist Du Schoen," a tune from a 1932 Yiddish-language musical comedy that later became the hit that launched the Andrews Sisters' career in 1937.

BEN POLLACK AND HIS ORCHESTRA, Deep Jungle (Columbia, December 28, 1933). The opener is a variation of the cadenza, shared by Yank Lawson, trombonist Benny Morton, and clarinetist Matty Matlock, and played over an atmospheric tom-tom beat. Lawson and the tom-tom return for a final coda.

ROY ELDRIDGE ensembles, **Minor Jive** (Jazz Archives, 1937, and September 9, 1939; Decca [originally World Transcriptions], November 1943). Eldridge puts "King of the Zulus" through some remarkable and innovative paces, each one progressively faster. This was his favorite among the Armstrong classics—the first and last of these performances are from studio transcriptions, the 1939 from a broadcast.

ROSETTA HOWARD, Plain Lenox Avenue (Decca, June 14, 1939). The song moves to the relative minor for a patter section, and Barney Bigard plays his solo over a vamp.

WINGIE MANONE & HIS ORCHESTRA, In the Barrel (Bluebird, June 19, 1939). Wingie (RCA's spelling) provides a humorously literal spin on Armstrong's "Yes! I'm in the Barrel." The record opens with a trumpet cadenza, and the vamp continues, behind a dialogue about Wingy's wearing a barrel until his tailor's alterations are completed.

LOUIS ARMSTRONG AND DUKE ELLINGTON, It Don't Mean a Thing (Roulette, April 3, 1961). Ellington opens with the familiar piano vamp, but Armstrong decides that it's a cue for "King of the Zulus" instead. His brief chorus concludes as the song begins.

The foregoing list is not complete. Since the "Gouge" cadenza was modular in nature, it was plugged into other compositions on unexpected occasions, becoming an important and recurring element of jazz vocabulary. We can no longer ask Charlie Green, Louis Armstrong, Jabbo Smith, Jack Teagarden, and other principals about their inspirations, motivations, and other reasons for perpetuating something that had no name and was more a musical device than a fixed melody. Elusive as that notion is, it nevertheless inspired some strong performances—and there are undoubtedly further examples, waiting for astute listeners to spot them.

This essay is based on an informal survey of recordings that echo the Charlie Green chorus in one form or another. Phonodisc sightings aren't always reliable as historic landmarks, since they reflect only a part of the milieu in which jazz—or any music—was made. Still, records are indispensable snapshots, and enough of them can preserve an overall sense of what was taking place as they were being made. Without the opportunity to ask Green and others who made them, it's hard to form conclusions about why his solo, in its original and evolved incarnations, popped up in so many places. But the records show that it did, and perhaps subsequent study will reveal how and why.

NOTES

Special thanks to David Sager, Mark Berresford, Dan Morgenstern, Robert Bamberger, and Tom Tsotsi, who have given the matter some thought and come up with several of the above sightings. Richard Sudhalter offered an especially thoughtful critique. An earlier version of this article appeared in VJM, Autumn and Winter, 1999 (numbers 115 and 116).

1. Both "Gouge" songs were included in Handy's fascinating book *Blues* (New York: Albert & Charles Boni, 1926, 142-47).
2. Walter C. Allen, *Hendersonia: The Music of Fletcher Henderson and His Musicians: A Biodiscography* (Highland Park, NJ: self-published, 1973), 113.

A CREATIVE APPROACH TO MULTI-TONIC CHANGES: BEYOND COLTRANE'S HARMONIC FORMULA

Masaya Yamaguchi
Edited by Jay Sweet

In jazz circles, multi-tonic changes are often referred to as "Coltrane changes" because John Coltrane, one of the first practitioners of the multi-tonic harmonic concept, based the changes of "Giant Steps" on a descending augmented triad. This chord is a symmetrical group of three notes with limited possibilities for transposition.

Many of our concepts about multi-tonic changes come from the work of David Demsey. In both *Annual Review of Jazz Studies*[1] and *Down Beat*,[2] Demsey defined the harmonic structure of multi-tonic changes as being a harmonic root motion pattern that moves at the interval of a major or minor third. Although Demsey's work is a pioneering effort, I believe that his definition of multi-tonics can be developed further. The purpose of this article is to define multi-tonic changes as a harmonic root motion pattern that consists of note groups of limited transposition and to explore other possibilities.

I. GIANT STEPS: THE MODEL FOR MULTI-TONIC CHANGES

Early in 1959, Coltrane began to experiment with chord progressions in his innovative composition "Giant Steps." His "Giant Steps" changes have been considered the first experiment with minimized multi-tonic changes in jazz. However, in looking at the bridge of Rodgers and Hart's 1937 composition "Have You Met Miss Jones?" (Example 1), we notice a harmonic similarity to that of "Giant Steps." As with "Giant Steps," the bridge of "Have You Met Miss Jones?" tonicizes the keys of B♭, G♭, and D, which enharmonically outline a D augmented triad.

"Giant Steps" outlines descending E♭ augmented and B augmented triads in the first eight measures (Example 2). The second eight bars of the tune are based on an ascending E♭ augmented triad. The augmented triad (1 3 #5) is unique in that it divides an octave into three major thirds. This equal division places the augmented triad into a symmetrical pitch class set that limits its transposition to only four possibilities.[3] In looking at "Giant Steps," we have already pointed out that Coltrane organizes the piece through E♭ and B

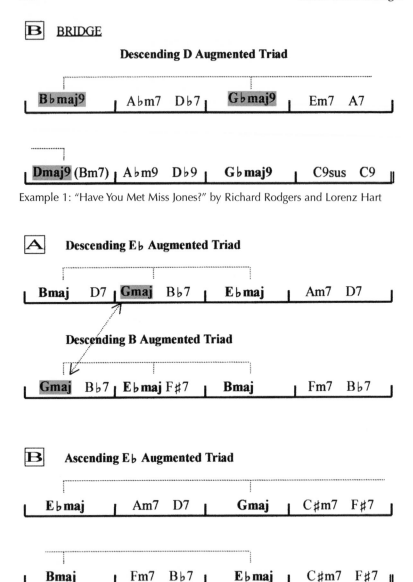

Example 1: "Have You Met Miss Jones?" by Richard Rodgers and Lorenz Hart

Example 2: "Giant Steps," by John Coltrane

augmented triads. It is important to keep in mind that these triads are inversions of each other; that is, they have the same pitches.

In improvising on the harmonic complexity and fast tempo of "Giant Steps," Coltrane often uses the 1st, 2nd, 3rd, and 5th pitches of the major scale, creating a pentatonic fragment (Example 3). In fact, Coltrane's pentatonic improvisation in "Giant Steps" was by itself a significant achievement. In *John Coltrane: His Life and Music*, Porter further underlines this point:

> Musicians on all instruments have taken the so-called pentatonic patterns that he [Coltrane] used on "Giant Steps" and applied them to all kinds of chord

Example 3: "Giant Steps," by John Coltrane (1st solo chorus)

progressions. Over a rapid rate of harmonic change, musicians play one such pattern over each chord. Over a slow-moving piece harmonically, such as a blues or modal pieces, they may play a sequence of four-note patterns that implies faster harmonic activity, enriching what might otherwise be moments of stasis — in this case they are learning from what Coltrane did in the two years following "Giant Steps." . . . In this way, Coltrane's innovation becomes a part of the mainstream, a skill that anyone can learn.[4]

As Porter points out, Coltrane's use of pentatonics has influenced many improvisers. His solos over later compositions, such as his 1964 recording of "Pursuance" (Part III of *A Love Supreme*), provide further evidence of interest in pentatonic improvisation. It is important to notice how Coltrane often ignores playing the root of a chord in order to free himself for further pentatonic possibilities, a procedure that creates a "polypentatonic" approach (Example 4). It is also important to note that Coltrane's pianist McCoy Tyner (with whom Coltrane worked throughout much of the 1960s) also developed an original pentatonic technique along with Coltrane. Tyner's improvisation on "Passion Dance" (1967) shows alternating pentatonic scales against an F7sus4 chord (Example 5). While Tyner voices an F7sus4 chord in his left hand, his right juxtaposes contrasting pentatonic collections. In looking at measures 137–40 of "Passion Dance" (Example

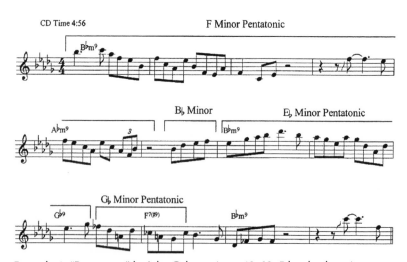

Example 4: "Pursuance," by John Coltrane (mm. 49–60; 5th solo chorus)

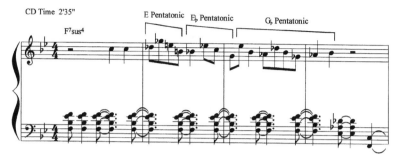

NOTE: Left-hand voicing consists of 1 4 ♭7 (in F).

Example 5: "Passion Dance," by McCoy Tyner (mm. 117–20)

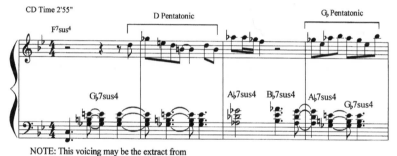

NOTE: This voicing may be the extract from
D Pentatonic: F♯, B, E = 3 6 2 of Dmaj

Example 6: "Passion Dance," by McCoy Tyner (mm. 137–40)

6), we see how Tyner further develops right-hand pentatonicism over a left hand with parallel sus4 chords.

II. FURTHER EXPLORATION OF MULTI-TONIC CHANGES: COLTRANE'S "SUPERIMPOSITION" CONCEPT

Coltrane's exploration into multi-tonic changes (M.T.C.) is summarized in Example 7.[5] Coltrane's harmonic explorations can be analyzed in several ways, but I will concentrate on "superimposition." Let us begin with "Fifth House," which is based on the Cole Porter standard "What Is This Thing Called Love?" (The title "Fifth House" comes from Coltrane's interest in astrology and the Tadd Dameron tune "Hot House," which is also based on

Song Title	Compositional Basis	M.T.C. Code
Giant Steps	Coltrane's Original	**M.T.C. 2b-1**
Countdown	Tune Up (Eddie "Cleanhead" Vinson) [NOTE: Often misattributed to Miles Davis]	**M.T.C. 2a-1**
Fifth House	What Is This Thing Called Love? (Cole Porter) Hot House (Tadd Dameron)	M.T.C. 2a-1 Superimposed
Satellite	How High the Moon (Morgan Lewis / Nancy Hamilton)	M.T.C. 2b-1
26-2	Confirmation (Charlie Parker)	M.T.C. 2b-1
Exotica	I Can't Get Started (Vernon Duke / Ira Gershwin)	M.T.C. 2b-1
Body And Soul	Body and Soul (John Green / Edward Heyman)	M.T.C. 2b-1 Re-harmonized
But Not For Me	But Not for Me (George & Ira Gershwin)	M.T.C. 2b-1 Re-harmonized
The Night Has A Thousand Eyes	The Night Has a Thousand Eyes (Jerry Brainin / Buddy Bernier)	M.T.C. 2a-1 Re-harmonized
Grand Central	Coltrane's Original	M.T.C. 2b-1 modified Superimposed
Limehouse Blues	Limehouse Blues (Douglas Furber / Philip Braham)	M.T.C. 2a-1 modified Superimposed
Summertime	Summertime (George Gershwin / DuBose Heyward)	M.T.C. 2a-1 Superimposed
Central Park West	Peace (Horace Silver)	M.T.C.5 modified [I → ♭ III→VI→V→ I → ♭ III → I → I]

Example 7: Coltrane's exploration into multi-tonic changes

the chord changes of "What Is This Thing Called Love?" and is frequently associated with Charlie Parker.[6])

In comparing Parker's improvisation on "Hot House" (Example 8) and Coltrane's improvisation on "Fifth House" (Example 9), we can get a sense of Coltrane's harmonic techniques. On "Fifth House," Coltrane's choice of notes implies his own harmonic changes over a C pedal point—a technique often called "superimposition."

Although the A, B, and D sections of "Fifth House" are played over a pedal point (as shown in Example 10), Coltrane superimposes "Coltrane changes" over the pedal. He also develops an improvisational concept using scale tones 1, 2, 3, and 5, which create a pentatonic fragment, similar to his improvisations on "Giant Steps" and "Countdown." Coltrane continues to use his harmonic formula, but inverts the scale tones 1, 2, 3, and 5 to 2, 1, 3, and 5 over the A♭ chords of "Fifth House" (at m. 6 and m. 14). Although this inversion appears in "Fifth House," it does not ap-

Example 8: "Hot House," by Tadd Dameron (improvisation by Charlie Parker)

pear in his "Giant Steps" solo.[7] Coltrane continued to develop his technique of superimposition in such compositions as "Grand Central" (Example 11) and "Summertime" (Example 12). The use of multi-tonic changes allows the ear to accept the sound of the superimposed harmonies.

Example 9: "Fifth House," by John Coltrane

Example 10: "Fifth House," by John Coltrane ("C" pedal point)

Example 11: "Grand Central," by John Coltrane (mm. 58–61)

Example 12: "Summertime," by George Gershwin and DuBose Heyward (improvisation by John Coltrane; mm. 43–44)

III. MULTI-TONIC CHANGES

Earlier, I pointed out that "Coltrane changes" are based on augmented triads and symmetrically grouped notes. In the following passage from *Down Beat*, Coltrane speaks about his note-grouping concept:

> I could stack up chords—say, on a C7, I sometimes superimposed an E♭7, up to an F#7, down to an F. That way I could play three chords on one. . . . I thought in groups of notes, not of one note at a time. I tried to place these groups on the accents and emphasize the strong beats—maybe on 2 here and on 4 over at the end. I would set up the line and drop groups of notes—a long line with accents dropped as I moved along.[8]

An example of this superimposition technique can be seen in a passage excerpted from "Moment's Notice" (Example 13), in which Coltrane uses scale tones 1, 2, ♭5, and ♭6, which can be transposed in six different ways. Porter labels the phrase as "Coltrane's Favorite Formula from 1958."[9] We can be fairly certain that Coltrane noticed the nature of the symmetrically grouped notes.

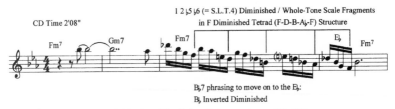

Example 13: "Moment's Notice," by John Coltrane (mm. 70–73)

Before we discuss further possibilities, we should clearly define multi-tonics. As we have seen earlier, we can define them as note groupings within their original key structures that project harmonic root motions of note groups of limited transposition. For instance, the chord changes of "Giant Steps" can be regarded as a typical example of multi-tonic changes because of the use of the augmented triads. With these points in mind, I have established a systematic method to explore all the possibilities of multi-tonic changes (Example 14).[10]

If one is creating tunes using multi-tonic changes, a coherent key scheme based on note groupings of limited transposition must exist. In further developing Coltrane's innovations, tenor saxophonist Joe Lovano has also used multi-tonics in his compositions. The bridge of Lovano's "Sleepy Giant" (Example 15) is a good example of multi-tonic changes using a "diminished tetrad."[11] Coltrane's "Central Park West" (Example 16) is another clear example of multi-tonic changes using a diminished tetrad. Although based on an augmented and diminished key sequence, Lovano's composition "Emperor Jones" (Example 17) is composed with a methodical multi-tonic plan.

In looking at "Emperor Jones" in relation to "Giant Steps," we see that Lovano chose to use II–V chord progressions that relate to the *previous* tonic chord (i.e., B♭maj7, then Cm7–F7). Such a practice should be labeled as "modified."

In analyzing Lovano's composition "In the Land of Ephesus" (Example 18), we can see that the chord progression fits almost perfectly into our chart (Example 14) under M.T.C. 3b-2 (based on 1 4 ♭5 7). If the final A♭maj7#11 were changed to Amaj7, it would meet all of the requirements of M.T.C. 3b-2.

"In the Land of Ephesus" seeks to capture the fact that Lovano's compositional scheme is nearly based on M.T.C. 3b-2. That is, M.T.C. 3b-2 consists of 1 4 ♭5 7, which is classified as a subset of limited transposition (S.L.T.)—in this case, S.L.T. 3.[12] S.L.T. 3 is limited to six possibilities of

2 note

S.L.T. 1 1 ♭5 (= Tritone)

S.L.T. 1 is limited to six possibilities of transposition.

Multi-Tonic Change 1	Dm7	D♭7	G♭maj	G7	Cmaj
(M.T.C.)			♭V		I

3 note

S.L.T. 2 1 3 ♭6 (= Augmented Triad)

S.L.T. 2 is limited to four possibilities of transposition.

M.T.C. 2a-1	Dm7	E♭7	A♭maj	B7	Emaj	G7	Cmaj	"Countdown"
			♭VI		III		I	Descending C Aug

M.T.C. 2a-2	Dm7	B7	Emaj	E♭7	A♭maj	G7	Cmaj	
			III		♭VI		I	Ascending E Aug

M.T.C. 2b-1	Bmaj	D7	Gmaj	B♭7	E♭maj	"Giant Steps"
	♭VI		III		I	Descending E♭ Aug

M.T.C. 2b-2	Gmaj	G♭7	Bmaj	B♭7	E♭maj	
	III		♭VI		I	Ascending G Aug

4 note

S.L.T. 3 1 ♭2 ♭5 5

  1 4 ♭5 7

S.L.T. 3 is limited to six possibilities of transposition.

M.T.C. 3a-1	Gmaj	D♭7	G♭maj	A♭7	D♭maj	G7	Cmaj	Des. 1 ♭2 ♭5 5
	V		♭V		♭II		I	

M.T.C. 3a-2	Fmaj	D♭7	G♭maj	G♭7	Bmaj	G7	Cmaj	Asc. 1 ♭2 ♭5 5 (in F)
	IV		♭V	×	VII		I	

M.T.C. 3b-1	Bmaj	D♭7	G♭maj	C7	Fmaj	G7	Cmaj	Asc. 1 4 ♭5 7
	VII		♭V		IV		I	

M.T.C. 3b-2	D♭maj	D♭7	G♭maj	D7	Gmaj	G7	Cmaj	Des. 1 4 ♭5 7 (in D♭)
	♭II	×	♭V		V	×	I	

Example 14: Multi-tonic changes: A new theory based on "the subsets of limited transposition," copyright 1999 by Yamaguchi, Masaya. *Continued on next page.*

transposition, as S.L.T. 4: 1 2 ♭5 ♭6. As indicated, Lovano uses S.L.T. 4 in the tail of M.T.C. 3b-2 as a twist: the root motion of Emaj7#11–D7#11–A♭ maj7#11–B♭maj7#11 is, in fact, made of 1 2 ♭5 ♭6 (S.L.T. 4). In other words, Lovano's compositional scheme of "In the Land of Ephesus" interchanges S.L.T. 3 with S.L.T. 4 in its harmonic formula. It is important to recognize that the first four chords of "In the Land of Ephesus" imply a "third related" cycle: B♭maj7–D7, and so on.

4 note (continued)

S.L.T. 4   1 2 b5 b6
             1 3 b5 b7

S.L.T. 4 is limited to six possibilities of transposition.

M.T.C. 4a-1	Abmaj	Db7	Gbmaj	A7	Dmaj	G7	Cmaj	Des. 1 2 b5 b6
	bVI		bV		II		I	
M.T.C. 4a-2	Emaj	Db7	Gbmaj	F7	Bbmaj	G7	Cmaj	Asc. 1 2 b5 b6 (in E)
	III		bV		bVII		I	
M.T.C. 4b-1	Bbmaj	Db7	Gbmaj	B7	Emaj	G7	Cmaj	Des. 1 3 b5 b7
	bVII		bV		III		I	
M.T.C. 4b-2	Dmaj	Db7	Gbmaj	Eb7	Abmaj	G7	Cmaj	Asc. 1 3 b5 b7 (in D)
	II		bV		bVI		I	

S.L.T. 5   1 b3 b5 6   (= Diminished Tetrad)

S.L.T. 5 is limited to three possibilities of transposition.

M.T.C. 5a-1	Amaj	Db7	Gbmaj	Bb7	Ebmaj	G7	Cmaj	Des. 1 b3 b5 6
	VI		bV		bIII		I	
M.T.C. 5a-2	Ebmaj	Db7	Gbmaj	E7	Amaj	G7	Cmaj	Asc. 1 b3 b5 6 (in Eb)
	bIII		bV		VI		I	

Example 14, *continued*

 BRIDGE

Ascending Eb Diminished Tetrad

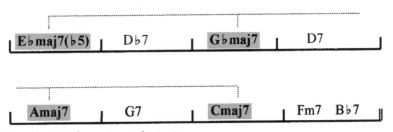

Example 15: "Sleepy Giant," by Joe Lovano

B Diminished Tetrad

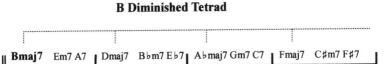

Example 16: "Central Park West," by John Coltrane. *Continued on next page.*

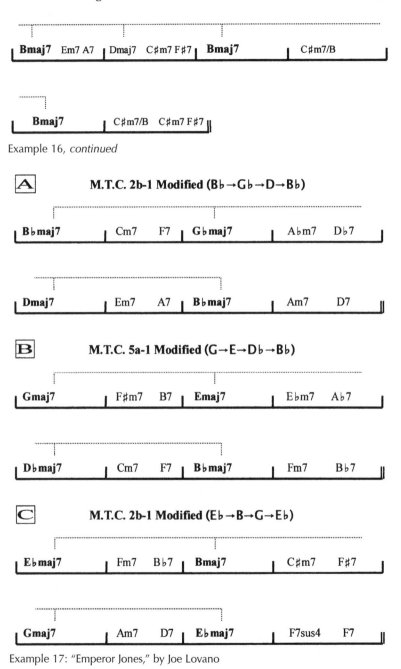

| Bmaj7 | Em7 A7 | Dmaj7 | C♯m7 F♯7 | Bmaj7 | | C♯m7/B |

| Bmaj7 | | C♯m7/B | C♯m7 F♯7 |

Example 16, *continued*

A   **M.T.C. 2b-1 Modified (B♭→G♭→D→B♭)**

| B♭maj7 | | Cm7 | F7 | G♭maj7 | | A♭m7 | D♭7 |

| Dmaj7 | | Em7 | A7 | B♭maj7 | | Am7 | D7 |

B   **M.T.C. 5a-1 Modified (G→E→D♭→B♭)**

| Gmaj7 | | F♯m7 | B7 | Emaj7 | | E♭m7 | A♭7 |

| D♭maj7 | | Cm7 | F7 | B♭maj7 | | Fm7 | B♭7 |

C   **M.T.C. 2b-1 Modified (E♭→B→G→E♭)**

| E♭maj7 | | Fm7 | B♭7 | Bmaj7 | | C♯m7 | F♯7 |

| Gmaj7 | | Am7 | D7 | E♭maj7 | | F7sus4 | F7 |

Example 17: "Emperor Jones," by Joe Lovano

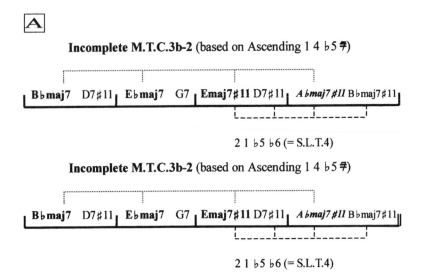

NOTE: The fact that the final chord in the sequence nearly meets the requirements, but does not do so exactly, is represented by the crossed-out numeral 7.

Example 18: "In the Land of Ephesus," by Joe Lovano

IV. COMPOSITION AND RE-HARMONIZATION (SUPERIMPOSITION/SUBSTITUTION) TECHNIQUES WITH MULTI-TONIC CHANGES

Coltrane's multi-tonic innovations imply further possibilities. My composition "Steps of the Giant" serves as an example of how these techniques may be extended (Example 19).

Compared to the structure of "Giant Steps" (based on M.T.C. 2b-1), "Steps of the Giant" can be seen as based on the opposite contour (descending/ascending) in chord changes (and melodies): M.T.C. 2b-2. We should not overlook that "Steps of the Giant" is still based on augmented triads (S.L.T. 2). Having made this distinction, we may further observe that my composition "Cortlandt St." (Example 20) is based on Lovano's "In the Land of Ephesus," i.e., 1 4 ♭5 7 and 1 ♭2 ♭5 5 (S.L.T. 3). Also notice the complete M.T.C. 3b-2 in the first four measures of "Cortlandt St."

In general, multi-tonic changes should aim at setting up more static chords, i.e., tonics. This principle leads to the table of possible chord changes, shown in Example 21.[13]

Example 19: "Steps of the Giant," by Masaya Yamaguchi

A

Complete M.T.C.3b-2 (based on Ascending 1 4 ♭5 7)

| B♭maj7 | D7♯11 | E♭maj7 | G7 | Emaj7 | E♭7♯11 | Amaj7 | B♭maj7 |

♭2 1 ♭5 5 (= S.L.T.3)

Incomplete M.T.C.3b-2 (based on Ascending 1 4 ♭5 7̸)

| B♭maj7 | D7♯11 | E♭maj7 | G7 | Emaj7 | B7♯11 | *Fmaj7* | B♭maj7 |

4 1 ♭5 7 (= S.L.T.3)

NOTE: The fact that the final chord in the sequence (i.e., Fmaj7) nearly meets the requirements, but does not do so exactly, is represented by the crossed-out numeral 7.

Example 20: "Cortlandt St.," by Masaya Yamaguchi

I → I

M.T.C. 2b-1 (expanded)	Ebmaj	Gb7	Bmaj	D7	Gmaj	Bb7	Ebmaj	"Giant Steps"
	I		bVI		III		I	

M.T.C. 2b-2 (expanded)	Ebmaj	D7	Gmaj	Gb7	Bmaj	Bb7	Ebmaj	
	I		III		bVI		I	

II b → I

M.T.C. 3b-2	Dbmaj	Db7	Gbmaj	D7	Gmaj	G7	Cmaj	
	bII	X	bV		V	X	I	overlaps

II → I

M.T.C. 4b-2	Dmaj	Db7	Gbmaj	Eb7	Abmaj	G7	Cmaj
	II		bV		bVI		I

Cf. II-V-I	M.T.C. 1	Dm7	Db7	Gbmaj	G7	Cmaj		
	M.T.C. 2a-1	Dm7	Eb7	Abmaj	B7	Emaj	G7	Cmaj
	M.T.C. 2a-2	Dm7	B7	Emaj	Eb7	Abmaj	G7	Cmaj

III b → I

M.T.C. 5a-2	Ebmaj	Db7	Gbmaj	E7	Amaj	G7	Cmaj
	bIII		bV		VI		I

III → I

M.T.C. 2a-2	Dm7	B7	Emaj	Eb7	Abmaj	G7	Cmaj
			III		bVI		I

M.T.C. 2b-2	Gmaj	Gb7	Bmaj	Bb7	Ebmaj
	III		bVI		I

M.T.C. 4a-2	Emaj	Db7	Gbmaj	F7	Bbmaj	G7	Cmaj
	III		bV		bVII		I

IV → I

M.T.C. 3a-2	Fmaj	Db7	Gbmaj	Gb7	Bmaj	G7	Cmaj	
	IV		bV	X	VII		I	overlap

V b → I

M.T.C. 1	Dm7	Db7	Gbmaj	G7	Cmaj
			bV		I

Example 21: Multi-tonic changes as superimposition techniques. *Continued on next page.*

Multi-tonic changes are also useful for re-harmonizing standards in which static chord progressions occur, as we may observe in my re-harmonization of "Stella by Starlight" (Example 22). It will be necessary, at this point, to explain 1 b2 b5 5 (S.L.T. 3) and 1 2 b5 b6 (S.L.T. 4). In the re-harmonization of the bridge, the first four measures are based on a descending 1 b2 b5 5 note group (S.L.T. 3) in C minor (i.e., V→V→II–I superimposed on the original V–I, or G+ to Cm). The second four measures of the bridge consist of a descending 1 3 b5 b7 (inverted 1 2 b5 b6, which is S.L.T. 4) note group in Bb major (i.e., bVII→V–III–I superimposed on the original bVII–I, or Ab7 to Bbmaj7).

V → I

M.T.C. 3a-1	Gmaj	Db7	Gbmaj	Ab7	Dbmaj	G7	Cmaj	
	V		bV		bII		I	

VIb → I

M.T.C. 2a-1	Dm7	Eb7	Abmaj	B7	Emaj	G7	Cmaj	"Countdown"
			bVI		III		I	
M.T.C. 2b-1	Bmaj	D7	Gmaj	Bb7	Ebmaj			"Giant Steps"
	bVI		III		I			
M.T.C. 4a-1	Abmaj	Db7	Gbmaj	A7	Dmaj	G7	Cmaj	
	bVI		bV		II		I	

VI → I

M.T.C. 5a-1	Amaj	Db7	Gbmaj	Bb7	Ebmaj	G7	Cmaj
	VI		bV		bIII		I

VIIb → I

M.T.C. 4b-1	Bbmaj	Db7	Gbmaj	B7	Emaj	G7	Cmaj
	bVII		bV		III		I

VII → I

M.T.C. 3b-1	Bmaj	Db7	Gbmaj	C7	Fmaj	G7	Cmaj
	VII		bV		IV		I

Example 21, *continued*

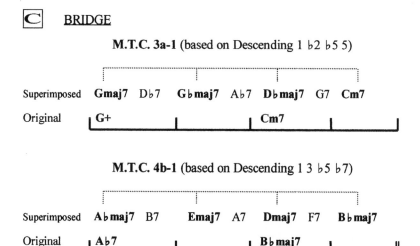

C **BRIDGE**

M.T.C. 3a-1 (based on Descending 1 b2 b5 5)

Superimposed	**Gmaj7** Db7	**Gbmaj7** Ab7	**Dbmaj7** G7	**Cm7**
Original	G+		Cm7	

M.T.C. 4b-1 (based on Descending 1 3 b5 b7)

Superimposed	**Abmaj7** B7	**Emaj7** A7	**Dmaj7** F7	**Bbmaj7**
Original	Ab7		Bbmaj7	

Example 22: "Stella by Starlight" (in Bb), by Victor Young (re-harmonized by Masaya Yamaguchi)

CONCLUSION

To expand expressive possibilities and give his music a unique harmonic voice, John Coltrane, using material derived from Nicholas Slonimsky, devised the changes of "Giant Steps." The harmonic structure of "Giant Steps" has influenced generations of improvisers, composers, and students of jazz. I hope that the multi-tonic concept discussed in this article will assist readers in understanding the harmonic structures of compositions inspired by "Giant Steps" as well as deepen their grasp of harmonic possibilities implied by the subsets of limited transposition.

APPENDIX: "THE SUBSETS OF LIMITED TRANSPOSITION"

An earlier form of this table appeared in *The Complete Thesaurus of Musical Scales* (New York: Charles Colin Publications, 2000). Reproduced by permission as Example 23.

---

2 note
S.L.T. 1   1   ♭5   = Tritone
          S.L.T. 1 is limited to six possibilities of transposition.
3 note
S.L.T. 2   1   3 ♭6   = Augmented Triad
          S.L.T. 2 is limited to four possibilities of transposition.

---

4 note
S.L.T. 3   1 ♭2 ♭5   5
              1   4 ♭5   7

          S.L.T. 3 is limited to six possibilities of transposition.

S.L.T. 4   1   2 ♭5 ♭6
              1   3 ♭5 ♭7

          S.L.T. 4 is limited to six possibilities of transposition.

S.L.T. 5   1 ♭3 ♭5   6   = Diminished Tetrad
          S.L.T. 5 is limited to three possibilities of transposition.

---

6 note
S.L.T. 6   1 ♭2   2 ♭5   5 ♭6
              1 ♭2   4 ♭5   5   7   = M.T.L. 5
              1   3   4 ♭5 ♭7   7

          S.L.T. 6 is limited to six possibilities of transposition.

S.L.T. 7   1 ♭2 ♭3 ♭5   5   6
              1   2   4 ♭5 ♭6   7
              1 ♭3   3 ♭5   6 ♭7

          S.L.T. 7 is limited to six possibilities of transposition.

Example 23: The subsets of limited transposition. *Continued on next page.*

S.L.T. 8   1 b2 3 4 b6 6

        1 b3 3 5 b6 7   = Augmented

S.L.T. 8 is limited to four possibilities of transposition.

S.L.T. 9   1 2 b3 b5 b6 6

        1 b2 3 b5 5 b7

          1 b3 4 b5 6 7

S.L.T. 9 is limited to six possibilities of transposition.

S.L.T. 10   1 2 3 b5 b6 b7   = Whole Tone   = M.T.L. 1
S.L.T. 10 is limited to two possibilities of transposition.

---

8 note

S.L.T. 11   1 b2 2 b3 b5 5 b6 6

      1 b2 2 4 b5 5 b6 7   = M.T.L. 4

        1 b2 3 4 b5 5 b7 7

          1 b3 3 4 b5 6 b7 7

S.L.T. 11 is limited to six possibilities of transposition.

S.L.T. 12   1 b2 2 3 b5 5 b6 b7

      1 b2 b3 4 b5 5 6 7

        1 2 3 4 b5 b6 b7 7   = M.T.L. 6

        1 2 b3 3 b5 b6 6 b7

S.L.T. 12 is limited to six possibilities of transposition.

S.L.T. 13   1 b2 b3 3 b5 5 6 b7   = M.T.L. 2

      1 2 b3 4 b5 b6 6 7   = Diminished
S.L.T. 13 is limited to three possibilities of transposition.

---

9 note

S.L.T. 14   1 b2 2 3 4 b5 b6 6 b7

      1 b2 b3 3 4 5 b6 6 7

      1 2 b3 3 b5 5 b6 b7 7   = M.T.L. 3

S.L.T. 14 is limited to four possibilities of transposition.

10 note

S.L.T. 15   1 b2 2 b3 3 b5 5 b6 6 b7

      1 b2 2 b3 4 b5 5 b6 6 7   = M.T.L. 7

      1 b2 2 3 4 b5 5 b6 b7 7

      1 b2 b3 3 4 b5 5 6 b7 7

      1 2 b3 3 4 b5 b6 6 b7 7

S.L.T. 15 is limited to six possibilities of transposition.

NOTE: M.T.L.= The Modes of Limited Transposition <by Olivier Messiaen>

Example 23, *continued*

NOTES

I would like to express my gratitude to David Demsey for his inspiration, to Lewis Porter for his encouragement, and to Jay Sweet and Henry Martin for their help in editing this article.

1. David Demsey, "Chromatic Third Relations in the Music of John Coltrane," *Annual Review of Jazz Studies* 5 (1991): 145–80.
2. David Demsey, "Pro Session: 'Earthly' Origins of Coltrane's Third Cycles," *Down Beat* (July 1995): 63.
3. It might be clearer to say that C+ inverts to E+, which inverts to G#+.
4. Lewis Porter, *John Coltrane: His Life and Music* (Ann Arbor: University of Michigan Press, 1997), 295.
5. For further details of "M.T.C. Code," see the chart of Multi-Tonic Changes in Example 14.
6. Note that Coltrane also recorded "Hot House" on alto saxophone in 1946.
7. More noteworthy is the configuration of 2 1 3 5 occurring in both solos: Parker at m. 18 and Coltrane at m. 6 and m. 14. These configurations of 2 1 3 5 may be a coincidence.
8. John Coltrane in collaboration with Don DeMicheal, "Coltrane on Coltrane," *Down Beat* (September 29, 1960): 26–27.
9. Lewis Porter, *John Coltrane: His Life and Music* (Ann Arbor: University of Michigan Press, 1997), 134–35.
10. For further details of "note groups of limited transposition," please refer to *The Complete Thesaurus of Musical Scales* (New York: Charles Colin Publications, 2000). Or see the appendix (Example 23).
11. A tetrad is a four-note chordal group in thirds.
12. See "The Subsets of Limited Transposition" in the appendix (Example 23).
13. Compare Example 21 to the chart of Multi-Tonic Changes (Example 14).

SELECTED BIBLIOGRAPHY

Baker, David. *The Style of John Coltrane: A Musical and Historical Perspective.* Lebanon, IN: Studio 244, 1980.

Coltrane, Alice, ed. *The Music of John Coltrane* (lead sheets). Milwaukee: Hal Leonard, 1991.

Coltrane, John, in collaboration with Don DeMicheal. "Coltrane on Coltrane." *Down Beat* (September 29, 1960): 26–27.

Demsey, David. "Chromatic Third Relations in the Music of John Coltrane." *Annual Review of Jazz Studies* 5 (1991): 145–180.

———. "Pro Session: 'Earthly' Origins of Coltrane's Third Cycles." *Down Beat* (July 1995): 63.

———. *Artist Transcription Series: John Coltrane Plays Giant Steps.* Milwaukee: Hal Leonard, 1996.

Kynaston, Trent. "Pro Session: Joe Lovano's Solo on 'Emperor Jones.'" *Down Beat* (May 1992): 64–65.

Lovano, Joe (no transcriber listed). *Artist Transcription Series: Joe Lovano.* Milwaukee: Hal Leonard, 1995.

Messiaen, Olivier. *The Technique of My Musical Language.* Paris: Alphonse Luduc, 1944.

Porter, Lewis. *John Coltrane: His Life and Music.* Ann Arbor: University of Michigan Press, 1997.

Ricker, Ramon, and Walt Weiskopf. *John Coltrane: A Player's Guide to His Harmony.* New Albany, IN: Jamey Aebersold, 1991.

Sher, Chuck, ed. *The New Real Book.* Vol. 2, *C-Vocal Version.* Petaluma, CA: Sher Music Co., 1991.

Simpkins, Cuthbert Ormond. *Coltrane: A Biography.* New York: Herndon House, 1975. Reprint, Baltimore: Black Classic Press, 1975.

Slonimsky, Nicholas. *Thesaurus of Scales and Melodic Patterns.* New York: Coleman-Ross, 1947, 160–168.

———. *Perfect Pitch: A Life Story.* New York: Oxford, 1988, 173–180.

Yamaguchi, Masaya. *The Complete Thesaurus of Musical Scales.* New York: Charles Colin Music Publications, 2000.

———. "Pro Session: Note Groups of Limited Transposition: A Key to Unlocking Multitonic Possibilities." *Down Beat* (September 2000): 70.

White, Andrew. *Trane 'n Me: A Treatise on the Music of John Coltrane.* Washington, D.C.: Andrew's Musical Enterprises, 1981.

JAZZ QUARTET:
A SONNET SEQUENCE

Mark Haywood

PRELUDE

To four jazz masters let us pay our dues:
To him whose vision's locomotive power
His name with new significance imbues
And which, not once derailed, engenders our
Unending debt of gratitude; to one
Whose name alike denotes his gift and shows
How far ahead[1] he strides of those who un-
inspiredly contest his skill; to those
Twin pianistic giants last who hold
Respectively a priesthood justly earned
By genial greatness, and a touch of gold
Like that of Midas, effortlessly learned.
And let that pipe which England's bard made sing[2]
Now dignify our fourfold offering.

NOTES

1. As in the album title *Miles Ahead*.
2. The Shakespearean sonnet form. See my *"Monkishness:* A Sonnet Sequence,"
   Annual Review of Jazz Studies 10, for an explanation of my interest in pre-
   senting jazz research in this poetic form.

JOHN COLTRANE: *GREENSLEEVES*[1]

"With courtly curtsies and with gracious bows
Come let us step into this stately dance
Where thoughts of pure decorum but arouse
Reciprocated modesties." But ans-
wers Trane with screaming pressure like a sei-
zure, like an apoplexy made to rend
The mask, to let the heart of hearts beat free

And with one blow deceptive arts to end.
"How strange this dance, that now bids me fulfill
The inner prompting that I hid." Then coun-
ters Trane, the victor's palm in sight, until
Through force of truth he sacks the truthless town.
"My lady, see how peacefully depart
The mists that clouded once my loving heart."

NOTE

1. On *Africa/Brass*, Impulse AS-6. This sonnet presents the alternating moods of
   Coltrane's performance as an apparent conflict. The stately artifice of the old
   melody is represented as the inhibition of emotion, and this is repeatedly torn
   apart by the cutting honesty of Coltrane's horn, which wears its heart on its
   sleeve. In the end emotion is victorious and the voice of modesty is won over,
   yet, since the emotion is that of love, it transpires that there never was a conflict after all. I have tried to capture Coltrane's ultimate peacefulness here, as
   well as to suggest how it is so often misconstrued amid his passionate playing.

MILES DAVIS: *SO WHAT*[1]

As when, from sleep's oppressive chains unbound,
We wake with dim-lit consciousness, just so
A dark, primeval somnolence of sound
Subsists 'til well-known structures[2] overthrow
This drowsy world with clearer thought. As we,
Then wakeful, face the prospect of this morn,
With quiet, pleasant expectation, see
How with relaxed composure Miles's horn
Swings into action. Yet what day is known
Within whose calm there never once arose
Some altered tenor,[3] like a storm cloud blown
This way and that before the evening's close?
This day that ends as it at first began –
How does it differ from the life of Man?

NOTES

1. On *Kind of Blue*, Columbia CL1355.
2. The famous "So What" chords.
3. The more pressured mood exerted by the alto and tenor of Adderley and
   Coltrane.

THELONIOUS MONK: *BLUE MONK*[1]

With stern interrogatory intent
The question twice is posed (more pressing in
Its iteration),[2] but, on mischief bent,
The child concludes his answer[3] with a lin-
gering quip, a disyllabic codicil, which rude
Impertinence the questioner resents
And twice again with ever angrier mood
Demands a straight reply.[4] The child repents,
Repeating, now without addenda wry,
The answer given before,[5] or else appears
Repentant, for when dealt a third chasti-
sement by his interlocutor[6] he jeers
With utterances well designed to storm
The other's obsolescent sense of form.[7]

NOTES

1. This sonnet addresses the actual 12-bar melody of "Blue Monk."

2–7. The remaining note references in the sonnet are cross-referenced in the musical example.

OSCAR PETERSON: *GEORGIA ON MY MIND*[1]

Give ear to that reflectiveness[2] which paves
The tranquil way to Georgia; Georgia which
With reminiscence's nostalgic waves
Is sweetly[3] brought to mind, until more rich
And mellow melancholies start to steer
The pining spirit as, a second time,[4]
Is contemplated Georgia's song. Give ear
To how it is this reverie sublime
Then makes transition (like a bridge[5] of fair
And elegant proportion) to where cries
Of heartfelt misery seem set to tear
With pain the very blueness of the skies.
How strangely then the whole of Georgia's bliss
Symmetrical appears[6]—give ear to this.

NOTES

1. On *Night Train*, Verve 2352 067.
2. During Peterson's four-bar introduction and the first A section of the AABA song form.
3. Cf. the song's lyrics: "Georgia, Georgia, . . . an old sweet song . . . as sweet and clear as moonlight through the pines."
4. The second A section of the AABA form, with its richer harmonies.
5. After the B section, or bridge, of the tune, Peterson opens up in the following A section with a full-blooded bluesy feel.
6. Peterson adds a final iteration of the A section plus a four-bar coda to make a perfectly symmetrical "intro + AABAA + coda" whole.

ERIK WIEDEMANN'S CAREER AND WORKS: THE STORY OF A MAJOR FIGURE IN DANISH JAZZ RESEARCH AND CRITICISM

Fabian Holt

Dr. Erik Wiedemann, professor emeritus, a Danish jazz critic and scholar for over 50 years, died on March 2, 2001, at the age of 70. Wiedemann was one of Denmark's most intelligent, original, and influential jazz critics and scholars.

This article is written on the occasion of Wiedemann's death, but it is not an obituary. Rather, it is an outline of Wiedemann's career and writings with a broad perspective. It provides analytical summaries of his two major books with a focus on important historical, cultural, and ideological relations and influences. The article includes a complete bibliography. Some of his writings have international importance, and we shall see that his career and the ideas he articulated are related to important themes and debates in the history of both Danish and international jazz criticism and research.

In personal terms, I feel an obligation to write this article. I was his only colleague in jazz research in the Department of Musicology at the University of Copenhagen.[1] My personal relations with him will be touched upon at the end of the article, but by way of introduction, I should like to mention that he made me more aware of the qualities of learning from other people, respecting other people, and at the same time trying to develop one's own style and ideas. This ideal is valuable as a personal and scholarly ethic, as I hope to show on the following pages.

CRITIC AND SCHOLAR: DISCURSIVE STRATEGIES AND GENERATION GAPS

To begin with, I should like to emphasize that Wiedemann was both a critic and a scholar. These two parallel and sometimes overlapping activities are essential to an understanding of his career and writings. In Wiedemann's works, criticism and academic research were sometimes able to meet, but he was aware of the differences between these genres.[2] If we examine the history of jazz research, we find that important work has been done by authors who were also critics (e.g., Marshall Stearns, André Hodeir, and Gunther Schuller), and up to about 1960 the distinction between criticism and research was fluid. The field of academic jazz research had not even been established. If a certain level of methodology is accepted as a fundamental criterion of academic research, then we might even say that academic jazz research only came of age in the 1970s or, in a strict sense, perhaps not even before the mid-1990s, when Krin Gabbard, Scott DeVeaux, and others opened the path to an interdisciplinary jazz research that does not differ on the methodological level from other disciplines in the humanities and the social sciences. Even if Gabbard's two anthologies from 1995 have been criticized, we have to admit that they helped to call forth the new interdisciplinary tendency in jazz research, which seems to be a most effective strategy.

We also find that the field of jazz research has drawn extensively on criticism; we might even say that jazz research developed from criticism. Nevertheless, the dialogue between these two fields of intellectual activity can still be improved to the advantage of both. Critics often think of scholars as being too academic—i.e., too abstract, philosophical, and distanced from the musical experience. On the other hand, it has almost become a cliché in academic circles to dismiss earlier jazz criticism, although such writing is the most important literary source for today's jazz scholar. Even the most qualified writers, Schuller for instance, have been criticized for conceiving of jazz as fine art by European standards and for being unreflective about canon strategies and their ideological implications.

As Mark Tucker has pointed out, Schuller and others (in Denmark, Wiedemann) had good reasons for their conception of jazz: jazz writers have always had to show that jazz was worth serious attention, and they had to be constructive. To be deconstructive would only obstruct their attempts at legitimization. Tucker is also right in stating that there is an unpleasant ambiguity about the fact that the deconstructionists of the younger generation turn their back on the founding fathers, who have contributed to the legitimization process so instrumental in the acceptance of jazz studies at universities—a process that has made it possible for new generations to make a living teaching jazz in academia. Whereas I subscribe to a moderate poststructuralist agenda, I think that some of the criticism of Schuller's generation is unfair. And although I generally appreciate Gabbard's writings, I feel that Mark Tucker has a point when he objects to some of the rhetoric in Gabbard's "The Jazz Canon and Its Consequences" (first published in 1993 and later, in a slightly altered version, as an introductory article to *Jazz among the Discourses*, the second of the two anthologies):[3]

The great underlying tension in Gabbard's argument comes from a persistent clash between now and then: on the one hand he acknowledges the recently elevated status of jazz and makes a bid for renovating scholarly approaches to the subject; on the other he strenuously critiques writers whose efforts at legitimating jazz helped its status rise in the first place. . . .

. . . scholars identified with the new jazz studies might consider taking steps on their own that will help advance the cause. They need to discover that they have a usable literary past that includes not just Bakhtin, Benjamin, and Cixous but also Hodeir, Schuller, and Williams.[4]

I apologize for quoting Tucker at length and for going so far with these general reflections, but, as I hope to show, they are crucial for our understanding of the history of jazz criticism and jazz research and the place of Wiedemann's writings within that history.

Though several years younger, Wiedemann can in many ways be regarded as a Danish equivalent to Hodeir (1921–), Schuller (1925–), and particularly Stearns (1908–66). Wiedemann's research on the historical, aesthetic, and social aspects of jazz is very much in line with Stearns's writings and, like Stearns, he is a founding father of jazz research (in Denmark). It might be added that Wiedemann did a translation of Stearns's 1956 *The Story of Jazz*. Though Wiedemann had no formal education in music theory (he took his doctoral degree in musicology as an independent study project) and did not write technical musical analyses as Hodeir or Schuller did, he shared many of their ideas. Like Stearns, Hodeir, and Schuller, Wiedemann was dedicated to the legitimization of jazz as an art form. Therefore, he also thought that jazz should enjoy the same respect, and could be studied on the same intellectual level, as the traditional, canonized arts (classical music, literature, theater, and art).

Wiedemann began to collect jazz records in 1945, and in 1948, while still in his teens, he began his career as a jazz critic. From early on he was able to fascinate readers with his writings and took great pains to articulate his ideas of jazz as an art form. He wrote in the national newspaper *Information* from 1951 until his death. He wrote books from 1953 on, scholarly articles from 1957 on, and freelanced at Danish National Radio from 1949 to 1976. In terms of its left-wing orientation and focus on intellectuals and art, *Information* was located within approximately the same cultural, symbolic space as that which Pierre Bourdieu assigned to French papers like *Le Monde* and the weekly *Le Nouvel Observateur*.[5]

It is hard to overestimate the importance of Wiedemann's investment in the legitimization process. Of course he had a genuine interest in jazz. It was for him not just a medium for dealing with cultural identity in general. But the legitimization project was deeply rooted in his psyche, and he resented the tendency to subsume jazz under the category of "popular music." In his newspaper writings, he complained about things that obstructed contemplative listening, such as noise from the audience and activities at the bar. At the opening of a new club (Copenhagen Jazz House) in 1991, he praised the establishment for placing the bar in a room separate from the music.

Another informative example is his radio career. When Wiedemann began to work at Danish National Radio, all jazz activities took place within the "entertainment" section. Wiedemann and other jazz critics worked side by side with journalists who played popular music from commercial hit lists. These journalists functioned as disc jockeys who primarily played records and supplied short, superficial comments in between, whereas the jazz staff spent much more time in preparation through careful listening and reading about the music and its history. In addition, the jazz staff was regarded as elitist. To be in the same section and professionally categorized (in regard to pay, too) with the happy-go-lucky journalists was absurd and frustrating for the jazz staff, who worked hard and had a deeper, more existential relationship to their music. Because of the gradual acceptance of jazz in general and the work of the jazz critics in particular, an independent department for jazz was later established at Danish National Radio along with the formation of a national big band. The Danish Radio Big Band was formed in 1964 and still exists.[6]

To sum up a few general points: it may be hard to imagine precisely what the conditions of jazz criticism were like in terms of the cultural acceptance of jazz before, say, 1960, but it is nevertheless important that we be aware of our history and the conditions of the founding fathers of jazz criticism and jazz research. Deconstruction can be a useful intellectual tool on an epistemological level, but it should be used with care and not as a weapon against colleagues. One of the basic problems in this debate is not specific to the field of jazz; it is the problem of a generation gap between "old" and "young" jazz scholars, and it is an important task in these years to bridge this gap, if only to preserve knowledge and improve the dialogue and continuity in the field of jazz research.

WIEDEMANN AND THE COPENHAGEN JAZZ SCENE

Erik Wiedemann was born in Copenhagen and lived there his whole life, except for a few years in a boarding school in the city of Soroe, less than

50 miles away. Needless to say, he knew Copenhagen and especially the history of its jazz scene as few others did. He was an expert on both early and modern Danish jazz history. This expertise is documented in his dissertation on jazz in Denmark, 1920–50, and in his countless articles in *Information,* from which a substantial portion of Danish jazz history could be extracted. His knowledge of the Danish jazz scene is also evident in an article (in English) on the history of the important jazz club Café Montmartre, which existed from 1959 to 1994 but had its heyday in the 1960s. We will return to the dissertation in a moment; but, in order to understand Wiedemann's career in historical perspective, it is relevant to mention that jazz came to Denmark in the 1920s, blossomed in the early 1930s, and reached its peak during World War II. As in America, the broad popularity of jazz declined after 1945, and the jazz scene changed in other ways, too. Modernist jazz criticism and its conception of jazz as fine art began to gain real influence in these years. From an international perspective, the formation of modernist jazz criticism and its "victory" over the traditionalist paradigm is marked by Hodeir's *Hommes et problemés du jazz* in 1954.[7]

Although the Danish jazz scene diminished in those postwar years, it blossomed again in the 1960s, and Wiedemann had the opportunity to become an influential critic and to document a vital part of Danish and international jazz history. He got firsthand experience from other European countries where he participated in festivals and had contact with colleagues, and from 1967 on he visited America, especially New York City, almost every year.

In the 1950s and the following two or three decades, Wiedemann commented on the jazz scene in Copenhagen. One example is his article on Café Montmartre.[8] Because of the milieu and conditions at this club, many famous American jazz musicians chose Copenhagen as their residence and base of operations in Europe: Stan Getz, Dexter Gordon, Ben Webster, Kenny Drew, Oscar Pettiford, and, in the early 1960s, avant-garde musicians such as Cecil Taylor, Albert Ayler, Archie Shepp, and Don Cherry. Among the reasons many American musicians chose Copenhagen as their base of operations was the decline in popularity of jazz in the United States because of the emergence of rock and the fact that black musicians felt less subject to racial discrimination in Denmark's capital. The presence of these American musicians had a huge impact on the Danish jazz scene. For young Danish musicians, to play with these prominent Americans was an invaluable education.

Wiedemann was one of the main originators of the Danish Jazz Society, which came into existence in 1956. One of its goals was precisely to improve the cultural status of jazz. The society has been important to the Danish jazz scene, especially to the musicians. Wiedemann was later involved in cultural politics as a member of the Danish National Music Council for two periods (1976–1979 and 1979–1983).[9]

ACADEMIC CAREER: FROM LITERATURE TO MUSIC

Wiedemann's criticism gained respect early on and is still respected for its high standards. His approach to jazz was sometimes described as scholarly or intellectual, but such opinions certainly depend on one's point of view. He was without doubt reflective and critical, he dealt with aesthetics, and he was strongly influenced by European art and literary criticism. From the perspective of Susan Sontag's distinction between a hermeneutics of art and an erotics of art, his criticism has elements of both; he could be interpretative, analytical, and passionate at the same time.[10]

Wiedemann was not particularly theoretically minded. He thought that theory should not take precedence over direct musical experience. Wiedemann did not write on abstract philosophical subjects. Rather, he focused on a methodological level close to the observational and descriptive, but with a broad perspective on the music. Wiedemann could write about music in a precise and somewhat intuitive way without being explicitly theoretical. Within this style, his writings are on a high level even in an international perspective. One of the special qualities of his criticism and research has to do with his linguistic talent and background as a literary scholar. His writing is distinguished by his subtle, tasteful use of figurative language. In the 1960s he also worked as a literary critic, especially of modern American literature.

In 1960 Wiedemann earned a Ph.D. in comparative literature with a dissertation on the European art novel, 1860–1900.[11] From 1960 to 1963 he worked at the National Discographical Collection in Denmark. His career in musicology did not begin formally until 1972 (he was then 41), when he was appointed a teacher in the history and aesthetics of jazz. In 1978 he obtained a permanent position as associate professor and held this chair until he retired in 2000.[12] He became a member of the Internationale Gesellschaft für Jazzforschung in 1970 (a year after the society was founded), and from 1977 on he was a member of the Danish Musicological Society.

It is worth noting that Wiedemann began his career as a jazz scholar in musicology about the same time as jazz entered musicological institutions in other Western countries. Like many other universities, theUniversity of Copenhagen had one teacher who specialized in jazz and one who specialized in classical music but was interested in jazz and taught it once in a while. Throughout his 28 years in the Department of Musicology in Copenhagen, Wiedemann was the only specialist in jazz and rock. Jazz of course held his main interest. He lectured very little on rock and never published any research in the field, although he supervised theses on rock, blues, and other kinds of music. In the early 1990s, popular music studies were taken over by specialists who did not work in jazz.

Wiedemann's open-mindedness and interest in different cultural phenomena were reflected in his writings on such diverse subjects as European and American literature, Danish and American jazz from all periods in jazz history, jazz musicians' use of marijuana, rock music, "twelve-tone jazz," and so on. He was no stranger to European fine art, both literature and art history (for several years he was married to the art critic and author Maria Marcus). In the late 1960s and early 1970s, he embraced some of the new rock music and was one of the first Danish rock critics. On a trip to America for two months in the summer of 1967, he participated in a "love-in" in San Francisco. Although 10 to 20 years older than the average participant in the student revolt of the 1960s, he was adaptive and open to the new ideas. In 1976 he wrote the article "Songs of the Vipers" on jazz musicians' use of marijuana from the beginning of jazz up to about 1950. He never became a hippie or a Marxist, though! His interest in rock had diminished considerably by the 1970s, but he had a long-lasting respect for certain kinds of rock and folk-rock, for instance Bob Dylan, The Velvet Underground, Jimi Hendrix, Frank Zappa, and Joni Mitchell.[13]

A HISTORY OF JAZZ

Two major works in Wiedemann's oeuvre deserve closer attention. The first is his comprehensive jazz history *Jazz og jazzfolk* (jazz and jazz people), published in 1958. It is structured in three large and two small concluding chapters. The first chapter, "The History of Jazz" (50 pp.) is an outline of the history of jazz in three periods: early (1890–1917), classic (1928–44), and modern (1945–). As readers might guess from these historical terms and the title of the book, Wiedemann was heavily influenced by Hodeir's 1954 book.[14]

Wiedemann's book has original perspectives, and there is no doubt that he had studied the music painstakingly. In this opening chapter on the history

of jazz, he combines description of concrete facts about the music with interpretations of historical, aesthetic, and social aspects. He gives a pedagog-
ical survey of each period and discusses difficult questions in a fairly simple, intuitive way. Like Hodeir, he compares the history of jazz to that of
European classical music and tells us that jazz underwent the same artistic
development (from primitive folk music to complex, fine art) within a much
shorter time span. He uses the same canon strategy as Hodeir and many
other modernists: since European classical music has the highest cultural
status, it is useful to understand jazz as an art music similar to European art
music, primarily on a discursive level. However, Wiedemann, being more
aware than other modernists of the special qualities of jazz, emphasizes, perhaps even more than Hodeir, the differences between the two. Let me quote
from the very first page:

> Jazzen er en ung musik, yngre end en del nulevende mennesker og nogenlunde
> jaevnaldrende med vort aarhundrede. Den synes helt at hoere vor tid til, og det
> saa meget mere som den foerst er kommet til vor bevidsthed efter 1. verden-
> skrig, den, der mere end noget andet markerer overgangen til den tidsalder, vi
> foeler som moderne: filmens og flyvningens, radioens og relativitetsteoriens,
> atomteknikkens epoke. . . . Jazzen er en saadan ny kunstnerisk form, affoedt af
> et behov, som ingen af de gamle kunstarter helt har kunnet tilfredsstille. . . .
> Den har hverken de aeldre formers aarhundredgamle erfaring eller deres tradi-
> tionsbestemte autoritet—til gengaeld har den ungdommens livskraft og friere,
> mere uhildede syn paa tingene.

> Jazz is a young music, younger than a number of now living people and about
> the same age as our century. It seems to belong completely to our time, and
> this is seen very much by the fact that it has only entered our mind after the
> First World War—something that more than anything else marks the transition
> to the age we feel as modern: the film and the aircraft, the radio and the the-
> ory of relativity, nuclear technology. . . . Jazz is such a new art form, born of
> a need that none of the other established arts were able to satisfy. . . . It has
> neither the centuries-old experience of the older art forms nor their authority
> of tradition—it has, in turn, the vitality of youth and a free, more unbiased
> view of things.[15]

Let us pay attention to the vital spirit and the fascination with the music that
is articulated in these lines (some of it inevitably lost in the translation). The
vitality is probably emanating from both the author and the culture he describes. To be sure, jazz had a special topicality and vital modern character
up to the 1960s that has gradually diminished. It has been replaced by a new
historical situation that looks very much like the cultivation of tradition that
we know from the traditional European arts: the repertory bands and the vo-

luminous space occupied by CD reissues today are significant signs that jazz has partly entered an imaginary museum. The historical nature of jazz has changed profoundly, undoubtedly affected by the passing of a generation of venerated musicians and critics.

The aforementioned observations by Wiedemann convey notions of cultural and historical emancipation. These ideological elements show the influence from the early jazz reception in Denmark among an influential group of left-wing intellectuals to the jazz reception of the 1930s affiliated with the broad Danish cultural movement called "kulturradikalismen" (culture radicalism). This movement reacted against traditional bourgeois values; it advanced ideas of bodily and sexual liberation, spontaneity, and musical improvisation. The Danish author Tom Kristensen elaborated on the metaphor of the body in the article "Jubel over jazzen" (delight at jazz) in 1928:

> [M]an skal hoere med hele Kroppen, ligesom Jazz skal spilles med hele kroppen. . . . Her har vi nu gaaet i flere Aarhundreder og kun haft Udtryk i Ansigtet. Kroppen doede under Jakke og Vest, Benene under Benklaederne, Foedderne i Stoevlerne. Haenderne kunde ganske vist bruges til Gestikulation, og her i vort moralske Norden blev overdreven Gestikulation opfattet som Affektion, som noget latterligt. Foedderne kunde vi kun bruge til at sparke med.

> [O]ne must hear with the whole body, just as jazz must be played with the whole body. . . . For centuries we have had only facial expression. The body died under jacket and waistcoat, the legs under pants, the feet in boots. The hands could, of course, be used for gesticulation, and here in our moral North [Scandinavia], gesticulation was considered an affectation, something ridiculous. The feet were good for kicking.[16]

Jazz was the ideal music to accompany this movement, and it was defended by proponents like Poul Henningsen (1894–1967), Bernhard Christensen (1906–), Astrid Goessel (1891–1975), Torben Gregersen (1911–), and particularly Sven Moeller Kristensen (1909–). The latter was a well-known professor of literature and wrote the first knowledgeable Danish book on jazz, *Hvad Jazz er* (What jazz is) in 1938. Though much less radical, this book anticipates some of Panassié's ideas about authenticity in *The Real Jazz* (1942).[17] *Hvad Jazz er* is the most important Danish book on jazz before Wiedemann's 1958 history of jazz.

With this historical background, it should be no surprise that Wiedemann was deeply influenced by Sven Moeller Kristensen. Wiedemann basically shared Kristensen's idea that jazz was a vital cultural force in the modern world with an emancipating, irrational, bodily, spontaneous character that had been lost in European culture, even if he did not share the primitivist ideology of Kristensen and his generation. Wiedemann later developed the idea of emancipation in his 1982 dissertation, drawing on Max Weber's theory of rationalization in Western culture. In this dissertation Wiedemann wrote that Kristensen's *Hvad Jazz er* would have made him well known on the international jazz scene had it been published in English, and suggests that it was not until Hodeir's 1954 work that a book on jazz, in any language, attained the same analytical level.[18]

When Hodeir entered the scene in the late 1940s, Wiedemann was deeply impressed and reacted against some of the ideas in the writings of Kristensen and other traditionalist jazz critics. Wiedemann followed Hodeir's writings during his time as editor of *Jazz Hot* (1947–50) with great attention and embraced Hodeir's modernist position.[19] He once told me that reading Hodeir's articles in *Jazz Hot* was like going to school. One of the main points in the modernist reaction against the traditionalists was the rejection of the concept of racial authenticity, the notion that blacks had an innate musical talent and were superior to whites on biological grounds. Another was the reaction against the primitivist ideology. (For further discussion of this complex issue, see a great work by Bernard Gendron: *Between Montmartre and the Mudd Club: Popular Music and the Avant-garde* [Chicago and London: University of Chicago Press, 2002, especially chapters 1, 6, and 7].)

Returning to Wiedemann's jazz history, we find the second chapter ("What is jazz?" 47 pp.) is a systematic description of the characteristics of jazz with reference to repertoire and the musical parameters: harmony, melody, sound, rhythm, improvisation, and arrangement. This chapter shows Wiedemann's analytical interest, especially at the empirical-observational level.

The third chapter ("The musicians in jazz," 61 pp.) is a survey of the important musicians' careers and styles. Again, this chapter shows Wiedemann's empirical interest and attests to his painstaking study of jazz history. The last two chapters are along the lines of essays: Chapter Four ("Jazz and its conditions," 15 pp.) is concerned with the cultural status of jazz. It concludes that like other art forms jazz should be taken seriously and is worthy of academic research. Here, Wiedemann's notion of art is heavily influenced by the European tradition of autonomous aesthetics. Social and musical aspects are dichotomized.

The final chapter ("Jazz and us," 9 pp.) addresses the reception of jazz and elaborates on the notion of emancipation and bodily experience. Most notably he develops a comfortable narrative that combines two basic elements of non-European and European culture: the bodily, rhythmic experience does not exclude aesthetic experience of form (a traditional aesthetic concept); they can go hand in hand, and in this way jazz can be both an art form with high cultural status and at the same time can be emancipating, bodily, and irrational.

THE RECEPTION OF JAZZ IN DENMARK, 1920–50

The peak of Wiedemann's academic career was his 1982 dissertation on Danish jazz. In Denmark, he was the first doctor in jazz research, and he was subsequently nicknamed "Dr. Jazz." The dissertation is titled *Jazz i Danmark—i tyverne, trediverne og fyrrerne* (Jazz in Denmark in the twenties, thirties, and forties) and consists of three volumes. The first volume is the main part of the study: a comprehensive cultural history of the jazz scene in Denmark for the three decades mentioned in the title. The other two volumes provide various kinds of information (Volume II) and musical examples on cassette tapes (Volume III). It is a great work both in scope (741 pp. of text) and in content. He worked full time on the dissertation for five years (1975–80) and during this period also built up a collection with the help of a research assistant. This collection is called Arkiv for Dansk Jazzforskning (Archive of Danish Jazz Research) and has now been taken over by the Royal Library in Copenhagen. It contains recordings, books, photographs, printed music, concert programs, taped interviews, scrapbooks, and other kinds of material.

The subject of the study is jazz in Denmark, 1920–50, with emphasis on the reception of jazz. The basic questions addressed are: How did Danes receive jazz? How did they react to the music, how did it influence their social life, and how did they integrate jazz into their society? These questions have an international, comparative perspective, with particular bearing on the relations between Denmark and America. In addition, the work can be considered a case study of how jazz was received in a western European country.

Hypothetical answers to these questions are developed with help from Morroe Berger's and Neil Leonard's studies of the reception of jazz in America.[20] Wiedemann agrees with Berger's conclusion that the negative reactions to jazz primarily had to do with social and not musical causes—that jazz was rejected largely because of white Americans' racial images of blacks.[21] Wiedemann finds that this thesis holds for Denmark, too. Europeans were not far behind white Americans as far as racial stereotypes and primitivist ideology were concerned, as evidenced by the delay in the appearance in Denmark of the first black American musicians until the mid-1920s (the first band to give a taste of American jazz was the Sam Wooding Orchestra, which played for a week in Copenhagen in September 1925). The relatively few black visitors could not be the only reason for the negative reaction to jazz in the 1920s, and, with inspiration from his American colleagues, Wiedemann also points to differences between jazz and classical music. The classical tradition has had a dominant position for centuries, much stronger than in America, just as the division between high and low culture has been much more strongly entrenched in European culture. Thus, we might conclude that many negative reactions towards jazz stemmed from both musical and social causes, and that these two are, ultimately, inseparable.

Wiedemann assumes that the development of the reception of jazz in Denmark was similar to American conditions with respect to the general change from rejection in the 1920s to gradual acceptance in the 1930s. This assumption is developed from Leonard's findings, as you might have guessed, but there are a few differences. He acknowledges Leonard's discovery of a general tendency towards acceptance and Leonard's rich perspective on the many circumstances that influenced the reception of jazz. He does not employ the whole body of Leonard's theory, which includes a shift towards traditional standards, the importance of symphonic jazz for legitimization, and, notably, the rise of a new break with the now conventionalized culture. This theory builds on a kind of phase model that can be formalized in the key words "innovation → rejection → modification → acceptance → new innovation."[22]

Wiedemann's method of investigating these assumptions and theoretical perspectives is all-encompassing and nonselective. Although he chooses not to omit anything, he does emphasize certain aspects. Thanks to this approach, we have a very broad and thorough documentation of this period in Danish jazz. It covers nearly all aspects of the jazz scene, including the creation of the music; concise analyses of important pieces; information on musicians, clubs, books, journals, critics, and films; and many other topics. One of the benefits of this approach is that it provides us with solid and rich information that can be used for further studies and interpretations.

Wiedemann's dissertation, however, is not simply an account of the events, but a combination of documentary research and cultural history. After the introduction and an outline of the purpose, the main body begins with a chronological survey. The second part (27 pp.) deals with the prehistory of jazz in Denmark. The Danish public had contacts with African

American music, albeit secondhand, starting in the 1860s,with minstrel shows and other visiting black performers like the Fisk Jubilee Singers in 1895. In 1903 John Philip Sousa's band introduced the cakewalk and the saxophone in Denmark. The prevailing attitudes towards these black performers were racist, and the music was largely considered vulgar and primitive.

The third part (65 pp.) covers the 1920s, a decade when jazz came to Denmark and a jazz scene was established. The most important pioneer was the bandleader and saxophonist Valdemar Eiberg. After him there were saxophonist Kai Ewans (a key figure during all three decades), trombonist Peter Rasmussen, and violinist Otto Lington, who introduced symphonic jazz in 1930. Throughout the 1920s and 1930s, jazz musicians played in dance halls, restaurants, and nightclubs, one result being that they had to play popular music, too. As to the importation of American jazz, the Original Dixieland Jazz Band's records came to Denmark in late 1919, and visiting jazz orchestras began to arrive in 1923. There were many visits during the period 1927–32.

The fourth part of Wiedemann's work (117 pp.) covers the 1930s. The jazz scene became more established and organized, and jazz became more accepted, though racist attitudes were still common. In 1931 the Danish hot club movement started with the Jazz Music Association in Copenhagen. Three books on jazz were published in 1929, 1934, and 1938, and three journals appeared in 1934 and 1935. We have already looked at the proponents of jazz and their ideas on the preceding pages. The most important musicians played in Erik Tuxen's band (1932–36), and a new trend toward professionalism among soloists in the late 1930s was represented by violinist Svend Asmussen, pianist Leo Mathisen, and guitarist/bassist Niels Foss. The importation of American records began in earnest in the early 1930s; many great soloists visited Denmark during that decade, as we shall see.

The fifth part (84 pp.) covers the wartime years 1940–45. Social conditions during the war had a great impact on the jazz scene. On the one hand, this period marked a culmination of the growth of jazz in Denmark. To a hitherto unparalleled extent, jazz musicians could live by playing jazz and did not have to play much commercial music. One of the main reasons for the new appreciation of jazz was that it had become an anti-Nazi, anti-German symbol. On the other hand, the Danish jazz scene was isolated. Danish musicians could not travel abroad, and the importation of American records was interrupted. Not until 1950 did important bebop records become available.

The sixth part (43 pp.) covers the postwar years 1945–49, generally a time of reconstruction. Instead of leading to the definitive integration of jazz, it became the end of an era; the jazz scene would not regain its vitality until around 1960. Some of the reasons were changing sensibilities, club owners' demand for more popular music, and the fact that jazz no longer had the status of being anti-German, i.e., a symbol of national identity. The jazz scene drastically diminished, and many musicians went to Sweden, Switzerland, the Netherlands, and the American zone in Germany.

The seventh part of the work is a short essay (8 pp.) on general aspects of the reception. One of the salient points is that governmental institutions did little to support jazz or listen to its proponents, who were attempting to improve the status of jazz. Wiedemann criticizes the educational system and Danish National Radio for being conservative and ignorant. The final part (7 pp.) describes the practical aspects of the dissertation project, including institutional affiliations, research assistants, and funding.

To give a brief outline of the valuable information contained in the last two volumes, I will present some of the main components in the form of a list:

Volume II
- 238 biographies (31 pp.), primarily of Danish musicians, but also of writers, promoters, and other persons on the jazz scene.
- A list of Danish bands and their personnel (28 pp.).
- A list of visitors from abroad (22 pp.), including Sam Wooding in 1925 and 1930, Josephine Baker in 1928, 1932, 1933, and 1938, Louis Armstrong in 1933 and 1949,[23] Coleman Hawkins in 1935, Alberta Hunter in 1935, 1936, and 1938, Joe Venuti in 1934, Benny Carter in 1936,[24] Adelaide Hall in 1937, Fats Waller in 1938, Duke Ellington in 1939, Don Redman in 1946, and Dizzy Gillespie in 1948.
- A comprehensive discography (112 pp.) of jazz recordings in Denmark, 1924–49.
- A list of 44 films in which Danish musicians participate or Danish films with jazz as part of the film score or soundtrack (8 pp.).
- Two lists of printed music (6 pp.), the first covering jazz-related popular music (cakewalks, rags, etc.), 1901–19, the second covering jazz, 1932–49.
- A bibliography of jazz-related books, articles, and journals (3 pp.).
- A list of the names of the 43 people Wiedemann interviewed in the course of his research (2 pp.).
- A chronological list of melodies (30 pp.) and index of names (9 pp.).

Volume III

Volume III consists of three tapes with 59 recordings: 4 from the 1920s, 16 from the 1930s, 32 from the war years, and 7 from the second half of the 1940s. Wiedemann writes that this selection reflects the importance of the periods concerned. I should like to point out 8 significant jazz recordings available on these tapes in order to refer readers without detailed knowledge of the subject to a manageable body of material:[25]

- Valdemar Eiberg and His Jazz Orchestra: "I've Got a Cross-Eyed Papa" (HMV X 2122, August 27, 1924), Eiberg (C-mel, leader)
- Otto Lington (v) & Leo Mathisen (p): "Wild Cow" (Columbia J 26, January 3, 1929), with a 32-bar solo by Mathisen, who was to become the most popular musician during the war
- Erik Tuxen and His Orchestra: 'Koebenhavner Rhapsodi I' ("Copenhagen rhapsody I") (Polyphon XS 50201, January 16, 1933), with elements of Ellington's mood pieces
- Kai Ewans's Dance Orchestra (as, leader): "Honeysuckle Rose" (Odeon D 382, Spring 1939)
- Svend Asmussen and His Quintet (v): "Some of These Days" (Odeon D 408, August 16, 1940), the best-selling record during the war.[26] We can hear the influence of Joe Venuti on Asmussen's playing.
- Boerge Roger Henrichsen (p) & Niels Foss (b): 'Praeludium i C' (HMV X 6877, July 30, 1942), an interesting duo piece by two leading instrumentalists inspired by the Ellington-Blanton duets from 1939 and 1940
- Kjeld Bonfils (p solo): 'Marokko' (Odeon D 1001, December 15, 1943), an example of Bonfils's modern piano style, with African influences
- Peter Rasmussen's Septet (tb): "Copenhagen Jive" (private recording, February 27, 1948), a blues by one of the leading groups of the time, and one of the few to absorb elements of bebop[27]

After he delivered his dissertation, Wiedemann did not do any further research on jazz in Denmark before 1950. He felt that he had to do something else and concentrated on Duke Ellington and his music. Ellington's music was Wiedemann's favorite, and this preference is reflected in his writings and his relatively large collection of Ellington records. One of his best articles on Ellington is "Duke Ellington: The Composer," which is the result of the painstaking effort typical of Wiedemann's writings.[28] One of the things he did not live to finish was a large Ellington project begun in the late 1980s. The aim of this project was to do a complete thematic catalog of every Ellington composition. It was meant to be finished in 1999, the year of Ellington's centennial, but for several reasons it was delayed. I hope his Ellington material, which has been collected and cataloged over thousands of hours (with help from research assistants), will be of use to other scholars some day.

ON A PERSONAL NOTE

I got to know Erik Wiedemann in 1996 as adviser on my M.A. thesis. I found him a warm and open-minded person—extremely knowledgeable about jazz history. Though there were differences between us in age (42 years) and academic style, we were fond of each other and had a relationship based on mutual respect. When he left this world, he had a private collection of 5,553 records, almost 3,000 CDs, 1,295 books, and about 30 periodicals. He encouraged me to apply for a Ph.D. scholarship with a jazz subject and was adviser on this project, too. When he died, he had read the draft of my dissertation and had made many valuable comments. I am sorry that he cannot see the final version. Above all, I miss him very much as a dear colleague and friend.

Lewis Porter was probably right in 1991 when he wrote that Wiedemann was not known to the mainstream of jazz scholars.[29] But he was known to André Hodeir, Dan Morgenstern, Mark Tucker, and many other Ellington experts. Wiedemann's influence in Denmark is beyond comparison. Let me conclude with a reference to one of his articles on Lester Young, in which he quotes Lee Konitz: "How many people Lester influenced, how many lives!"[30] I think the same can be said of Erik Wiedemann's influence on the Danish jazz world in the second half of the twentieth century and especially on the audiences that read his criticism in *Information* and heard him on the radio.

NOTES

I should like to thank Franz Krieger at the University of Music and Dramatic Arts in Graz for encouraging comments during the writing process. I also thank Birgit Wiedemann, Erik's widow. For comments on the article, I am grateful to Niels Krabbe, head of the Department of Music and Theater at the Royal Library in Copenhagen, and, at the University of Southern Denmark in Odense, music librarian Frank Büchmann-Moeller and English professor Christen Kold Thomsen. Krabbe was a close friend of Wiedemann and his colleague for more than 20 years at the music department at the University of Copenhagen.

1. I want to avoid irrelevant autobiographical information, but let me add that I was his doctoral student and the only person familiar with his private collection. The collection has been an important source for this article.

2. Even if an author's own opinion is no proof of what he actually does, see Wiedemann's early distinction between criticism and academic research in Wiedemann 1958a, 179–80.

3. Krin Gabbard. "The Jazz Canon and Its Consequences." *Annual Review of Jazz Studies* 6. Ed. Edward Berger, David Cayer, Dan Morgenstern, and Lewis Porter, 1993: 65–98. Krin Gabbard: "Introduction: The Jazz Canon and Its Consequences." *Jazz among the Discourses*. Durham and London: Duke University Press, 1995, 1–28.

4. Mark Tucker. Review of *Representing Jazz*. Ed. Krin Gabbard; and *Jazz among the Discourses*. Ed. Krin Gabbard. *Journal of the American Musicological Society* 51/1 (Spring 1998): 143 and 148.

5. Pierre Bourdieu. *Distinction : A Social Critique of the Judgement of Taste*. New York and London: Routledge, 1979/1984, 440–53.

6. "The Danish Radio Jazz Group" (1961–86) was also sponsored by the Danish government but less closely associated with the radio operation (Erik Wiedemann. "Radioens Big Band" and "Radiojazzgruppen." *The New Grove Dictionary of Jazz*. Ed. Barry Kernfeld. New York: Macmillan, 1998/1996, 1012).

7. The English translation was published in 1956, and though it is very useful, it is not quite a satisfactory translation, as Hodeir remarked a year after in *Jazz Hot* # 125 in a response to his American critics: "Je m'étonne qu'avant de mettre en cause la traduction de David Noakes. . . . ils n'aient pas eu le souci de se référer au texte original" (from "Lettre sur le blues, l'improvisation et l'essence." Reprinted in André Hodeir. *Jazzistiques*. Roquevaire: Parenthèses, 1984, 51. For English translation: "Letters on the Blues: Improvisation, and the Essence." *Toward Jazz*, New York: Da Capo 1962/1986, 57–62).

8. Wiedemann 1996a.

9. The National Music Council (Danish "Statens Musikraad") is a Danish equivalent to the National Endowment for the Arts in the U.S.

10. I am thinking of Sontag's famous essay "Against Interpretation." Susan Sontag. *Against Interpretation and Other Essays*. New York and London: Anchor Books, 1966/1990, 3–14. She writes: "Today is such a time, when the project of interpretation is largely reactionary, stifling. . . . To interpret is to impoverish, to deplete the world—in order to set up a shadow world of "meanings." . . . What is important now is to recover our senses. We must learn to *see* more, to *hear* more, to *feel* more. . . . The function of criticism

should be to show *how it is what it is*, even *that it is what it is*, rather than to *show what it means* [italics in original]. In place of a hermeneutics we need an erotics of art." (Ibid., 7 and 14.)

11. Wiedemann 1960a.
12. The Danish word for his position was "lektor."
13. Wiedemann 1976.
14. In his article on the 1949–50 Capitol recordings by Miles Davis's nonet, Wiedemann concludes with a strong recommendation of Hodeir's chapter on Davis and cool jazz as further reading and acknowledges that it has been a substantial help for his article (Wiedemann 1957b). See André Hodeir. *Hommes et problémes du jazz.* Paris: Au Portulan, chez Flammarion 1954, 144–68.
15. Wiedemann 1958, 5.
16. Quoted from Wiedemann 1982, I, 120.
17. Sven Moeller Kristensen later wrote another book within the same tradition-alist paradigm: *Jazzen og dens Problemer* (Jazz and its problems) from 1946. Cf. Hugues Panassié. *The Real Jazz.* New York: A. S. Barnes and Com-pany, 1942. According to Leonard Feather, the term "Crow Jim" was coined by Barry Ulanov (Leonard Feather. *The Book of Jazz: A Guide to the Entire Field.* London: Arthur Barker, 1957/1961, 49).
18. Wiedemann 1982, I, 223–24. I should add that Sargeant's book from 1938 is at least one exception (Winthrop Sargeant. *Jazz: Hot and Hybrid.* Lon-don: E. P. Dutton & Co. Inc., 1938/1959).
19. For a concise summary of the conception of jazz in Sven Moeller Kris-tensen's book and its mixture of ideas connected to traditionalist jazz criti-cism and the Zeitgeist of the culture-radical movement in the 1930s, see Wiedemann 1982, I, 236–37.
20. Morroe Berger. "Jazz: Resistance to the Diffusion of a Culture Pattern." *The Journal of Negro History* XXXII (October 1947). Reprinted in *American Music: From Storyville to Woodstock.* Ed. Charles Nanry. New Brunswick, NJ: Transaction Books, 1972, 11–43. Neil Leonard. *Jazz and the White Americans.* Chicago: The University of Chicago Press, 1962.
21. Berger 1947/1972, 39 (see previous note).
22. See Leonard 1962, 154–56.
23. On October 19, 1933, Armstrong was received by 5,000–10,000 fans at the central railway station in Copenhagen (Wiedemann 1982, I, 153). See also Armstrong's own account: Louis Armstrong. *Swing That Music.* London and New York: Longmans, Green and Co., 1936, 112.
24. Cf. Morroe Berger, Edward Berger, and James Patrick. *Benny Carter : A Life in American Music*, I (Studies in Jazz No. 1), Metuchen, NJ, and London: Scarecrow Press, 1982, 149–54.
25. For a complete list of the recordings on the three tapes, see Wiedemann 1982, II, 274–76. For practical reasons, I have listed the band names in English only. The recordings of well-known American melodies reflect the influence of American jazz.

26. Wiedemann 1982, I, 314.
27. Wiedemann 1982, I, 352.
28. See Wiedemann 1991a.
29. Wiedemann 1991d, 285.
30. Ibid.
31. Christian Braad-Thomsen (ed.). *Jazzen i blodet. Udvalgte artikler 1951–2000 (Jazz in the Blood. Selected articles 1951–2000)*. Copenhagen: Glydendal, 2001. (This note references a citation in the following paragraph.)

CHRONOLOGICAL AND ANNOTATED BIBLIOGRAPHY

The following bibliography is complete, excluding publications in newspapers and magazines. It would simply take up too much time and space to include the thousands of reviews and articles that were published in *Information*. An anthology of this material was published in fall 2001.[31] As for magazines, some of the most important contributions can be found in *Jazzinformation* (1950), *Musikrevue* (1954–61), and *Jazz Revy* (1961–65). For obvious reasons I have left out a couple of articles that were later published as part of his 1982 dissertation.

Wiedemann was coauthor and coeditor of three encyclopedias (1953, 1962a, and 1969). All three are listed because they are quite different in spite of what their titles may suggest. The first is *Jazzens Hvem-Hvad-Hvor*. The second is a thoroughly revised and enlarged version with the same title. The third is, again, a thoroughly revised and enlarged edition (except for the omission of 400 biographies) with the title *Musikkens Hvem-Hvad-Hvor: Jazz*.

For articles from the yearbook *Jazz-aarbogen* (1957–61), only the first item (1957a) is supplied with a translation of the book title and the information that it was published by the Danish Jazz Society.

For publications in English, a capital letter "E" is added in brackets in the far-left margin right after the year of publication. The Danish titles are translated in parentheses.

1953. Erik Wiedemann, John Joergensen, Sven Moeller Kristensen, eds., with a contribution from Boerge Roger Henrichsen. *Jazzens Hvem-Hvad-Hvor (Politikens Jazzleksikon)* (Who's who of jazz [Politiken's dictionary of jazz]). Copenhagen: Politikens Forlag. The first Scandinavian handbook on jazz, with more than 700 biographies.

1957a. Erik Wiedemann. "Omkring William Schiöpffe" (On William Schiöpffe). *Jazz-aarbogen* (The jazz yearbook), published by the Danish Jazz Society. Copenhagen: Aschehoug: 37–40.

1957b. Erik Wiedemann. "Miles Davis' store forsoeg" (Miles Davis's great attempt). *Jazz-aarbogen*: 84–99. A musical analysis of the 1949–50 Capitol recordings by Miles Davis's nine-piece band, the so-called "Birth of the Cool" recordings.

1958a. Erik Wiedemann. *Jazz og jazzfolk* (Jazz and jazz people). Copenhagen: Aschehoug.

1958b. Erik Wiedemann. "Mens vi venter paa . . ." (While we are waiting for . . .). *Jazz-aarbogen*: 31–43.

1958c. Erik Wiedemann. "Dansk jazz-diskografi 1945–58" (Danish jazz discography, 1945–58). *Jazz-aarbogen*: 71–84.

1958d. Erik Wiedemann. "Jazz i Massey Hall" (Jazz at Massey Hall). *Jazz-aarbogen*: 91–96. An article on the historic Parker-Gillespie-Powell-Mingus-Roach concert, May 15, 1953, in Toronto, with analyses of the recordings.

1959a. Erik Wiedemann. "Lester Young—II : Efterkrigsaarene" (Lester Young II: The postwar years). *Jazz-aarbogen*: 20–29.

1959b. Erik Wiedemann. "Hoejt at flyve—Charlie Parkers Savoy-indspilninger 1944–48" (Flying high: Charlie Parker's Savoy recordings 1944–48). *Jazz-aarbogen*: 82–96.

1959c. Erik Wiedemann. "Dansk jazz-diskografi 1958–59" (Danish jazz discography, 1958–59). *Jazz-aarbogen*: 102–05.

1960a. Erik Wiedemann. *Den europaeiske kunstnerroman o. 1860–o. 1900* (The European art novel c. 1860–c. 1900). Ph.D. diss., University of Copenhagen.

1960b. Erik Wiedemann. "Ind i 60'erne" (Into the '60s). *Jazz-aarbogen*: 65–71.

1960c. Erik Wiedemann. "Dansk jazz-diskografi 1959–60" (Danish jazz discography, 1959–60). *Jazz-aarbogen*: 91–96.

1961. Erik Wiedemann. "Dansk jazz-diskografi 1960–61" (Danish jazz discography, 1959–60). *Jazz-aarbogen*: 91–95.

1962a. Erik Wiedemann and John Joergensen, eds. *Jazzens Hvem-Hvad-Hvor* (Who's who of jazz), rev. and enl. ed. Copenhagen: Politikens Forlag. Contains almost 1,800 biographies.

1962b. Erik Wiedemann and Maria Marcus, trans. *Historien om jazzen* (The story of jazz), by Marshall Stearns, in Danish translation. Copenhagen: Gyldendal.

1966. Erik Wiedemann, ed. *Ny amerikansk prosa* (New American prose). Copenhagen.

1967a. Erik Wiedemann. "Jøden som kulturhelt" (The Jew as cultural hero). *Perspektiv* 5–6, 13th Year: 89–96.

1967b. Erik Wiedemann. "Fra amerikansk til dansk" (From American to Danish). Perspektiv 5–6, 13th Year: 154–57.

1969. Erik Wiedemann, John Joergensen, Arnvid Meyer, and Steen Nielsen. *Musikkens Hvem-Hvad-Hvor: Jazz.* (Who's who of music: Jazz). In collaboration with the Danish Jazz Society. Copenhagen: Politikens Forlag.

1975 [E]. Erik Wiedemann. "Une Minute Mystique de Jazz: Some Remarks on the Conditions of Collective Improvisation." *Musik & Forskning* (Music and research) 1: 95–106.

1976 [E]. Erik Wiedemann. "Songs of the Vipers." *Musik & Forskning* 2: 116–30.

1982. Erik Wiedemann. *Jazz i Danmark—i tyverne, trediverne og fyrrerne : en musikkulturel undersoegelse* (Jazz in Denmark: in the twenties, thirties and forties: A music cultural study). 3 vols. Doctoral diss. Also published in book form. Copenhagen: Gyldendal, 1982.

1983. Erik Wiedemann. "En anden slags musikhistorie? Musikken i et holistisk perspektiv" (Another kind of music history? Music in holistic perspective). Lecture given at the 9th Nordic Meeting of Music Scholars, 1983. *Dansk Aarbog for Musikforskning*: 35–42.

1985. Erik Wiedemann, ed. *Konference om Nordisk Jazzforskning: Jazz : historie, samtid, metoder: rapport fra den 2. konference om nordisk jazzforskning 26.–29. april 1984 i Koebenhavn* (Conference on Nordic jazz research: Jazz: History, present, methods: Report on the 2nd conference on Nordic jazz research, April 26–29, 1984, in Copenhagen), with a summary in English. Copenhagen: C. A. Reitzels Boghandel A/S.

1986a. Erik Wiedemann. "Duke Ellington som komponist—en indkredsning" (Duke Ellington as composer: An outline). *Musik & Forskning* 11, 1985–86: 77–90.

1986b. Erik Wiedemann. "Nogle Ellington-fund" (Some new discoveries of Ellington manuscripts). *Musik & Forskning* 11, 1985–86: 91–98.

1987a. Erik Wiedemann. "Kompositioner af Duke Ellington—et supplement" (Compositions by Duke Ellington: A supplement). *Musik & Forskning* 12, 1986–87: 149–62.

1987b. Erik Wiedemann. "Duke Ellington og Danmark 1950–1973" (Duke Ellington and Denmark, 1950–1973). Den tredje nordiske konferansen om jazzforskning (The third Nordic conference on jazz research). [Editor not listed.] Oslo: Norsk Jazzarkiv: 15–18.

1988 [E]. Thirty-six articles in *The New Grove Dictionary of Jazz* on Danish musicians and bands, including articles on Bernhard Christensen, Valdemar Eiberg, Bent Fabricius-Bjerre, Ib Glindemann, Leo Mathisen, Marilyn Mazur, Palle Mikkelborg, Radioens Big Band, John Tchicai, and Mads Vinding. See the full list in "Appendix 2: List of contributors," *The New Grove Dictionary of Jazz*. Ed. Barry Kernfeld. New York: Macmillan. One-volume edition 1996: 1357.

1991a [E]. Erik Wiedemann. "Duke Ellington: The Composer." *Annual Review of Jazz Studies* 5: 37–64.

1991b [E]. Erik Wiedemann. "Duke in Denmark: A Discographical Excursus." *Annual Review of Jazz Studies* 5: 65–80. Printed in a Danish version in *Musik & Forskning* 13, 1988.

1991c. Erik Wiedemann. "En ukendt musical af Duke Ellington : Paa sporet af *Man with Four Sides*" (An unknown musical by Duke Ellington: On the scent of *man with four sides*). *Musik & Forskning* 16, 1990–91: 145–53.

1991d [E]. Erik Wiedemann. "Lester Young: The Postwar Years." In *A Lester Young Reader*. Ed. Lewis Porter. Washington and London: The Smithsonian Institution Press: 285–91. Translation of Wiedemann, 1959a.

1993. Erik Wiedemann. "Musik i doedens skygge : Duke Ellington og hans tre Sacred Concerts" (Music in the shadow of death: Duke Ellington and his three sacred concerts). *Musik & Forskning* 18, 1992–93: 63–74.

1995. Erik Wiedemann. "Jazzforskning i Danmark" (Jazz research in Denmark). *Musik & Forskning* 20, 1994–95: 101–07. This article entails a complete list of Danish M.A. theses with subjects related to jazz. The first is from the mid-1950s. By December 1994, 62 theses had been written. They are listed in thematic order. Most of them are works on a single musician, i.e. biographical.

1996a [E]. Erik Wiedemann. "The Montmartre, 1959–76: Towards a history of a Copenhagen jazz house." *Musik & Forskning : Music in Copenhagen: Studies in the Musical Life of Copenhagen in the 19th and 20th Centuries*: 274–93. Also printed in a Danish version, Copenhagen, 1997.

1996b. Erik Wiedemann. "25 aar i skoven" (25 years in the forest). In *Det Danske Jazzcenter 25 Aar*. Ed. Cim Meyer. Roennede: The Danish Jazz Center: 68–70. This article is a remembrance of the career of Arnvid Meyer, an old friend of Wiedemann and an important figure on the Danish jazz scene for several decades. Meyer was founder of the Danish Jazz Center, which is situated in a forest in the countryside; thus the title.

1996c. Erik Wiedemann. "Tolvtonemusik og jazz: en indkredsning" (Twelve-tone music and jazz: An outline). In *Festskrift Jan Maegaard*. Ed. Mogens Andersen, Niels Bo Foltmann, and Claus Roellum Larsen. Copenhagen: Engstroem & Soedring: 139–47.

1998. Erik Wiedemann. "Jazz." In *Den Store Danske Encyklopaedi* X. Copenhagen: Gyldendal: 48–50.

BOOK REVIEWS

Max Harrison, Eric Thacker, and Stuart Nicholson, *The Essential Jazz Records, Volume 2: Modernism to Postmodernism* (London and New York: Mansell, 2000, 889 pp., $82.95 cloth, $41.95 paperback)

Reviewed by Lawrence Kart

One had high hopes for *The Essential Jazz Records, Volume 2: Modernism to Postmodernism*, if only because one of its three coauthors, Max Harrison, is among the best critics jazz has ever had, with a broad range of sympathies, acute analytical gifts, and the ability to grasp and vividly express the essential aesthetic issues. To borrow a phrase from the book's introduction, he is one of the "few great contemporary listeners," and we have been benefiting from his work for almost half a century. An Englishman, Harrison began writing about jazz for *Jazz Monthly* in 1955, and later, on classical music, for *The Times of London* and *Gramophone*. A selection of his jazz pieces was published as *A Jazz Retrospect;*[1] *The New Grove Gospel, Blues, and Jazz*[2] includes the brilliant main article on jazz that he contributed to the 1980 revision of *The New Grove Dictionary of Music and Musicians*, and he has played an increasingly prominent role in the series of books that have preceded the one under review — *Jazz on Record: A Critical Guide to the First 50 Years: 1917–1967* (with Albert McCarthy, Alun Morgan, Paul Oliver, and others);[3] *Modern Jazz: The Essential Records, 1945–70* (with Alun Morgan, Michael James, Jack Cooke, and Ronald Atkins);[4] and *The Essential Jazz Records, Volume 1: Ragtime to Swing* (with Charles Fox and Eric Thacker).[5]

The best of those books was the second, *Modern Jazz: The Essential Records, 1945–70* — not only because all the participants (frequent contributors to the late, lamented *Jazz Monthly*), were gifted, knowledgeable critics of broad sympathies but also because there were five of them. This made it much more likely, in view of the fact that 200 different records (i.e., entire long-playing albums, not individual recorded performances) were dealt with in 131 pages (individual entries averaging about 500 words), that each man would be writing about something he wanted to address and that no recording calling for comment would lack a sound commentator. *The Essential Jazz Records, Volume 1: Ragtime to Swing*, which dealt with some 250 records in entries that often were of considerable length (there were 552 pages of text) had only three coauthors, and neither the sound but sometimes rather stolid Eric Thacker nor Charles Fox, broadly experienced but perhaps by this stage in his career too often the genial phrasemaker, were up to the level that Harrison and his collaborators had reached in *Modern Jazz: The Essential Records, 1945–70*. And, perhaps inevitably, there were times here when one felt that a particular writer was dealing with a particular recording only because he had drawn the short straw.

Before he died in 1997, Thacker contributed many entries to *The Essential Jazz Records, Volume 2*, and his virtues and flaws remain the same; while he rarely puts a foot wrong when it comes to judging the value of an individual work or its place in the historical scheme, his moments of genuine critical illumination are uncommon. Further, though the breadth of Thacker's sympathies was admirable, he seems to have been more at home writing about the jazz of the 1920s and 1930s than he was writing about, say, Ornette Coleman or Albert Ayler. Replacing Fox, who died in 1991, is critic and journalist Stuart Nicholson, author of biographies of Ella Fitzgerald, Billie Holiday, and Duke Ellington. The role Nicholson plays in this book is, in my view, a near-disastrous one; the reasons for that estimate should become clear below. As for Harrison, brilliant though he often is, he also is something of a professional iconoclast—an enemy, so it seems, of received opinion in all its forms. (A typical Harrison remark: "Though by no means its only sign of virtue, this [recording] is the kind of music that has never found much favour with jazz fans, still less with those who write for them" [709].) However habitual Harrison's oppositional stance might be, it can yield valuable results—for example, his discussions in *The Essential Jazz Records, Volume 1* of the Chicagoans and the Red Nichols– Miff Mole axis, his reconsideration of the Casa Loma Orchestra, and his detailed, definitive refutation of the too commonly held view that the Louis Armstrong of the late 1930s to mid-1940s was a lesser artist than the Armstrong of the Hot Five and Hot Seven recordings. But Harrison's iconoclasm, and the tone of exasperated sarcasm that so often accompanies it, can become quite rigid at times; and as these traits proliferate in *The Essential Jazz Records, Volume 2*, they begin to threaten the intellectual coherence of the entire enterprise.

I wish it had been possible for me to deal with this book wholesale and head-on. But having lived with it for more than a month now, and having tried and failed to write about it in that manner, I've had to adopt a more piecemeal approach. Here, then, are examples, good and bad, of what in my view makes *The Essential Jazz Records, Volume 2* a book that is both stimulating and deeply disappointing.

- Three examples of Harrison at his gem-cutter best. On Art Tatum: "Other features of his work . . . were the packing of so much music, not just a lot of notes, into short time lengths and—another aspect of the same thing—his often compositional shaping of each performance as a whole instead of as simply an episode of open-ended improvisation on the chords. It was all done with an ease so extreme as to suggest ironic detachment" (12). On Dizzy Gillespie: "Restless in attack, his style was dramatic, full of sharp contrasts which created a dynamic sense of insecurity in listeners. . . " (17). On Jimmy Giuffre: "A whispering barker who offered amazing reductions . . . ." (371).
- An example of how Harrison's need to sneer can lead him to make remarks that border on willful inaccuracy: "[Fat's Navarro's] dates with 'Lockjaw' Davis, an arch vulgarian who subsequently found his true *metier* as a cog in Basie's ponderous latter-day machine . . . ." (39). Harrison is free to dislike the music of both Davis and the latter-day Count Basie band (long a Harrison bugaboo); what he is not free to do is imply (as he surely does here) that the 1946 recordings that Davis made with Navarro are at all representative, even of Davis's early work. A full two years before this, with Cootie Williams, the young Davis stands revealed as a callow but earnest Ben Webster disciple; on his recordings with Navarro the tenor saxophonist clearly is attempting to emulate (undoubtedly for commercial reasons) nascent R & B gestures. The titles of two of the pieces —"Hollerin' and Screamin'" and "Stealin' Trash" —would seem to be good clues to what was going on.
- Nicholson proclaims that Charlie Parker, "even in live performance, seldom played more than three choruses" (61). It would have been nice if he had been aware of the album *Charlie Parker—The Apartment Sessions,* discussed by Thacker, who notes "the exuberant continuum of invention which [Parker] threads through 15 or so choruses of a fast *Little Willie Leaps* . . . . " (54), or this passage from Carl Woideck's *Charlie Parker: His Music and Life:* "When Parker and Strings played in nightclubs, they sometimes modified the arrangements to allow Parker multiple choruses of unbroken improvisation (reportedly as long as fifteen minutes). . . . "[6] Another example of Nicholson's taste for making dubious sweeping generalizations: Instancing Max Roach's

"singularly detached," "boorishly metronomic" playing behind Thad Jones on "Thedia" from the album *The Magnificent Thad Jones* and speculating that this may have been a reaction on Roach's part to Clifford Brown's death two weeks before, Nicholson adds: "This unyielding and unsupportive aspect of his ensemble playing . . . is a criticism that can be levelled at Roach's drumming in general" (103). But, surely, it is quicksilver, polyrhythmic responsiveness that is the essence of Roach's style—as could be confirmed by anyone who has listened to, say, Roach behind Brown and Sonny Rollins on such performances as "Pent-Up House," not to mention virtually all the recordings Roach made with Parker. One can attempt to argue that this commonly held view is false, but one can't, especially in a book of this sort, merely assert the opposite.

- An example of Thacker at his best, with empathy leading to understanding, then to illumination: "Clarity of tonguing and light sound . . . go with subtle control of minute contrasts within [tenor saxophonist J.R.] Monterose's melodic syntax: a sense of interior dialogue and of a passion which increases, though with a wry deceptiveness" (114). Again, one wishes that Thacker were engaged to this degree more often.

- Harrison writes of a 1955 recording by composer-arranger-tenor saxophonist Jack Montrose (not the same man as J.R. Monterose): "Both Montrose and [baritone saxophonist Bob] Gordon were unfortunate. Pointedly ignored by writers on jazz, they have gone unmentioned in histories, have been dealt with perfunctorily in works of reference or omitted altogether, and their records have not been much reissued . . . . Montrose played for many years in non-jazz situations . . . . He was on Frank Butler's *The Stepper* . . . in 1977 but did not make another record under his own name until . . . 1986. And musicians pretend that the good or bad opinions of writers on jazz make no difference!" (164). Yes, those "good or bad opinions" make some difference. But does Harrison really believe that the shape of Montrose's career (or that of any jazz musician of Montrose's era who possessed comparable musical goals and gifts) could have been significantly altered if he had been praised more often by jazz writers, or that it was the lack of good notices that led Montrose to work in Las Vegas show bands for several decades?[7]

- Discussing the composer-arrangers who wrote for the Boyd Raeburn Orchestra, Harrison refers to "the obscure Tommy Talbot" (204). The still-active Tom Talbert—who has several albums (both reissues and recent recordings) in print—might be less obscure in the future if his last name had been spelled correctly here. Also, Bert Howard (256) is Bart Howard, Gunter Hempel (451) is Gunter Hampel, Irwin Helfer (757) is Erwin Helfer, Michael Brecker (752) attended Indiana University, not Indiana State, and despite two sneering *sics* from Harrison, "Shubert" is spelled correctly in the title of the album *Mel Torme Swings Shubert Alley* (265). (Shubert Alley, the center of Manhattan's theater district, is named after the theater-owning family, not the composer of *Die Winterreise*.) Then there is Harrison's assertion that Eddie Sauter's writing for strings on Stan Getz's *Focus,* which he notes critic Martin Williams has described as "derivative of Bartok," in fact bears "no stylistic resemblance" [to Bartok] at all" (382)—to which he adds in an arch footnote: "Bartok's influence here . . . can be heard by those who do not know the composer's work yet not by those that do" (811). But the first piece on *Focus,* "I'm Late, I'm Late," is clearly based on the second movement of Bartok's *Music for Strings, Percussion, and Celesta*, a fact that is confirmed in the liner notes of the compact disc reissue of *Focus* by Jacob Glick of the Beaux Arts String Quartet, the first chair violist on the album.[8]

- How do the authors of *The Essential Jazz Records, Volume 2: Modernism to Postmodernism* regard the jazz avant-garde? That is among most the important questions one could ask of a book that covers the period 1941 to the present, for the nature and quality of that music and its relationship to the rest of jazz remain a fierce bone of contention—rivaled only by the contentiousness over the nature and quality of jazz-rock and over the jazz neoconservatism exemplified by Wynton Marsalis. (Jazz-rock is dealt with here almost exclusively by Nicholson, a fervent advocate of the genre, on grounds that rather indiscriminately mingle the aesthetic with the economic and the sociopolitical—see his comments below on the Don Ellis Orchestra. Marsalis's music is discussed only once, dismissively, by Nicholson, who deals with it in a manner that again seems less aesthetic than sociopolitical—"in the context of jazz as a whole," he writes, "it appeared as a narrow elitism") (739).

- As for the avant-garde, Nicholson begins to lay his cards on the table here: "[Don] Ellis was among the first jazz musicians to realize that a rapprochement with popular culture was necessary to invigorate jazz as much as to retain its audience. . . . " (225). And he continues, with these remarks: "For many, free jazz became the anthem that screamed rejection of racial inequality. . . . This inevitably posed problems of critical evaluation, free jazz sometimes weighing more heavily on critics' consciences than their pleasure centres and a certain critical discretion preceded valour lest posterity marked the denigrator of a new Picasso or Joyce. . . . For several years free jazz remained impaled on the barriers of sociopolitical issues, part rhetoric, part artifice. . . . " (553). And these: "European freedom, with its arcane preoccupation with the radical and, one might unkindly add, the marginal . . . " (569). " [I]f there is one thing that jazz has always needed, it is a flourishing avant-garde, if only to keep the mainstream honest. . . . " (581). The values on display here are vulgarly journalistic at best, complete with imputations of bad faith (Nicholson knows what is going on in other people's "pleasure centers" and whether or not responses to music are sociopolitical). Then there is the assumption that that which is radical and marginal (i.e., less than widely popular) is on the one hand not artistically vigorous, while, on the other hand, "a flourishing avant-garde" (of the nonradical sort?) is "always needed . . . if only to keep the mainstream honest."

Thacker makes no such general remarks about the avant-garde, and Harrison more or less retires from this part of the fray, though not before emitting this drastic encomium to Albert Ayler: "Even decades later, on listening to Ayler's courageous, bewitched, desperate music, we are haunted by the strange and disquieting impression that we are out on the very limits of the expressible, out on the last dangerous fringes where the ice of what we normally call art is so thin that we can almost see through into the depths below, into the mysterious thing-in-itself from which we abstract the all-too-human conventions of music" (502). But for reasons that Harrison nowhere explains, his interest in the post-Ayler avant-garde seems to be virtually nonexistent; aside from Anthony Braxton, John Zorn, and four European figures—Tomasz Stanko, Bernt Rosengren, Zbigniew Namyslowski, and Gyorgy Szabados—he deals with no post-Ayler avant-gardists in the book. There are some glancing remarks, though, that suggest that he and Nicholson agree on some points. Of Don Ellis's *How Time Passes* album, Harrison writes: "In reality several of these pieces . . . arrive at overall forms considerably more free and varied . . . than most of those found elsewhere in what in those years was called 'the New Thing'" (638). Of the John Mayer–Joe Harriott *Indo-Jazz Fusions* album, he writes: "The kind of exoticism represented here offered a viable alternative to free jazz in the 1960s even though, for reasons that had little to do with music, free jazz received nearly all the attention" (729). And expanding on the "exoticism as viable alternative" point, he writes of the mid-1950s Lighthouse All-Stars

recordings that featured Bob Cooper on oboe and English horn and either
Bud Shank or Buddy Collette on flute: "The permanent establishment of
these instruments in jazz was part of a general expansion of that music's
colouristic and textural resources . . . [that] in turn was part of an increase
in the expressive resources of jazz which can never be simply a matter of
expanded melodic, rhythmic and harmonic vocabularies" (438). One wel-
comes Harrison's focus on musical rather than sociopolitical matters, but
one wonders how exoticism, or an expansion of "colouristic and textural resources" that does not involve an expansion of "melodic, rhythmic and harmonic vocabularies," could possibly be a recipe for long-term aesthetic
success.

Again, Harrison's remarks merely hint at what his view of jazz's present
and future might be. And that brings us to what may be the book's most peculiar and frustrating omission,[9] for it deals with three key figures of the
jazz avant-garde—guitarist Derek Bailey, saxophonist Evan Parker, and the
late percussionist-bandleader John Stevens of the Spontaneous Music Ensemble (and such related figures as bassist Barry Guy, trombonist Paul
Rutherford, and percussionist Paul Lytton)—by, for the most part, not dealing with them at all. Whatever one thinks of the music of Bailey, Parker, et
al., it has been prominent for more than 30 years and remains widely influential. (Although the "European freedom" that Nicholson dismisses has
other points of origin, this music certainly runs parallel to it—a "type of
free improvisation [that]," in the words of critic Victor Schonfield, "has become accepted as a common language for an army of improvisers throughout the world."[10]) But Parker is mentioned only as a sideman on Peter
Brotzmann's "Machine Gun" (507), Bailey is referred to, once, by Nicholson as "an arcane visionary" (782), while Harrison also confines himself to
a lone remark, saying of a musician he admires that "he has even collaborated with Derek Bailey." Stevens and the others do not appear at all. And
yet in the March 1973 issue of *Jazz and Blues* Harrison wrote of the Spontaneous Music Ensemble: "The most notable thing was not this performance's varied sensuous impact but the way it established its own rules of
expression and organization. . . . [T]he threads are drawn together, trombone, bass and drum parts forming a unified texture wherein each line is
acutely responsive to the others. . . . The group here [on the album *Kary-
obin*] displays a perfectly individual method and style. . . . although the instrumental lines are unsparingly discontinuous the vitality of the whole is
such that everything finds a meaningful place. . . . "[11] Of course, Harrison
is free to change his mind, and it is possible he feels that this music has de-
cayed or gone astray, or both, or ought not to be regarded as jazz, or that

back in 1973 he was mistaken about its value. But one would think that he, and this book, owe us some response to this music other than Nicholson's seemingly market-oriented claim that it is "marginal."

- Nicholson seldom misses the opportunity to mention the presence of harmonic commonplaces (we are often told of ii–V–I sequences being resolved) and to outline a piece's chorus structure, e.g., this account of Wayne Shorter's "Dance Cadaverous": "It is a long, 64-bar composition with an ABAB[1] form, comprising four 16-bar sections: Intro (8 bars) + A (8 + 8) + B (8 + 8) + A (8 + 8) + B (8 + 8[1])"(335). But the point is what, other than Nicholson's having demonstrated that he can count and that he knows that ii–V–I sequences exist? As someone once said, "A difference, in order to be a difference, must make a difference." Nicholson himself proves the point when he nicely describes how Red Garland's "omitting the root of the chord from the bottom of some of the voicings he used to accompany soloists . . . particularly on dominant seventh chords . . . gave a feeling of harmonic ambiguity which suited [Miles Davis's] . . . horizontal style of improvising [and] also suited Coltrane's vertical approach . . . for a rootless dominant seventh chord can sound like two chords at the same time in certain circumstances . . . " (278).
- While discussing Davis's "Filles de Kilimanjaro," Nicholson states: "In bop and hard bop, complex themes were the province of the front line, while the accompaniment provided by piano, bass and drums followed established conventions of clarity and simplicity" (583). But as Jack Cooke said of Art Blakey and Horace Silver, in his classic formulation of the hard bop aesthetic in *Modern Jazz: The Essential Records, 1945–70:* "With Blakey . . . the high-hat . . . cymbal is introduced on the second and fourth beats . . . the [ride] cymbal beat is emboldened to match, and the various accents [are] raised to the degree of becoming strong, lengthy rhythmic designs in their own right, setting up in polyrhythmic opposition to the basic beat. Inevitably, this is a style in which the drummer no longer functions as accompanist pure and simple but often, and for long periods, becomes a contributor on the same level as the soloist, playing parallel with him, competing with him, sometimes even dominating him. . . . Silver was building the same kind of attacking method for the piano . . . and he and Blakey became a rare team of wit and ferocity. . . . "[12] Would it be too much to say that Cooke's description amounts to fact, not opinion? And what, then, does that make Nicholson's "in hard bop . . . the accompaniment

provided by piano, bass and drums followed established conventions of clarity and simplicity"?

In sum, *The Essential Jazz Records, Volume 2: Modernism to Postmodernism* is a deeply flawed work. In part that is because the task that the authors of this book and *The Essential Jazz Records, Volume 1: Ragtime to Swing* undertook—to provide "a critical survey of the whole field of recorded jazz . . . to see both the wood and specimens of significant individual trees" (x)—is such an inherently daunting one. Even so, the flaws of this project are finally those of the individuals involved—especially Nicholson the breezy pontificator and Harrison the professional iconoclast. I will, however, consult this book again for all that the other Max Harrison has to say about the many musicians he has so much to say about—Jimmy Giuffre, Gil Melle, Martial Solal, Charlie Parker, Dizzy Gillespie, Tadd Dameron, Conte Candoli, Wardell Gray, Fats Navarro, Bob Cooper, Lennie Tristano, Lars Gullin, and so on. Would that this Max Harrison were the only one.

NOTES

1. London: Quartet Books, 1976.
2. New York and London: Norton, 1986.
3. London: Hanover Books, 1968.
4. London: Hanover Books, 1975.
5. London: Mansell, 1984.
6. Ann Arbor: University of Michigan Press, 1996, p. 186.
7. A comparison between Montrose's career and those of two comparable figures, saxophonists Bill Perkins and Bud Shank, might help to explain why Harrison's "And musicians pretend that the good or bad opinions of writers on jazz make no difference!" is such a naïve and peculiar statement. Perkins, Shank, and Montrose all worked in the same West Coast milieu in the mid-to-late 1950s, all three received positive attention from a number of jazz writers and from their musical peers, and all three made recordings under their own names and as sidemen. None of them, however, made a *living* for any significant stretch of time as the leader of his own group; instead, the chief source of profitable work available to them was in Hollywood film studio and television industry orchestras. The multiply demanding lifestyle of studio work was, however, not to the taste of every jazz-oriented musician: Perkins left it to work as a tape editor in the recording industry, returning to the studios intermittently and with reluctance; Shank remained in the studios for many years, then moved to Port Townsend, Wash.; and Montrose chose

or took the Las Vegas show band option. One would imagine, then, that among the chief reasons Montrose made so few records after his mid-1950s moment in the sun, while Perkins and Shank have continued to record under their own names from time to time, was that Montrose simply was "off the scene"—working in another city, and one that is not a home to the recording industry, as Los Angeles is. Lack of favorable reviews from jazz writers had little or nothing to do with any of this.

8. Bill Kirchner, liner notes for *Stan Getz: Focus* (Verve 314-521-419).
9. Also peculiar and frustrating is the fact that Mischa Mengelberg's album *Change of Season*, which is devoted to music of Herbie Nichols, is discussed but not any of Nichols's own recordings.
10. Liner notes for *Evan Parker, London Air Lift* (FMP CD 89).
11. Harrison, Max, 1973, The Spontaneous Music Ensemble, *Jazz and Blues*, March 1973: 8–9.
12. London: Hanover Books, 1975, p. 69.

Edward Brooks, *The Young Louis Armstrong: A Critical Survey of the Early Recordings, 1923–1928* (Lanham, Md., and London: Scarecrow Press and Institute of Jazz Studies, 2002, 531 + xxxi pp., $85.00 cloth)

Reviewed by Randy Sandke

There is no doubt that the seminal work of Louis Armstrong, as both side-man and leader, is worthy of an exhaustive study such as this one. The period 1923 to 1928 was one of fervid and often startling development for Armstrong, and the musical ramifications of his innovations are still being felt. As Miles Davis noted, "You can't play nothing on trumpet that doesn't come from him."

Edward Brooks does a service to Armstrong scholars by listing in chronological order all the recordings Armstrong made within this period. Every entry begins with the band name as it appeared on the original recording, the personnel, the matrix and record numbers of the original 78 issue, the city in which the recording took place, the date, the take number, the key, and finally the metronome marking indicating tempo.

Following this, Brooks maps out the form for each selection. He lists the bar length of each introduction, theme, solo, etc. The performer of each section is duly spelled out, be it soloist, full, or partial ensemble. In the case of the King Oliver recordings Brooks also notes whether Armstrong or Oliver played the ensemble leads.

All of this information is valid and useful. It is also relatively cut and dried. Where Brooks leaves solid ground, taking his book into controversial territory, is in the analyses that conclude each entry. Along with a measure of thoughtful scholarship, I find an overabundance of questionable speculation born of equally questionable assumptions. Also, despite an attempt to apply the "learned" terminology of academic musicology, most of Brooks's musical observations are of a vague and general nature. He almost totally ignores any detailed description of Armstrong's rhythmic innovations, which are legion and crucial to the development of jazz. Writing of Armstrong without serious discussion of rhythm is like speaking of Monet without reference to color.

But by far the most troublesome aspect of this book is the patronizing and superior tone it assumes towards its subject. The sum total of Mr. Brooks's observations adds up to the conclusion that if Armstrong had applied himself to the trumpet more studiously, understood the fine points of musicology (as Brooks does), and been more esthetically sophisticated and less lazy, he would have produced much better recordings. Such an attitude tells us much more about the author than about Armstrong.

A large part of the problem with Mr. Brooks's approach is that he applies musical standards more appropriate to the classical tradition, or later forms of jazz, than to the jazz pioneers. One would make the same mistake in judging the quality of an African mask by the standards of Renaissance art. Much of the beauty of the music of King Oliver, and the Hot Fives and Sevens, lies in its unselfconscious and unfettered spirit. The music is not without its own sophistication, but it was at this stage essentially a folk music. Armstrong's genius lay in his ability to maintain the untrammeled feel of the old New Orleans style while almost single-handedly propelling jazz into ever greater realms of technical prowess and profound emotional expression.

To meticulously point out every mistaken chord, intonation problem, or fluffed note, as Brooks does, rather misses the point. The presence of a classically trained trombonist instead of Kid Ory would not have improved these records. The rawness—and at times even crudeness—of this music is part of its charm. It imparts a human quality that has always been part of the best of jazz, and one that is sorely lacking in the buffed and overly glossy popular music of our time. I am not implying that these recordings are beyond criticism, but merely that they should be judged by standards appropriate to their own esthetic.

Despite the fact that the Oliver recordings are almost universally recognized as among the most important in the history of jazz, Brooks harbors a low opinion of the band. "I would not rate Oliver higher than a very talented cornetist myself," he writes. Furthermore, "many of the [Oliver] tracks patently don't swing."

It is precisely King Oliver's relaxed phrasing and sense of swing, which was a total revelation to musicians of the early 1920s, that makes him a musical figure of inestimable significance and influence. Isham Jones insisted that his entire band visit the Lincoln Gardens to hear Oliver in person, and many others, including Bix Beiderbecke, Hoagy Carmichael, and Muggsy Spanier followed in short order.

How much of Armstrong's style was from Oliver is open to conjecture, but by his own admission the debt to his mentor was considerable. Oliver's use of mutes was truly revolutionary. Bubber Miley heard him in person one night in 1921 and the experience changed his life. Through Miley the pixie-and-plunger technique made its way into the Ellington band, a development that portended yet another revolution in jazz. To say that Oliver was nothing more than a highly talented cornetist betrays an astonishing ignorance of jazz history.

Brooks maintains that the Oliver band "still emphasizes the first and third beats in the bar," yet I detect a definite, though at times subtle, accent on two and four. He also feels that the rhythm section is often "leaden" and "devoid of swing"; I would say that they play with considerable drive, though one muted by the limitations of acoustic recording. It is true that they hadn't yet absorbed the looser rhythmic feel of Oliver and Armstrong, but aside from Bechet and Beiderbecke and a handful of others, no one else had by that time.

Brooks heaps unbridled scorn on Lil Hardin (the future Mrs. Armstrong): "Her music suffers from emotional anemia," he contends. "She is revealed as fussy, watery, and lacking in rhythmic drive. . . . Her unsympathetic attitude towards jazz is apparent from her limp piano in the solo choruses." Needless to say, Hardin was no great virtuoso and her playing is often heavy-handed. Nevertheless, Brooks's judgments are overly harsh. Hardin was one of the first jazz pianists on record who had to deal with the problem of maintaining rhythmic intensity after the ensemble drops out. This is a problem pianists are still acutely aware of. Her solution may not have been the most elegant, as the example of Earl Hines would soon show, but she is a gutsy player and one who deserves much more credit than Mr. Brooks is willing to give.

Even Armstrong himself is not spared verbal brickbats. In the book's introduction, Brooks states that his "enthusiasm for the early music of Louis Armstrong is boundless." That may be so, but his praise for Armstrong's music is constantly tempered by a steady stream of criticism of the most nitpicking, disparaging, and, to my mind, uninformed sort. Thus we are told that Armstrong's early efforts are "often gauche" and that his first recorded solo on "Chimes Blues" is "a diffident and recherché effort. . . . Really, he is not up to it; the responsibility is too much." This observation is reminiscent of James Lincoln Collier's remarks in his book *Louis Armstrong: An American Genius.* Both make a point of denigrating this solo, which is in fact simply a barely elaborated thematic statement. Nevertheless, Armstrong's personal stamp is all over it, with his characteristic phrasing and sound already evident. Brooks complains of the presence of "too many broken chords" but this is merely a function of the melody Armstrong is assigned to play. He also detects a "tendency towards jerkiness," which, like Collier's accusation that Armstrong "turns the beat around," is simply not born out by careful listening.

In some of Armstrong's recordings with Fletcher Henderson, Brooks notes "a depressing tendency to display the nonjazz skills of Howard Scott and Elmer Chambers." Most jazz writers agree that in fact Armstrong decisively improved the jazz skills of that entire band, and by extension the entire New York jazz fraternity of the mid-1920s.

Regarding Armstrong's many accompaniments to blues singers, Brooks often carps about insensitivity to the lyrics or mood of the performance. The fact that many of these records would be consigned to eternal obscurity were it not for the presence of Armstrong and the life he breathes into them does not deter the author. A typical entry reads: "[A]lthough the unimaginative piano suits the ingenuous vocal, some of Armstrong's filigree work tends to undermine its artless charm: after a restrained and appropriate introduction, his line often becomes too contrived for this species of blues. Also notice his antiphony in bars 7/8 of the last chorus, where he loses his melodic thread and produces an unattractively thin timbre."

Even Armstrong's renowned Hot Five and Hot Seven recordings are not immune from severe and unwarranted criticism. In "Melancholy Blues," his "breaks in the verse sound rushed and a little strained." His solo on "Twelfth Street Rag" is "full of fluffed pitches and the impression one is left with is that it is all beneath his dignity." "S.O.L." and "Gully Low Blues" lack "overall integrity as a result of the arbitrary tempo change." The former "is undermined by the jokey venality of the vocal," and the phrasing in the trumpet solo in the latter is "marginally more stilted" than the one from the preceding day. The epochal "Potato Head Blues" solo is "full of energy and fertile of ideas but falls short of the virtuosic."

Armstrong's stirring solo on "Ory's Creole Trombone" is "a little over ambitious. . . . It climaxes with some feral and unstable high register ululations." I must interject here that I find it disingenuous for writers such as Mr. Brooks to proclaim that Armstrong's later work grew increasingly stale while at the same time chiding him for his earlier bold experimentation. Even if Armstrong's technique fails to keep pace with his overheated imagination on some of these classic recordings, his intentions are clear and his daring is laudable. I am not the first to say that I would rather hear Armstrong miss a note than a thousand other trumpet players execute entire solos flawlessly.

In "Hotter Than That," which blazes with energy and invention from start to finish, Brooks finds that Armstrong's opening solo "comes to grief (partially) only in his uncouth effort following the chromatic triplet at the beginning of bar 6." In "Skip the Gutter," Armstrong "falls back in bar 24 on that old standby of the lazy or distracted improviser, the bugle call." His solo in "Two Deuces" is "unsettled and awkwardly phrased." On "Basin Street Blues" he "exploits his highest register, and inevitably attracts several mistakes in technique; he often sounds rushed in the early bars, not at ease with the fast lipping and fingering he has decided upon." On "Save It Pretty Mama," his "final cadential cliché is embarrassing in its banality." It is worth noting that Brooks praises Armstrong for playing essentially the same phrase at the conclusion of "Yes! I'm in the Barrel." In that instance, according to Brooks, Armstrong "treats us to a perfectly executed ascending chromatic-triplet run," though in fact the phrase consists mainly of sixteenth notes.

By now it must be obvious that I disagree with all of these so-called critical assessments. As I've already indicated, whatever lapses in technique that Brooks correctly identifies in Armstrong's playing do not detract one bit from my lifelong pleasure in listening to these recordings. There is a thrill of spontaneity, of being present at the moment of creation, that permeates all of them. They remain as fresh today, and in many ways as startling, as they were the day they were made.

Yes, it is easy enough to find fault with them. After all, the Armstrong small group recordings were often done early in the morning after a long night's work. The group was not a regular working band and had only an hour or so to rehearse the music before committing it to wax. However, the crucial question is: despite their occasional rough patches, what is it about these recordings that have made them so compelling to generations of jazz fans, including musicians, critics, and casual listeners alike? And how much light does Brooks shed on this all-important subject?

Take for instance Armstrong's remarkable scat vocal on "Hotter than That." The first 16 bars are made up of alternations between on-the-beat quarter notes and over-the-bar quarter-note triplets. Then for a full nine bars Armstrong superimposes a syncopated figure in three against the basic four-four pulse, which comes about as close to the opposing metrics of West African music as any example in jazz up to the present time. What does Brooks have to say on the subject? He offers only the bland and vague assessment that Armstrong "effects an astonishing extended pattern of rhythmic manipulation." He also misses the fact that this tune is a "Tiger Rag" derivative, and not merely "a popular song."

In "Savoy Blues," Brooks fails to take note of Armstrong's unusual and repeated use of the major instead of flatted seventh over the IV chords in his solos. This choice adds a sweetness and poignancy to the entire performance. Instead, Brooks mentions only a "wide range of moods" plus "a certain detachment." On the landmark recording of "Tight like This," the author feels compelled to bemoan the "inane erotic dialogue" at its outset. He detects that Earl Hines is "curbed . . . because of the restricted harmonic possibilities" in what is possibly the most adventurous piano solo of the era. And what of Armstrong's towering three-chorus solo? Brooks takes note of a "High Society" allusion early on which I confess entirely eludes me. The author then opines that the slow, measured opening phrase, immediately followed by one with faster notes, is a reference to the dual moods, somber and invigorating, of New Orleans funeral. This is a highly doubtful assertion at best. The second chorus "irrelevantly" hints at "'Egyptian' or 'Arab' music accompanying sand-dancers on the variety stage of the time." The last chorus includes some "cascading pathogenic arpeggios." According to my dictionary, "pathogenic" means capable of causing disease. I once had a friend who suffered a nosebleed at a Maynard Ferguson concert, but I have never heard of anyone taking ill from exposure to Armstrong's arpeggios.

Armstrong's stentorian a cappella opening to "West End Blues" has fascinated listeners for nearly 75 years. What makes this statement so compelling? I would say that much of its strength lies in an ingenious interplay between the simple and the complex, the straightforward and the ambiguous. Take the opening phrase: are those eighth notes or quarter notes? What is the basic pulse, or is there one? Is the first beat of the triplets in the second phrase a pickup or a downbeat? Are we in E♭ or C minor? And yet given all the uncertainty this introduction sounds somehow perfectly natural and immediately accessible. This is the kind of magic that only an artist of the first rank can produce.

What are Brooks's findings? That "its speed, accuracy (there are no mistakes), beauty of tone, and ascent to c'" determine it as virtuosic." Further observations bog down in generalities: it has "unstoppable rhythmic drive produced by syncopation and attack" and a "satisfying structure," "the melodic shapes are pleasing," and "the tempo is largely free." He offers some detail to back up these observations, but nothing that really qualifies as insight. He also fails to mention the descending sixteenth-note phrase in the final chorus, a phrase that echoes the introduction and helps tie the whole piece together.

All too often this book resorts to idle, solipsistic speculation that borders on meaningless claptrap. For instance: "It is significant that although Armstrong's Stompers' solos carried mordents, this Hot Seven solo contains none; this seems to be a deliberate attempt to avoid a grace often associated with sentiment or whimsy." Or: "The break . . . is an integral part of jazz and perhaps a metaphor for freedom or orgasm." In discussing the difference between pentatonic and major or minor scales Brooks tells us that "semitones can produce harmonic drive and a more personal feeling." It would follow that he finds Gershwin's "Summertime" lacking in personal feeling.

Many odd and eccentric assumptions are sprinkled throughout this book. For example, if a solo is relatively free of mistakes, Brooks surmises that it must have been worked out in advance. He informs us that the "triplet" eighth-note feel was introduced to jazz via Henry Busse's recording of the "Wang Wang Blues" with Paul Whiteman in 1920, and that white jazz musicians tend to use blue notes decoratively whereas black musicians use them expressively. (Jack Teagarden? Wild Bill Davison?)

He goes into great detail to prove that Armstrong attempted to imitate Beiderbecke on the Henderson recording of "Alone at Last," and the Savoy Ballroom Five recording of "No One Else but You." In my opinion, these claims are baseless. Armstrong and Beiderbecke were highly individualistic players, and although they admired each other greatly, their styles were poles apart. A case could be made that Beiderbecke may have been influenced by Armstrong via jam sessions both men participated in at the Savoy in Chicago during the fall of 1927 and summer of 1928. Some of Beiderbecke's solos with Frank Trumbauer from the spring of 1929, such as on "Louise," and "Wait Till You See Ma Cherie," and "I'm in Seventh Heaven" with Whiteman, show a new and sudden interest in high notes. However, this was a period of physical and emotional decline for Beiderbecke, and these recordings are far from his best. He may have been undergoing a phase of intense self-doubt, which could conceivably have led him to alter his style. But Armstrong was never one to question or substantially change his own basic approach.

Several facts are incorrectly stated in this book as well. Brooks hears triple tonguing on "Chimes Blues" which doesn't exist. I can categorically state that Armstrong never used triple tonguing in his life. (The supposed triple-tonguing that Gunther Schuller mentions (in his book *The Swing Era*) on the Victor recording of "Mahogany Hall Stomp"is in fact the result of alternate fingering.) The concluding two-cornet break in "Canal Street Blues" outlines a ♭VI chord (D♭ in the key of F), not a whole-tone scale, as Brooks asserts. Armstrong is the muted soloist throughout the Henderson recording of "T.N.T." despite Brooks's stubborn insistence that it is Joe Smith. The key for the Hot Five recording of "Struttin' with Some Barbecue" is A♭ and not B♭. This is significant because the author makes much of the notion that Armstrong's solo contains a high d''', which would have been the highest note he had recorded thus far. In fact the note is a c''', which he had played on record several times before. A "Big Butter and Egg Man" is a slang reference to a "big shot" and not to a "hayseed dairy trader." The "pop cymbals" (also known as "bacarabac cymbals") that Zutty Singleton employs are not "finger cymbals" and are in fact played with a stick. (The usual method of playing was to hold the contraption with the left hand and beat it with the right, though on some of these recordings

Singleton seems to have rigged it to a foot pedal and beat it with both hands.) The length of the chorus to "Yes! I'm in the Barrel" is 20 bars with a three-beat pickup and not 20½.

Brooks is fond of borrowing terms from classical music where appropriate and familiar jazz terms already exist. Thus "pickup" becomes "anacrusis," and "alternate fingerings" become "bariolage." An "improvised solo" is a "counter-melody" and a "straight mute" is called a "fixed mute." Sometimes terms are confused, as when Mr. Brooks mistakenly uses the word "tessitura" to mean "range." He also speaks of Armstrong's employing an "unusual tremolo." Since a trumpet is incapable of producing a tremolo, such a phenomenon would indeed be unusual! All of this adds up to unnecessary confusion for the reader, who must frequently guess at Brooks's true meaning.

One of the author's stated intentions is to "assist critical awareness with the object of drawing the reader closer to the musicians' minds." I think that this book shows us, in great and often numbing detail, the personal likes and dislikes of Edward Brooks, but fails to bring us any closer to a true understanding of the genius of Louis Armstrong. It is brimming with observations that aren't even of trivial importance. Consider the following reports on the amount of phlegm detectable in Armstrong's voice: "At this session, he seems to carry more surplus liquid in his throat than usual . . . the frog in his throat seems to have gathered more mucus . . . displays less excess throat liquid . . . his throat seems full of excess liquid again." In a line worthy of inclusion under the *New Yorker* heading "There'll Always Be an England," Brooks maintains that the last three notes of Armstrong's vocal on "Basin St. Blues" "appear to suggest the strain of evacuation."

As for more weighty esthetic matters, Brooks is, to paraphrase him, "not up to it; the responsibility is too much." I'm left wondering who the intended audience for this book is. People who already know and love these recordings will find that Brooks's opinions will not appreciably add to their delight or understanding. And it would be a pity for first-time listeners to be exposed to Armstrong's legacy through the distorting lens of an eccentric and egocentric musicologist. It is much better to go out and buy the recordings and form one's own opinions, free from prejudice.

The spirit of these great early recordings is one of school being out. Work's done, so let's relax, throw up our heels, and have a good time. The mood of Brooks's tome is school's back in session, so it's time to get back to work, sit up straight, tense up, and prepare to have your betters tell you how to think.

Jeff Sultanof, ed., *Miles Davis, Birth of the Cool: Scores from the Original Parts* (Milwaukee, WI: Hal Leonard, 2002, 167 pp., $24.95 paperback)

Reviewed by Henry Martin

It is a pleasure to report that the scores of the famous Miles Davis nonet recordings known collectively as *Birth of the Cool* have recently been published by Hal Leonard, in a folio edited by Jeff Sultanof. Even better, they are not transcriptions, but the scores themselves, as originally written (albeit with some reconstruction). Sultanof, in his introduction, describes how the discovery of the music came to pass:

> Sometime in 1995, Miles Davis' effects stored in a warehouse in Philadelphia were delivered to his estate lawyer. Those effects included three boxes of music, which were sent to Joe Muccioli of King Brand Music in New York to organize and evaluate. I was one of the first people to look through these boxes, and it is a day I will never forget. All of the scores that Gil Evans wrote for Miles' classic albums were there, as well as the session parts. While Joe and I sorted through the boxes, many of the original pencil-copied parts of the nonet library began turning up. All of the parts still existed for some pieces, and in others, enough parts were available to assemble versions that were relatively close to the originals (4).

An exciting find, indeed. Miles Davis had possession of the parts, but apparently not the original scores themselves. Famous for not wishing to revisit or recreate earlier stages of his career, Davis refused to lend the parts out or let them be copied. Sultanof created scores from these existing parts, including two pieces that were never recorded by the nonet in the studio, "Joost at the Roost" (Mulligan) and "Birth of the Cool Theme" (Evans). (The latter does exist as an aircheck from a nonet broadcast of September 4, 1948.)

Sultanof has done a fine job of bringing these scores to life. The layout is clean and clear, and the quality of the work superior. Still, this is not a scholarly edition, and so it raises questions regarding editing procedures, a topic that Sultanof treats only briefly in the introduction (4). For example, just what parts of what pieces did Sultanof in fact reconstruct?

The good news is that detailed answers to this and other questions will be forthcoming, because Sultanof is planning an article on the project for this journal. For this review, I e-mailed him a list of questions, to which he kindly responded. Quotations and summaries of his remarks, unless otherwise attributed, are from his e-mailed responses to my questions. As is usual, quotations and page references from the volume itself are given in parentheses with no further citations.

In his introduction, Sultanof succinctly summarizes the genesis and history of the *Birth* recordings. In the late 1940s, a group of musicians centered around Gil Evans began discussing ideas for a small band with charts like those Evans had been writing for the Claude Thornhill Orchestra, but with greater emphasis on bebop. Eventually, Miles Davis was brought into the project and a group was formed that was booked into the Royal Roost, where Davis had been performing with Charlie Parker. This engagement led to a signing of the band by Pete Rugolo for Capitol Records and, eventually, three recording dates: January 21 and April 22, 1949, and March 9, 1950. Upon release, the records generated little attention and sold poorly: "[H]owever, according to Rugolo, none of Capitol's modern jazz recordings [was] promoted properly and all of them suffered poor sales" (2).

> In 1954, Rugolo persuaded Capitol to release eight of the twelve sides on a 10" Capitol album called *Classics in Jazz—Miles Davis*. In 1957, eleven of the tracks were issued on a 12" album entitled *The Birth of the Cool*, the first time the famous phrase was coined describing the ensemble and its music. It was long assumed that producer Rugolo was responsible for the title, but he has denied this (2).

The mystery of the catchy *Birth of the Cool* phrase remains. Perhaps anonymous marketing personnel at Capitol came up with the title. Nonetheless, once collected on LP, the pieces took off—and have been available on record and CD continuously since 1957.

There are historical problems with attributions of the pieces to various composers and arrangers. For example, whereas "Deception" is credited to Miles Davis, Sultanof notes that "the majority of the parts are in Mulligan's hand." Similarly, "'Boplicity' is now acknowledged to have been written by Miles and Gil, and Evans wrote the arrangement." The latter has led to copyright claims on behalf of the Evans estate. Presumably, Sultanof will explore these and other issues of attribution in the forthcoming article.

An interesting paradox is that so many of the *Birth of the Cool* charts are uptempo or at least medium uptempo. One recalls the nonet's founding intention to bring "more bebop" to the basic sound of Evans's writing for the Thornhill band. Thornhill himself resisted suggestions by Evans to incorporate bebop into the band's library, because this was not his aesthetic interest. And so the antibop stance by Thornhill became a motivating factor in the founding of the "cool sound + bebop" workshop centering around Evans in the first place.[1]

The later celebrity of cool jazz and Davis himself surely had much to do with the unexpected popularity of the *Birth of the Cool* LP in 1957. The timbre of the LP is "cool," but its most ambitious charts also reveal the "birth" of the 1950s "third stream" clique. Gunther Schuller was the French horn player for the March 9, 1950, session; later, he and some of the *Birth* composer-arrangers became prominent in the more experimental directions of jazz. That is, just as the *Birth* recordings gave rise to the influential solo stylings of Gerry Mulligan, Miles Davis, Lee Konitz, and John Lewis, historical continuity also existed between the participants on those sessions and the leaders of the third stream avant-garde. Given that both the cool and the third stream movements have a common progenitor in the *Birth* recordings, it may not be hyperbolic to describe them as among the most important and influential series of recordings in jazz history.

The folio offers full score layouts of the selections contained in the *Birth of the Cool* LP with the exception of "Darn That Dream," with vocalist Kenny Hagood. Sultanof admits that he never cared much for the selection and wanted to be sure that there was room for "Joost at the Roost." Still, as the only vocal selection, this is a curious omission from an otherwise complete presentation.

The score layouts are in concert. Interestingly, this was the publisher's decision; Sultanof would have preferred to issue the volume with the parts transposed so that readers could "see how the parts lay for the instruments themselves." Sultanof also points out correctly that transposed scores were preferable in professional situations because copying fees were minimized. (With recent computer notation programs, transposition is easily automated when parts are extracted from the score, although they usually need to be edited for enharmonic spellings, page turns, computer glitches, and so on.)

Although Sultanof's points on the advantages of transposed scores are well taken, I believe that transposition is itself an out-of-date holdover from the early days of instrument building. How much more convenient it would be if all music appeared in concert! Except for the minority of players who double on differently sized instruments of the same family, musical life and discussion, and score preparation and correction, would be far less onerous. Concert scores are one way we can continue to move in this direction.

Nonetheless, given contemporary practice, concert scores and parts are not commercially viable. I queried Sultanof about whether Hal Leonard was planning to issue performance editions of the folio, and he replied that the publisher "has chosen not to prepare and sell parts to the 'Birth' pieces, the feeling being that 'combos do not sell.'"

In addition to the written parts for the scores, it is gratifying to note that the volume includes transcriptions of the improvised solos, mostly by Miles Davis, Gerry Mulligan, Lee Konitz, and J.J. Johnson. The solos were transcribed by Ron Duboff, although he is not credited in the publication. For the most part they are accurate, although I came across a few errors.[2]

A particularly pleasing feature of Sultanof's layout is that he avoided "D.S. al Coda" indications and the like, which make page flipping such a chore. As he writes, "In such pieces as 'Jeru' where the first playing of the head has a clear downbeat on the first measure, and the second playing has a tied note from the last bar, I opted to write everything out." Hence, the scores are easy to navigate and a pleasure to study.

One oversight was omitting the name of the arranger for each chart. Sultanof assumed that anyone consulting his edition would know who the arrangers were already, but of course that may not be the case. The composers are always credited, but in several instances the composers were not the arrangers. Sultanof intends to supply the arrangers' names to Hal Leonard in hopes that the publisher will add them to future printings.

As noted above, Sultanof will detail the philosophy and specifics of his editing practices in an upcoming article; hence, I will merely summarize these procedures, as clarified in his responses to my questions:

1. Sultanof generally leaves notes as they were written, even if they were changed for the recording—for example, "so people could see what Mulligan wrote."
2. But he does sometimes edit for the sake of simplicity: "Where notes could be re-spelled to eliminate an accidental, I did so (E naturals to E flats were changed to F flat-E flat)."
3. He occasionally edits rhythmic notation, as well: "I also correct the way rhythms are sometimes written. Gil Evans often wrote rhythms in ways that really confuse musicians to this day, which explains why the musicians at the Miles Davis Columbia albums had a hard time playing the music. The entire last section of 'Moondreams' is entirely re-notated in this folio to make it easier to read, as an example."
4. Sultanof generally leaves articulations and phrasings as they appeared on the original parts. "Some parts had slurs one way, others were different. I used my judgment to make them consistent, based on the recordings."
5. He adds chord symbols to piano parts with written-out chords.

As an editor for jazz-related publications of Hal Leonard and Warner Bros. for more than two decades, Sultanof has extensive experience in dealing with these matters, but such alterations to the music as notated should be made clearer. For future projects along these lines, perhaps Sultanof might consider working with a more scholarly publisher, for example the A-R Editions series, Music of the United States of America (MUSA), which is supported by the American Musicological Society. The MUSA series is highly eclectic and includes music of significant value that is not widely available; among its first 10 volumes are works of Irving Berlin, Ruth Crawford, Lou Harrison, and Fats Waller! Perhaps Sultanof might interest A-R Editions in a MUSA volume of *Miles Ahead*, *Porgy and Bess*, and *Sketches of Spain*, although securing copyright clearances would be a major burden—particularly for *Porgy and Bess*.

Though some of the *Birth* scores had been previously available (such as "Boplicity"), and though the remaining had been previously transcribed (some more than once), it is thanks to the persistent and careful efforts of Jeff Sultanof that we can now savor these scores in a consistently edited format and without musing over possible transcriptional inaccuracies. With Sultanof's promised follow-up article, moreover, we should be able to annotate our editions to reflect his own work more precisely. This folio provides a significant tool to jazz scholarship and considerably enhances our understanding of the composition and arranging concepts motivating the jazz vanguard of the late 1940s. Within the framework of a mainstream musical publication, Jeff Sultanof has provided us with a collection of scores of uncommon interest and importance.

Transcription errors:

"Move" (9), m. 42: Bb in trumpet run should be B♮.
"Budo" (37), m. 55: trumpet E♭ should be E♮; (39), mm. 81–82, baritone should be octave higher; (39), m. 83, first note of alto should be A♮, not A♭; (39), m. 88, alto's A♭ on fourth beat should be A♮.
"Venus de Milo" (78), m. 62: last three notes of bar in trumpet solo should be D♭–E♭–C rather than B–D♭–B; (79), m. 65, trumpet note should be F rather than G.
"Rouge" (99), m. 45: seventh note of alto solo should be E rather than F♯.
"Boplicity" (92), m. 78: C on beat 4 should be D; on same page, rehearsal (measure) number 85 should be 83.
"Israel" (67), m. 76: alto note on third beat should be C♯, not C.
"Rock Salt" [a.k.a. "Rocker"]: (136), m. 64, trumpet notes should be A♭, not A.

Software glitches:

"Move" (10), m. 56: overwritten naturals in trumpet part key signature.
"Budo" (37), m. 56: overwritten naturals in trumpet part key signature.
"Budo" (38), bottom system: barlines and overwritten naturals in baritone part.

I also spotted a typo at m. 65 of "Deception" (123), where the B♭ chord in the trumpet part does not agree with the C/G chord in the piano part. Sultanof notes that the trumpet chord is an error.

NOTES

1. The "Birth of the Cool" recordings can be compared to Evans's writing for Thornhill's group on the recently released CDs from The Jazz Factory: *Gil Evans—The Real Birth of the Cool—Studio Recordings* (JFCD-22801) *and Gil Evans—The Real Birth of the Cool—Transcription Recordings* (JFCD-22803).
2. The transcription errors are the more obvious ones I noticed in a quick read-through. I will not take issue with complicated passages that are more approximate, since transcription of the solos is not the principal purpose of the folio. Nonetheless, since it is so handy to have the solos to refer to, I list these corrections. Again, page numbers are in parentheses.

Noal Cohen and Michael Fitzgerald, *Rat Race Blues: The Musical Life of Gigi Gryce*; foreword by Benny Golson (Berkeley, CA: Berkeley Hills Books, 2002, 456 pp., $18.95 paperback)

Reviewed by Scott A. Carter

Rat Race Blues: The Musical Life of Gigi Gryce provides a thorough examination of the musical genius of one of jazz's underrated musicians. As sideman, leader, arranger, or educator (the profession he followed after his retirement as an active musician), Gryce always held himself to the highest of standards and helped those with whom he worked to elevate the level of their musicianship. During a career that lasted just over a decade, Gryce worked with some of the best musicians of the time, including Clifford Brown, Benny Golson, Quincy Jones, Lionel Hampton, Oscar Pettiford, and Tadd Dameron; this new entry into the growing canon of jazz biographies provides much-needed attention to Gryce's achievements.

Born George General Grice, Jr. (Grice was the original spelling of his surname), on November 28, 1925, in Pensacola, Florida, Gigi was the fifth of six children born to George and Rebecca Grice. All of the children would eventually become educators. Gryce's musical studies did not begin in earnest until his teenage years, when his high school was able to hire Raymond Sheppard through the Federal One music project division of the Works Progress Administration. Sheppard, an alto saxophone player, had worked with Noble Sissle and Jimmie Lunceford before leading his own dance band in the Pensacola area. Gryce's first lessons were on clarinet, but he soon switched to alto saxophone; and before graduating from high school in 1943, he was already working with Sheppard's dance band. The following year, Gryce was drafted into the U.S. Navy and joined the band at the Great Lakes, Illinois, training center, which was well known for its music program. Gryce was also able to further his studies at the Chicago Conservatory of Music.

After being discharged, Gryce moved to Hartford, Connecticut, and then to Boston, where he began studying composition with Alan Hovhaness at the Boston Conservatory of Music. He would eventually graduate in 1952 after spending time in Paris studying with Nadia Boulanger. This association ended prematurely, however, when Gryce returned to Boston because of personal problems. In addition to his studies, Gryce began to make contacts with both new and established musicians in Boston and New York. These experiences included the chance to work with one of his idols, Thelonious Monk, at the Hi-Hat in 1949. Among his musical acquaintances during these formative years were future luminaries Oscar Pettiford, Howard McGhee, Jaki Byard, and Horace Silver. It was through Silver that between 1951 and 1952 Gryce had six compositions premiered by Stan Getz, including one of his better-known compositions, "Hymn to the Orient."

In 1953 Gryce made his first commercial recording as a sideman with Max Roach before joining Tadd Dameron's band that summer in Atlantic City, New Jersey. During his tenure with Dameron, Gryce met Clifford Brown and Benny Golson. Gryce and Brown soon left to join Lionel Hampton's band to tour Europe that fall. Gryce's second European experience would prove more successful than the first, with Gryce, Brown, and bandmate Quincy Jones making some of their earliest recordings in Paris.

Over the next two years Gryce participated in projects with Art Farmer, Oscar Pettiford, and Charles Mingus's Jazz Composer's Workshop; but perhaps his most enduring achievement of this period was his activity on behalf of musicians' rights, particularly in the area of music publishing and ownership. In 1955, Gryce founded two publishing companies, Melotone and Totem, with Golson. As an appendix to the book, Cohen and Fitzgerald have provided a list of the holdings that constituted these companies. Gryce was very aware that many musicians were not being treated fairly with regard to royalty payments and other financial matters and encouraged colleagues (including Horace Silver, who would create his own publishing company) to take a more active role in the management of their music. Also in 1955, he published a two-volume folio of his compositions, *Modern Sounds,* in which he expressed his desire to create music "in the jazz idiom that has its roots in the traditional jazz language but which incorporates all of the advances in jazz theory and practice that have been made in the past ten years" (155).

Although many of the band projects with which Gryce became involved never amounted to more than a rehearsal or two, one of the more intriguing undertakings was the Oscar Pettiford Orchestra, which lasted from 1956 to 1957. This band consisted of two trumpets, two French horns, trombone, four reeds, harp, cello, piano, bass, and drums. Along with Lucky Thompson, Gryce composed and arranged for this modified big band—an undertaking that provided an extraordinary challenge and resulted in music of the highest caliber. After two LPs and a few performances, the band folded because of financial problems. Gryce's next group began to record in 1957 and during that year was presented on no less than six LPs. Called The Jazz Lab and co-led by trumpeter Donald Byrd, it helped establish Gryce as a player, composer, and arranger. In his words, the Jazz Lab was created "to both give the listener something of substance that he can feel and understand and also indicate to the oriented that we're trying to work in more challenging musical forms and to expand the language in other ways" (213–14). Usually performing as a quintet, the Jazz Lab at various times employed pianists Tommy Flanagan, Wynton Kelly, Hank Jones, and Wade Legge, bassists Wendell Marshall and Paul Chambers, and drummers Art Taylor and Osie Johnson. The repertoire consisted of many original compositions by Gryce and other members of the band and was a wonderful showcase for Gryce's arranging talents. After the demise of the Jazz Lab, Gryce focused his energy on arranging for record dates by various musicians, including the *Rich versus Roach* album, a Betty Carter album, and three recordings for Golson. After leading three record dates in 1960, Gryce formed his last band, the Orch-tette. This group, which recorded just once, focused heavily on new arrangements written specifically for its members. By the end of 1962, Gryce had retired from active playing.

Gryce's next life would begin a year later, but not before the dissolving of his two publishing companies. In the fall of 1963, Gryce began working as a substitute public school teacher. Having adopting the name Basheer Qusim after his conversion to Islam, Gryce would eventually be hired as the music instructor at Community Elementary School No. 53 in the Bronx. While there, he was able to establish a boys chorus and continued to compose for the groups he now taught. Gryce earned his Master's degree in education administration and supervision in 1978 at Fordham University and continued working towards a Ph.D. until his death in 1983. Later that year the public school at which he had taught was renamed in his honor.

The research conducted for this book provides answers to many questions that have arisen since Gryce's retirement, most of them initiated and encouraged by Gryce himself. Rumors concerning Gryce's relocating to Europe because of threats seem to have been inaccurate, although there is evidence that he was pressured by some publishing and recording companies to curtail his efforts on behalf of musicians' rights. Little had been known about Gryce's life after music, and although this book concentrates on Gryce's professional years, it does provide new information about his postjazz career. Fitzgerald and Cohen furnish well-documented examples of the efforts that Gryce put into his music, including college transcripts and many interviews with musicians and family that help the reader to understand what he wanted to accomplish. While the interviews provide firsthand accounts of how Gryce operated, their tendency to include long passages, sometimes as much as two and three pages, of transcribed interviews makes for tedious reading.

The authors' commentary on, and analysis of, Gryce's recordings are an excellent source for readers, whether they are familiar with his work or have just become interested in it. Cohen and Fitzgerald also offer thorough discussions of Gryce's original compositions and arrangements, but they provide only a few musical examples of his playing. Given the book's concentration on Gryce's talents as an arranger and composer, it would have been very helpful to students and scholars to see how Gryce handled challenges in orchestration such as his writing for the Oscar Pettiford Orchestra. The preface mentions plans to publish some of Gryce's works. One hopes these plans will soon come to fruition.

This book provides a thorough look at a musician who, while admired by his peers, is often only a footnote to the better-known musicians with whom he worked. With their exceptional research and detailed examination of Gigi Gryce, Fitzgerald and Cohen have brought much-needed attention to one of the most ingenious musical minds of his era.

John Chilton, *Roy Eldridge: Little Jazz Giant* (London and New York: Continuum, 2002, 400 pp., $39.95 cloth, $29.95 paperback)

Reviewed by Edgar Jordan

In a January 2003 online discussion conducted by the Jazz Journalists Association, the question was posed: Are we in the midst of a "golden age" of jazz biographies? Publishers, both trade and specialized, are producing books that chronicle the work of both major figures and lesser-known but important contributors. In addition, publishers are reprinting autobiographies, biographies, and histories, some of which have been unavailable for many years. Surprisingly, until now there has not been a comprehensive study of Roy Eldridge. It is fitting that John Chilton should fill this void. As a trumpet player himself and as author of exemplary biographies of Sidney Bechet and Coleman Hawkins among others, Chilton does not disappoint in his latest effort.

Roy Eldridge's legacy tends to begin with the notion that Louis Armstrong and Dizzy Gillespie must be linked in some way and that Eldridge is that link. Labeling someone a link between important historical figures may be considered a positive attribute, but it can also obscure important contributors and contributions. Eldridge is a major stylist in his own right, a progenitor of swing, and at times a controversial figure.

Eldridge is often singled out for his facility in the upper range of the trumpet. "Higher and faster" grabs the listeners' attention and can often overshadow many other aspects of a player's arsenal. Upon further exploration and more varied listening, one finds that Eldridge's complete musicianship and mastery of the technique essential to jazz music is ever present. He feigned modesty when talking about his blues playing, but his playing *and* singing of the blues revealed his authority and soulfulness in that genre as well. Eldridge, like many other musicians of his generation, was able to assimilate any musical situation or style with ease.

Chilton follows a standard chronological approach and includes concise yet aptly titled chapters like "A Bite at the Big Apple" and "Flying with the Hawk." What has become a standard feature of Chilton's books, "Roy on Record," is here an exhaustively annotated section discussing a sizable portion of Eldridge's discography. The notes to the chapters serve the additional function of a bibliography. A minor disappointment in the final index of selected recordings is the omission of LP, compact disc, or compilation titles, which would benefit readers unfamiliar with Eldridge's catalogue. Chilton does include many of these in the "Roy on Record" section, however.

Chilton first met Eldridge in 1958, and the two continued a relationship until the trumpeter's death in 1989. Much of the information in the book, therefore, comes from firsthand accounts, as well as from a wealth of information and interviews. Chilton's almost fifty years of experience as a trumpeter lends veracity to his commentary on many of the technical aspects of Eldridge's playing, embouchure, and equipment. Chilton describes a young Eldridge's trumpet experimentations: "In order to toughen his lip further, he cut small grooves in his mouthpiece rim and then rubbed the mouthpiece on a hard stone surface. This flattened the rim and broadened it, thus spreading the pressure he used to produce a note over a larger area of his lips. It was not an uncommon strategy in those days, usually producing a scar on the lips, which Roy said he felt quite proud of, thinking he now resembled a veteran trumpet player" (24). Chilton also gives detailed insight into Eldridge's further adapting his playing in 1944 as a result of having to replace his dental plate (154–55).

In chapter 1, Eldridge's early years in Pittsburgh are well chronicled and impressively presented, thanks in no small part to the use of a judicious amount of Eldridge's own commentary and anecdotes. Eldridge details his early musical forays (6), his mother's musical influence (5, 9) and his early models: Rex Stewart, Benny Carter, and Coleman Hawkins (10–12). Whereas Chilton is careful to highlight the obviously pertinent musical history of Eldridge, he skirts over much of his family history. Eldridge's parents' birthplaces are relegated to parenthetical references, a technique that Chilton uses often. Such details are important to Eldridge's upbringing and should in my view have been more prominently featured. Chilton offers significant information on Eldridge's father ("Alexander, like all of his brothers, was by trade a master carpenter" [4]; and "[he] was religious, and made sure Roy went to church regularly" [4]) but offers no other background beyond the fact that he was originally from Petersburg, Virginia (4). Were Alexander's relatives in Pittsburgh with his immediate family? What church did the family attend? Did Eldridge and his siblings ever visit Petersburg, Virginia—or Winston Salem, North Carolina, where his mother was born? (5). These details would provide a more complete impression of his family life.

On occasion, in moments of candor, Eldridge spoke about various encounters with racism. Chilton provides ample space for commentary on his experiences as a member of Gene Krupa's Band (117–18) and the controversies over articles written by Leonard Feather in which Eldridge felt he had been misrepresented (186–87, 188–89). "Interlude in Paris" discusses Eldridge's decision to stay in Europe after a Benny Goodman tour in 1950

(174), intimating that the decision was based on "the encroachment of bop"(177) as well as racism. However, the quote Chilton chooses does not seem to make the intended point: "Progress in music, yes, but no bloody revolution. A lot of people seem to think I'm against bop. I'm not, but it's no use plugging it when so many people just don't catch on. I believe music must have something that the fans can whistle. Sandwich a progressive number between two real tunes. That's the way to get them interested" (177). While Eldridge appears to make a distinction between bop and "real tunes," this is not the statement of someone running from the new music.

The final section, "Roy on Record," is far-reaching in scope. Here Chilton describes and analyzes a hefty portion of Eldridge's recorded works chronologically. The author's familiarity with the recorded material is impressive, and his approach is an inspiration to aspiring writers. Moreover, his passion for the music is evident. Unfortunately, even a writer as experienced and crafty as Chilton can run out of adjectives. The tone of the section becomes more that of an extended record review at times: "There are no moments of madness or of grandstanding; instead there is a series of solos offering a fascinating mixture of joy and sorrow"(381); "Tommy Turk, a speedy and powerful trombonist with a fruity tone . . . "(349). Chilton does not shy away from value judgements of the material at hand: "Good taste is sometimes in short supply but there is an abundance of excitement and a purposeful ending to what was a drawn contest" (358); "Again the pull of high altitude takes the two trumpeters away from the more fertile plateau" (363); "Jo Jones is the first to jettison good taste and things go downhill from there" (372). Chilton also quotes writer Alyn Shipton's opinion on recordings of Jazz at the Philharmonic: "Although there are many great moments in the recorded legacy of JATP, there is an almost equal number of vapid chase choruses, with soloists vying to play louder, higher and faster than one another—all of which may have been very exciting in a concert hall at the time, but make for extremely tedious listening today" (357). Chilton then proceeds to comment on some of the JATP recordings, which are already tainted in the reader's mind. While some of this commentary can be frustrating, the selection of recordings covered is wide-ranging and perfectly complements Eldridge's history as presented in earlier chapters.

Roy Eldridge: Little Jazz Giant is a welcome addition to the ever expanding array of jazz biographies. Chilton's praiseworthy research and evenhanded view of jazz music and the essential (and to some extent underappreciated) talents of Roy Eldridge should spur a "golden age" of rediscovery of a gifted musician.

CD-ROM REVIEW

Tom Lord, *The Jazz Discography*, version 3.3 [for PC: Windows 95 or higher; for Mac: OS9 or higher] (West Vancouver, BC: Lord Musical Reference, $277.00) [available from www.lordisco.com]

Reviewed by Edward Berger

The release of Tom Lord's work on CD-ROM is a milestone in the history of jazz discography; if ever a field were tailor-made for computerization, it is discography. By any measure it is an extraordinarily useful tool, providing users with nearly instantaneous searches that were previously either impossible or extremely time-consuming. Yet despite its undeniable virtues, *The Jazz Discography* can prove frustrating to experienced jazz researchers, and its undisguised appropriation of previous works raises a number of serious ethical questions.

The Jazz Discography was originally available in printed form in 26 volumes distributed by Cadence/NorthCountry. Well into the project, Cadence and Lord had a parting of the ways. As a result the first 25 volumes are sold through the distributor but the last volume, five index volumes, and the CD-ROM are marketed by Lord directly (www.lordisco.com). This rift may have repercussions beyond the marketing of the work, because Cadence was a major supplier of current discographical data for the project. Presumably, Lord will not have access to this information for future editions (beyond what is published in *Cadence* magazine, of course).

SCOPE

Lord describes his work (in the Introduction section of the Help menu):

The Jazz Discography is the most up-to-date general discography of all categories of recorded jazz, from 1896 to today. It is a complete single-source catalog which updates and replaces previously published individual category and limited time-period general discographies. Significantly, it is the first jazz discography to be published on CD-ROM, and the first ever to be compiled using a computer database.[1]

Lord adds: "The period covered by CD-ROM Version 3.3 is from 1896 to 2001 inclusive." This statement is misleading; only a very small portion of the discography contains material recorded as late as 2001. The CD-ROM contains virtually the same material (with some typos and inconsistencies corrected) found in the 26 printed volumes that were released over a 10-year period, 1992 to 2001. Because Lord started at the beginning of the alphabet, the termination dates of each volume vary from 1991 (vol. 1: A–BANKHEAD) to 2001 (vol. 26: WINTER–ZZEBRA).

A major advantage of the use of a database for a project of this type is the potential for constant updating. Purchase of this version of the CD-ROM entitles the buyer to future updates (promised annually) at half price.

FORMAT AND SEARCHES

The CD-ROM display retains the traditional discographical format used in the printed volumes, which will be comforting to those accustomed to using the standard jazz discographical reference works of the past. Information supplied for each of the 136,263 sessions in the database includes *Leader or Group Name*; *Album Title* (where applicable); *Personnel*; *Place and Date of Recording*; *Tune Titles* (with matrix numbers, if applicable); and *Label and Release Numbers* (78 and 45 rpm, LPs, and CDs).

What sets the CD-ROM apart, naturally, is its search capabilities. Basic artist searches may be done in two ways: by LEADER (24,351 entries) or by MUSICIAN (i.e., sideman) (754,132 entries). A leader search yields all recordings by a leader in chronological order. The sessions may be viewed in summary form (listing dates and Lord's assigned session numbers) or in detail, which displays all the data for that session in the standard discographical layout. The MUSICIAN search produces a similar display but includes all sessions of the selected artist, whether as leader or sideman. The results may be viewed chronologically or alphabetically by leader.

A TUNE INDEX produces a list of all tunes in the database (737,487 entries) and the number of sessions on which each title appears. A TUNE SEARCH shows full discographical entries for all recordings of the selected title. This display can be viewed either chronologically or alphabetically by leader.

A MULTIPLE SEARCH option permits searches combining up to three musicians and three tune titles. This feature enables a researcher to find out whether a particular artist ever recorded a certain tune or whether Artist "A" ever recorded with Artist "B."

A SEARCH BY DATE feature does not do what the title implies and is not explained anywhere in the documentation. The date search is possible only within another search (i.e., artist or tune). It is not possible to search for a date through the entire database, an operation that would enable one to find all recordings made on a specific date in jazz history. Although functional, the database does not provide many of the sophisticated features to which we have grown accustomed, particularly customized searches and reports. For example, there is no search by record label, a very useful approach for many aspects of discographical research.

Apart from the aforementioned "search by date" omission, the on-screen explanations are generally helpful if at times overly complicated, and navigation is easy to master simply through a bit of experimentation. One can easily print from any screen, a feature not present on earlier versions. Another added feature of Version 3.3 is the standardization of all performers' names and most song titles, which greatly aids in searching.

Lord deals effectively with "carryover" personnels (i.e., larger groups that remain essentially the same over a number of sessions). Traditionally, discographers have noted only the changes from session to session without repeating the full list. This practice saves space and enables users to readily see what changes have taken place. But such a method would not allow full indexing of all names for each session in a database system. Lord's listings follow the traditional method of tracking only the changes in personnel but include the full list of names in the database. One can view this list by simply pressing an icon denoting that a session contains an expanded carryover personnel. The system works well in theory but in practice results in many erroneous (or at the very least dubious) personnel listings. For example, Budd Johnson is correctly credited with one arranged title for Gene Krupa: "What's This?" (January 22, 1945, session # K4262-3). [Lord's note identifies him rather cryptically as "aj," presumably for Albert Johnson, his given name.] Yet Johnson is also listed as arranger in the personnel of Krupa's big band for 13 other sessions (beginning with November 11, 1944 [session K4254-3], through April 24, 1945 [session # K4267]), on which he played no role whatsoever. Furthermore, one of those sessions, that of March 8, 1945 (# K4265-3), is correctly listed as being by the "Gene Krupa Trio," yet Lord's "carryover" icon yields a full big band personnel, again including Johnson.

One positive note about the program's reliability: in over a year of constant use at the Institute of Jazz Studies, *The Jazz Discography* has never failed to function.

CONTENT

Unfortunately, the content is not always as reliable as the software. Anyone who has paged through *The Jazz Discography* will quickly discover its anomalies, idiosyncrasies, and out-and-out errors. Duplicate entries are a frequent problem. These often occur when a previously unissued session is later released but Lord fails to recognize the titles as being from one source, with the result that the material is listed twice. An example is Ornette Coleman's *Science Fiction* sessions of September 9, 10, and 13, 1971 (# C4489-3). Five unissued titles from these sessions later appeared on the *Broken Shadows* LP, but Lord treats them as a new session (C4497-3) with a different recording date even though the liner notes (Columbia FC38029) clearly identify these tracks as deriving from the *Science Fiction* sessions.

Another type of duplication occurs when Lord lists the same session under different leaders. For example *Phil Silvers and Swinging Brass* is listed once under Nelson Riddle (session # R3370-3), who was the composer-arranger-conductor, and again under Silvers (session # S6345-3).

Other common errors include transposed issue numbers, incorrect record company names (Lord sometimes confuses manufacturers or distributors with labels), inconsistent forms of label names (sometimes within the same session!), incorrect release information due to misalignment of issue numbers with song titles, and inconsistent use of notes (i.e., some refer to an entire session and others only to the tune title immediately preceding the note.). Overall, one gets the impression that Lord is more a collator than a researcher. He has collected massive amounts of data in a relatively short time from a variety of sources, often without applying critical judgment or even common sense.

SOURCES

Lord's copyright notice includes the standard wording: "The use of any part of this publication reproduced, transmitted, in any form by any means, electronic, mechanical, photocopying, recording, or otherwise, or stored in a retrieval system, without prior consent of the publisher is an infringement of the copyright law." Had Lord himself heeded this warning, *The Jazz Discography* would not exist. Discography, particularly comprehensive discography, is by its nature a cumulative endeavor, with new works building upon the base of knowledge established by earlier researchers, as well as by informal networks of current contributors. But the massive amount of material lifted by Lord verbatim from other works has crossed a line. In their exhaustive and meticulous study, "Comprehensive Discographies of Jazz, Blues and Gospel,"[2] Barry Kernfeld and Howard Rye discuss the question of discographical plagiarism, particularly by Bruyninckx and Lord, concluding that the latter " [i]n crucial respects . . . seems unqualified to be a jazz discographer. He certainly does not understand what constitutes plagiarism."[3]

U.S. Copyright Law states that one may not copyright "works consisting entirely of information that is common property and containing no original authorship (for example: standard calendars, height and weight charts, tape measures and rulers, and lists or tables taken from public documents or other common sources)."[4] Many colleges and universities have formulated detailed guidelines for students on what constitutes plagiarism. A typical statement is in a document prepared by The Writing Center at the University of Wisconsin-Madison, "Quoting, Paraphrasing and Acknowledging Sources," which defines the concept of "common knowledge":

> It is not necessary to document certain factual information considered to be in the public domain: e.g., birth and death dates of well-known figures, generally accepted dates of military, political, literary, and other historical events. In general, factual information contained in multiple standard reference works can usually be considered to be in the public domain. If, however, you use the exact words of the reference source, you must credit the source. If in doubt, be cautious and cite the source.[5]

Applying these guidelines to the world of discography, one need not credit any particular source for the recording date of Armstrong's "West End Blues," since it is available in countless works. But Lord has appropriated without attribution vast amounts of original information, particularly from the more detailed jazz bio-discographies. A typical example is the note following his entry for an unissued Coltrane performance of August 1, 1965 (Lord session # C4899-3): "The 'Untitled' has been mistaken for 'A love supreme' and 'Chasin' the Trane' but it has rather a similarity with 'Vigil' although it moves along different patterns." How did Lord know this? Did he listen to this item, and if he did, would he have recognized the underlying structure of this piece? It turns out he paraphrased (and none too accurately) a note from David Wild's *The Recordings of John Coltrane*: "65-0801a [the untitled piece] has been misidentified as 'A Love Supreme' and 'Chasin' the Trane'; it is however an unidentified modal composition quite similar to 'Vigil'. . . .[6] This is a particularly egregious case, since Wild's work is not even included in Lord's "bibliography."

As Kernfeld and Rye point out, Lord seems more naïve than devious. If he were the latter, he surely would have better attempted to disguise his borrowings. For example, in many instances Lord has not even bothered to correct the awkward syntax and grammar of non-native English-speaking discographers whose work he has used.

By Lord's own admission to Kernfeld,[7] 60 to 65 percent of *The Jazz Discography* was taken from Bruyninckx (who himself took freely from Jepsen), not to mention the copious copying from more specialized discographies. Apparently Lord sincerely believes that this wholesale use of material is absolved by his inclusion of a bibliography and by this brief statement, which follows his list of contributors: "And of course a deep bow to general discographers who have come before; Hilton Schleman, Charles Delaunay, Brian Rust, Jorgen Jepsen, Walter Bruyninckx and Erik Raben."[8]

This is not to say that Lord has added nothing to the work of these and other discographers. Just as Bruyninckx greatly expanded the coverage of Jepsen's *Jazz Records 1942–* (the termination date varies between 1962 to 1969, depending on the volume), Lord has pushed discographical coverage into the 1990s (and, in his final volume, into the new millennium)—far closer to the present than any of his predecessors. He has also made a major contribution in documenting CD releases of earlier material. Presumably, future updates will contain more original material because Lord will be traversing discographically uncharted territory.

Kernfeld and Rye concluded their comprehensive assessment of jazz discography by advising music librarians against purchasing Lord's work (then available only in printed form) on ethical grounds.[9] Although I sympathize with their position, the CD-ROM version is so useful a research tool that it is almost indispensable for any institution engaged in jazz research. Counterculture gadfly Abbie Hoffman may have provided the answer to this moral dilemma when he wrote *Steal This Book*. Perhaps the ultimate justice would be to borrow the CD-ROM and copy it. But that, of course, would be illegal.

NOTES

The author would like to thank John Clement and Michael Cuscuna for their help in compiling this review.

1. It should be noted that Walter Bruyninckx's discography is also being issued in CD-ROM format under the title *85 Years of Recorded Jazz* (with a coauthor: Domi Truffandier). *ARJS* will review this work when it is complete.
2. Barry Kernfeld and Howard Rye, "Comprehensive Discographies of Jazz, Blues and Gospel," parts one and two, *Notes* 51, no. 2 (December 1994): 501–547; no. 3 (March 1995): 865–891.
3. Kernfeld and Rye, "Comprehensive Discographies of Jazz, Blues and Gospel," part two, *Notes* 51, no. 3 (March 1995): 877. Incidentally, the Tom Lord of *The Jazz Discography* is not the author of the same name who compiled the excellent *Clarence Williams* discography (Chigwell, Essex, England: Storyville, 1976).
4. Website: http://www.copyright.gov/circs/circ1.html#wwp.
5. Website: http://www.wisc.edu/writing/Handbook/QuoWhatDocumented.html.
6. David Wild, *The Recordings of John Coltrane,* 2nd. ed. (Ann Arbor, MI: Wildmusic, 1979), p. 70.
7. Kernfeld and Rye, op. cit., part two, p. 879.
8. Although meticulously researched, Raben's noble effort at updating Jepsen, *Jazz Records 1942–1980,* suffers from a limited scope and a painfully slow rate of publication (7 volumes—to FRA in the alphabet—in a decade). The publisher, Karl Emil Knudsen, reports that vol. 8 will be published as a CD-ROM.
9. Kernfeld and Rye, op. cit., part two, p. 890.

JAZZ RESEARCH BIBLIOGRAPHY (2001–2002)

Keith Waters and Jason R. Titus

This is the second installment in an ongoing bibliography project. Articles contained in this bibliography are scholarly essays on jazz contained in journals not specifically devoted to jazz. This volume features articles that appeared in print during 2001–2002; the previous volume (11) of *Annual Review of Jazz Studies* contains articles that appeared in 1999–2000. Special thanks to Marin Marian Balasa, David Carson Berry, Barbara Bleij, Vincenzo Caporaletti, Geoffrey Collier, Krin Gabbard, Nicholas Meeus, Steven Pond, Bruce Boyd Raeburn, Marc Rice, Janna K. Saslaw, Gabriel Solis, Walter van de Leur, Eric Van Tassel, and others for items suggested for inclusion.

Suggestions for academic articles published in nonjazz journals after 2002 may be e-mailed to Keith Waters (watersk@stripe.colorado.edu) or Jason R. Titus (jason@jasontitus.com). Complete citations (date, volume and number, pages) would be appreciated.

Anderson, Iain. "Jazz Outside the Marketplace: Free Improvisation and Nonprofit Sponsorship of the Arts, 1965–1980." *American Music* 20/2 (Summer 2002): 131–167.

Ashley, Richard. "Do[n't] Change a Hair for Me: The Art of Jazz Rubato." *Music Perception* 19/3 (Spring 2002): 311–332.

Berry, David Carson. "The Popular Songwriter as Composer: Mannerisms and Design in the Music of Jimmy Van Heusen." *Indiana Theory Review* 21 (2000): 1–51.

Bleij, Barbara. "De Berklee-methode. Aantekeningen bij een jazzharmonieleer." *Tijdschrift voor Muziektheorie* 6/2 (May 2001): 131–136.

Busse, Walter Gerard. "Toward Objective Measurement and Evaluation of Jazz Piano Performance via MIDI-Based Groove Quantize Templates." *Music Perception* 19/3 (Spring 2002): 443–462.

Caporaletti, Vincenzo. Review of "Klassik analysiert jazz–und umgekehrt" by M. Drude and A. Engelbrecht. *Analisi. Rivista di Teoria e Pedagogia Musicale* 36 (2001): 38–39.

Caporaletti, Vincenzo. "Straight, No Real. Stratificazione metrica e modularità costruttiva in 'Straight, No Chaser' di Thelonious Monk." *Musica Theorica Spectrum* 2/3 (May/September 2002): 32–51.

Collier, Geoffrey L., and James Lincoln Collier. "A Study of Timing in Two Louis Armstrong Solos." *Music Perception* 19/3 (Spring 2002): 463–483.

Friberg, Anders, and Andreas Sundström. "Swing Ratios and Ensemble Timing in Jazz Performance: Evidence for a Common Rhythmic Pattern." *Music Perception* 19/3 (Spring 2002): 333–350.

Gabbard, Krin. "A Roundtable on Ken Burns's *Jazz*." (With Geoffrey Jacques, Bernard Gendron, Scott DeVeaux, and Sherrie Tucker.) *Journal of Popular Music Studies* 13/2 (Fall 2001): 207–25.

Gabbard, Krin. "Miles Passed, Miles Ahead." *Chronicle of Higher Education* 47/36 (May 18, 2001): B17–19.

Goodheart, Matthew. "The 'Giant Steps' Fragment." *Perspectives of New Music* 39/2 (Summer 2001): 63–95.

Halay, Benjamin. " 'Body and Soul' (1930). Musique de John Waldo Green, paroles de Robert Sour, Edward Heyman, et Franck Eyton." *Musurgia* 7/3–4 (2001): 131–143.

Horn, David. "The Sound World of Art Tatum." *Black Music Research Journal* 20/2 (Fall 2000): 237–257.

Iyer, Vijay. "Embodied Mind, Situated Cognition, and Expressive Microtiming in African-American Music." *Music Perception* 19/3 (Spring 2002): 387–414.

Jackson, Travis. Review of *The Birth of Bebop: A Musical and Social History* by Scott DeVeaux. *Journal of the American Musicological Society* 54/2 (Summer 2001): 405–412.

Jadunath, David. "An Interview with Hubert Laws." *Flutist Quarterly* 27/2 (Winter 2002): 36–41.

Janke, Berend. "Jazz in Lithuania." *European Meetings in Ethnomusicology* 8 (2001): 57–64.

Johnson-Laird, P.N. "How Jazz Musicians Improvise." *Music Perception* 19/3 (Spring 2002): 415–442.

Larson, Steve. "Musical Forces, Melodic Expectation, and Jazz Melody." *Music Perception* 19/3 (Spring 2002): 351–386.

Leeuwenberg, Boudewijn, Berend van den Berg, and Daniel Kaminski. Review of *Jazzharmonie aan de piano,* by Frans Elsen. *Tijdschrift voor Muziektheorie* 6/3 (November 2001): 238–243.

Levy, Claire. "From Imitation to Innovation: Ethnojazz from Bulgaria." *European Meetings in Ethnomusicology* 8 (2001): 51–56.

Madsen, Peter. "A Jazz Trombone Ensemble Discography." *International Trombone Association (ITA) Journal* 30/1 (January 2002): 28–29.

Marconi, Piero. Review of "La definizione dello swing. I fondamenti estetici del jazz e delle musiche audiotattili," by Vincenzo Caporaletti. *Musica Theorica* 1 (January 2002): 23–24.

Modirzadeh, Hafez. "Aural Archetypes and Cyclic Perspectives in the Work of John Coltrane and Ancient Chinese Music Theory." *Black Music Research Journal* 21/1 (Spring 2001): 75–105.

Mouellic, Gilles. "Improvisation: Le jazz comme modèle. Du 'bebop' au 'free jazz': Etude." *Musurgia* 7/3–4 (2000): 35–106.

Pond, Steven F. Review of *Jazz* by Ken Burns. *Ethnomusicology* 46/3 (Fall 2002): 552–556.

Pressing, Jeff. "Black Atlantic Rhythm: Its Computational and Transcultural Foundations." *Music Perception* 19/3 (Spring 2002): 285–310.

Raeburn, Bruce Boyd . "Early New Orleans Jazz in Theaters." *Louisiana History* XLIII/1 (Winter 2002): 41–52.

Ropers, Didier. "Improvisation: Le jazz comme modèle. Du 'bebop' au 'free jazz': Analyses." *Musurgia* 7/3–4 (2000): 107–129.

Roueff, Olivier. "Faire le jazz: la coproduction de l'expérience esthétique dans un jazz-club." *Revue de Musicologie* 88/1 (2002): 67–94.

Saslaw, Janna K. "Far Out: Intentionality and Image Schema in the Reception of Early Works by Ornette Coleman." *Current Musicology* 69 (Spring 2000): 97–117.

Sipa, Alexandru. "Mircea Tiberian's Thoughts about Ethnojazz." *European Meetings in Ethnomusicology* 8 (2001): 65–72

van de Leur, Walter. "The 'American Impressionists' and the 'Birth of the Cool.'" *Tijdschrift voor Muziektheorie* 6/1 (February 2001): 18–26.

Van Tassel, Eric. "What Jazz Teaches Musicians: An Appreciation of Jazz Can Inform Early Music Performance Practice." *Early Music America* 6/3 (Fall 2000): 23–29.

Waddeland, Carl Haakon. " 'It Don't Mean a Thing If It Ain't Got That Swing' — Simulating Expressive Timing by Modulated Movements." *Journal of New Music Research* 30/1 (March 2001): 23–38.

Weist, Steve. "Remembering the King: A Tribute to James Louis 'J.J.' Johnson, 1929–2001," "An Interview with J.J. Johnson," and "J.J. Johnson's Trombone Solo on 'Now's the Time.'" *International Trombone Association [ITA] Journal* 29/4 (Fall 2001): 38–50.

BOOKS RECEIVED

Compiled by Vincent Pelote

Following is a list of recently published or republished books added to the archives of the Institute of Jazz Studies. Books are listed alphabetically by title, with the primary title in full capitals.

ART BLAKEY: Jazz Messenger, by Leslie Gourse (Schirmer Trade Books, 2002)

BASS LINES: A Life in Jazz, by Coleridge Goode and Roger Cotterrell (Northway Publications, 2002)

BENNY CARTER: A Life in American Music, 2 vols., by Morroe Berger, Edward Berger, and James Patrick [2nd edition] (Scarecrow Press, Inc., 2002)

BESSIE, by Chris Albertson [revised and expanded] (Yale University Press, 2003)

BILL EVANS: Everything Happens to Me—A Musical Biography, by Keith Shadwick (Backbeat Books, 2002)

CASTLES MADE OF SOUND: The Story of Gil Evans, by Larry Hicock (Da Capo Press, 2002)

THE CAT ON A HOT THIN GROOVE, by Gene Deitch [jazz cartoons] (Fantagraphics Books, 2003)

CHORD CHANGES ON CHALKBOARD: How Public School Teachers Shaped Jazz and the Music of New Orleans, by Al Kennedy (Scarecrow Press, Inc., 2002)

CONTEMPORARY CAT: Terence Blanchard with Special Guests, by Anthony Magro (Scarecrow Press, Inc., 2002)

COOKIN': Hard Bop and Soul Jazz, by Kenny Mathieson (Canongate Books, 2002)

CUBAN FIRE: The Story of Salsa and Latin Jazz, by Isabelle Leymarie (Continuum, 2002)

DEEP IN A DREAM: The Long Night of Chet Baker, by James Gavin (Alfred A. Knopf, 2002)

DRUMMIN' MEN: The Heartbeat of Jazz: The Bebop Years, by Burt Korall (Oxford University Press, 2002)

DUKE'S DIARY: The Life of Duke Ellington, 2 vols., (Part One, 1927–1950; Part Two, 1950–1974), by Ken Vail (Scarecrow Press, Inc., 2002)

THE EARLY SWING ERA, 1930 TO 1941, by Dave Oliphant (Greenwood Press, 2002)

FAITH IN TIME: The Life of Jimmy Scott, by David Ritz (Da Capo Press, 2002)

FEELING MY WAY: A Discography of the Recordings of Eddie Lang, 1923-1933, by Raymond F. Mitchell (Self-published, 2002)

FROM AFRICA TO AFROCENTRIC INNOVATIONS SOME CALL "JAZZ," 4 vols.: Vol. 1, chs. 1–4) The Afrocentric Roots of "Jazz" and African Music in the Americas (Antiquity–1910); Vol. 2, chs. 5–8, The Evolution of Classic "Jazz" Forms (1910–1950); Vol. 3, chs. 9–12, The Creation of Fire, Fusion and Reconstructive Modern Styles (1950–2000); Vol. 4, An Encyclopedia of Music, Musicians and Recordings (appendices for Chs. 1–12), by Karlton E. Hester (Hesteria Records & Publishing Co., 2000)

GOOD VIBES: A Life in Jazz, by Terry Gibbs, with Cary Ginell (Scarecrow Press, Inc., 2003)

HARD BOP ACADEMY: The Sidemen of Art Blakey and the Jazz Messengers, by Alan Goldsher (Hal Leonard Corporation, 2002)

JAZZ: A Critic's Guide to the 100 Most Important Recordings, by Ben Ratliff (Times Books, 2002)

JAZZ AND DEATH: Medical Profiles of Jazz Greats, by Frederick J. Spencer, M.D. (University Press of Mississippi, 2002)

JAZZ IN NEW ORLEANS: The Postwar Years Through 1970, by Charles Suhor (Scarecrow Press, 2001)

JAZZ NOIR: Listening to Music from *Phantom Lady* to *The Last Seduction*, by David Butler [jazz in films] (Praeger, 2002)

A JAZZ ODYSSEY: The Life of Oscar Peterson, by Oscar Peterson, with editor and consultant Richard Palmer (Continuum, 2002)

JAZZ MY LOVE, by Giuseppe Pino [photographs] (Schirmer/Mosel, 2002)

JAZZ VOYEUR, by Gerardo Cañellas [photographs] (Lunwerg Editores, 2002)

JELLY'S BLUES: The Life, Music, and Redemption of Jelly Roll Morton, by Howard Reich and William Gaines (Da Capo Press, 2003)

JOHNNY VARRO DISCOGRAPHY, compiled by Gerald Bielderman (Self-published, 2002)

JUST FOR A THRILL: Lil Hardin Armstrong—First Lady of Jazz, by James L. Dickerson (Cooper Square Press, 2002)

LATIN JAZZ: The Perfect Combination/La Combinación Perfecta, by Raúl Fernández (Chronicle Books, 2002)

A LIFE IN THE GOLDEN AGE OF JAZZ: A Biography of Buddy DeFranco, by Fabrice Zammarchi and Sylvie Mas (Parkside Publications, Inc., 2002)

LOOKING FOR FRANKIE: A Bio-Discography of the Jazz Trumpeter Frankie Newton, by Bob Weir and John Postgate (Self-published, 2003)

A LOVE SUPREME: The Story of John Coltrane's Signature Album, by Ashley Kahn (Viking, 2002)

MEL TORMÉ: A Chronicle of His Recordings, Books and Films, by George Hulme (McFarland & Company, Inc., 2000)

NORMAN GRANZ: The White Moses of Black Jazz, by Dempsey J. Travis (Urban Research Press, Inc., 2003)

NOTES FROM A JAZZ LIFE, by Digby Fairweather (Northway Publications, 2002)

OSCAR PETERSON: A Musical Biography, by Alex Barris (Harper Collins, 2002)

PAUL WHITEMAN: Pioneer in American Music, Vol. I: 1890–1930, by Don Rayno (Scarecrow Press, Inc., 2003)

Q: The Autobiography of Quincy Jones, by Quincy Jones (Doubleday, 2001)

RAT RACE BLUES: The Musical Life of Gigi Gryce, by Noal Cohen and Michael Fitzgerald (Berkeley Hills Books, 2002)

ROY ELDRIDGE: Little Jazz Giant, by John Chilton (Continuum, 2002)

THE SONG FOR ME: A Glossary of New Orleans Musicians, by Brian Wood (Self-published, 2003?)

SO WHAT: The Life of Miles Davis, by John Szwed (Simon & Schuster, 2002)

STAN GETZ: Nobody Else But Me, by Dave Gelly (Backbeat Books, 2002)

STARDUST MELODIES: A Biography of Twelve of America's Most Popular Songs, by Will Friedwald (Pantheon Books, 2002)

STARDUST MELODY: The Life and Music of Hoagy Carmichael, by Richard M. Sudhalter (Oxford University Press, 2002)

TONIGHT AT NOON: A Love Story, by Sue Graham Mingus (Pantheon Books, 2002)

UNDERNEATH A HARLEM MOON: The Harlem to Paris Years of Adelaide Hall, by Iain Cameron Williams (Continuum, 2002)

WHAT IS THIS THING CALLED JAZZ?: African American Musicians as Artists, Critics, and Activists, by Eric Porter (University of California Press, 2002)

YONDER COME THE BLUES: The Evolution of a Genre, by Paul Oliver, Tony Russell, Robert M.W. Dixon, John Godrich, Howard Rye (Cambridge University Press, 2001)

THE YOUNG LOUIS ARMSTRONG ON RECORDS: A Critical Survey of the Early Recordings, 1923–1928, by Edward Brooks (Scarecrow Press, Inc., 2002)

ABOUT THE EDITORS

EDWARD BERGER, associate director of the Institute of Jazz Studies, is active as a record producer and photographer. He is coauthor of the recently revised and updated *Benny Carter: A Life in American Music* and author of two other works in the Scarecrow Press Studies in Jazz Series.

DAVID A. CAYER was a founding coeditor of the *Journal of Jazz Studies*, the predecessor of *Annual Review of Jazz Studies*, in 1973 and has been affiliated with the Institute of Jazz Studies since 1965. In 1991, he retired from Rutgers University as associate vice president for academic affairs.

HENRY MARTIN, associate professor of music at Rutgers University–Newark, is a composer and music theorist. He is also founder and chair of the Special Interest Group in Jazz Theory of the Society for Music Theory. His *Charlie Parker and Thematic Improvisation* is no. 24 in the Studies in Jazz Series. Wadsworth/Schirmer recently issued his jazz history text (coauthored with Keith Waters), *Jazz: The First Hundred Years*.

DAN MORGENSTERN, director of the Institute of Jazz Studies, is a jazz historian and former editor of *Down Beat*. His many publications include *Jazz People*, and he has won six Grammy awards for album notes. He has been a vice president of the National Academy of Recording Arts and Sciences, a jazz panelist for the Music Program of the National Endowment for the Arts, and a teacher of jazz history at Brooklyn College, New York University, the Peabody Institute, and Rutgers.

GEORGE BASSETT studied music theory with Milton Babbitt and Claudio Spies, among others, at Princeton University. For over 20 years he has sung in and arranged for the jazz-, folk-, standards-, and rock-oriented vocal group Cahoots along with his wife, Nancy Wilson (no, not that one).

ABOUT THE CONTRIBUTORS

SCOTT A. CARTER graduated from the University of North Carolina at Chapel Hill with a degree in music. He is a recent graduate of the Master's Program in Jazz History and Research at Rutgers University in Newark, where he wrote his thesis on Max Roach's *Freedom Now Suite*.

BEN GIVAN recently completed a Ph.D. in music theory at Yale University and is currently a visiting assistant professor at Skidmore College.

MARK S. HAYWOOD lives in England, holds a Ph.D. in classics from Liverpool University, and currently coordinates staff training at a college of Further Education in Birmingham. He has had two books of popular piano music and various jazz research papers published and has a particular interest in the sonnet form as a means of expression.

FABIAN HOLT, Ph.D., is assistant professor of music at the University of Copenhagen, Denmark, and has specialized in jazz and cultural theory (aesthetics, sociology, representation, etc.). He has written an M.A. thesis on the jazz records from the German ECM label and a dissertation on "cool" jazz in the 1920s and 1930s with an attempt to reconceptualize conventional ideas of hot and cool jazz in relation to racial issues. He is currently working on a book on generic boundaries in American popular music, tentatively titled "Theorizing Popular Music Genres in the Wake of Postmodernism."

EDGAR JORDAN has a degree in music from the University of North Carolina at Chapel Hill, where he studied trumpet with James Ketch. He is a recent graduate of the Master's Program in Jazz History and Research at Rutgers University in Newark, where he wrote his thesis on Roy Eldridge.

LAWRENCE KART was assistant editor of *Down Beat* in 1968–69 and wrote regularly on jazz for the *Chicago Tribune* from 1977 to 1988. A collection of his work, *Jazz in Search of Itself,* is forthcoming from Yale University Press.

NORMAN MEEHAN is the head of jazz studies at Massey University in Wellington, New Zealand. He has published articles discussing jazz styles and improvisation, and his forthcoming book on Paul Bley, *Time Will Tell*, is to be published by Berkeley Hills Books in 2003.

VINCENT PELOTE is the head of collection services/sound archivist at the Institute of Jazz Studies. He has compiled discographies of Billie Holiday, Lionel Hampton, and the Commodore label. He contributed to *The Oxford Companion to Jazz,* and has written many LP and CD program notes on jazz guitar, Mary Lou Williams, Benny Carter, Johnny Smith, and others. Mr. Pelote has contributed book and CD reviews to the *ARSC Journal.* He is one of the hosts of the radio program "Jazz from the Archives," on WBGO-FM, National Public Radio, in Newark.

SCOTT REEVES is an associate professor of music at The City College of New York and also teaches at the Juilliard School of Music. He is the author of two highly regarded jazz improvisation texts, *Creative Jazz Improvisation* and *Creative Beginnings*, both published by Prentice-Hall, and is a published composer of music for jazz ensemble. As a trombonist and alto flugelhornist, he appears on recordings with Kenny Werner, James Williams, and the Anthony Braxton Orchestra, has appeared in concert with Ron Carter, Clark Terry, John Patitucci, George Garzone, and many others, and performs regularly at NYC venues such as Birdland and the Knitting Factory with the Dave Liebman Big Band and the Chico O'Farrill Afro-Cuban Jazz Orchestra.

RANDY SANDKE is a professional trumpeter who has recorded three albums of Louis Armstrong–related material. Five of his transcriptions of classic Armstrong recordings were published by Warner Music for Jazz at Lincoln Center and the Smithsonian. His book, *Harmony for a New Millenium,* was published in 2002 by Hal Leonard Music. Mr. Sandke recently recorded the trumpet solos for the New York production of *Ma Rainey's Black Bottom.* His most recent CD, *Inside Out,* was named one of the ten best jazz albums of 2002 by *Jazz Times* magazine. He produced two concerts for the 2003 JVC Jazz Festival; and *The Subway Ballet,* an extended composition for big band by Mr. Sandke, had its premiere this year at Dick Hyman's "Jazz in July" concert series.

TAD SHULL, Ph.D., is a tenor saxophonist and writer living in New York City. He has several discs on the Criss-Cross label, including *In the Land of the Tenor* and *Deep Passion*. He also has many publications on European politics and is now working on French intellectuals' and critics' views of jazz.

DICK SPOTTSWOOD was a founder of the journal *Bluegrass Unlimited* in 1966 and is the author of *Ethnic Music on Records* (University of Illinois Press). He is the producer of many archival reissues and a radio host whose eclectic *Dick Spottswood Show,* a.k.a. "The Obsolete Music Hour," may be heard via www.wamu.org.

JASON R. TITUS holds degrees in music from the Eastman School of Music, Indiana University of Pennsylvania, and Louisiana State University. He is currently a Ph.D. student in music theory at Eastman. His research interests include the chord voicings of Thelonious Monk and the modal jazz of Miles Davis.

KEITH WATERS is assistant professor of music theory at the University of Colorado at Boulder. He has published articles pertaining to jazz improvisation and analysis, and his book, *Jazz: The First Hundred Years,* coauthored with Henry Martin, was recently published by Wadsworth/Schirmer. As a jazz pianist, he has performed throughout the United States and Europe, as well as in Russia, and has performed in concert with James Moody, Bobby Hutcherson, Chris Connor, Sheila Jordan, Buck Hill, and others. He has been featured in *Jazz Player* magazine. His most recent recording is with the Jon Metzger Quartet for VSOP Records.

MASAYA YAMAGUCHI is a guitarist who received an M.A. in jazz performance from the City College of New York. He is also the author of *The Complete Thesaurus of Musical Scales, Symmetrical Scales for Jazz Improvisation,* and *The Pentatonicism in Jazz: Creative Aspects & Practice* (all from Charles Colin Music Publications), of *John Coltrane Plays Coltrane Changes* (Hal Leonard Corporation), and of the Coltrane-centered article "Note Groups of Limited Transposition: A Key to Unlocking Multitonic Change Possibilities" (*Down Beat,* September 2000).

ABOUT THE INSTITUTE OF JAZZ STUDIES

The Institute of Jazz Studies of Rutgers, the State University of New Jersey, is a unique research facility and archival collection, the foremost of its kind. IJS was founded in 1952 by Marshall Stearns (1908–1966), a pioneer jazz scholar, professor of medieval English literature at Hunter College, and the author of two essential jazz books: *The Story of Jazz* and *Jazz Dance*. In 1966, Rutgers was chosen as the collection's permanent home. IJS is located on the Newark campus of Rutgers and is a part of the John Cotton Dana Library of the Rutgers University Libraries.

IJS carries on a comprehensive program to preserve and further jazz in all its facets. The archival collection, which has more than quadrupled its holdings since coming to Rutgers, consists of more than 100,000 sound recordings in all formats, from phonograph cylinders and piano rolls to video cassettes and laser discs; more than 5,000 books on jazz and related subjects, including discographies, bibliographies, and dissertations; and comprehensive holdings in jazz periodicals from throughout the world. In addition, there are extensive vertical files on individuals and selected topics, a large collection of photographs, sheet music, scores, arrangements, realia, and memorabilia.

IJS serves a broad range of users, from students to seasoned scholars, authors, and collectors. The facilities are open to the public on weekdays by appointment. In addition to students, scholars, and other researchers, IJS routinely assists teachers, musicians, the media, record companies and producers, libraries and archives, arts agencies, and jazz organizations.

For further information on IJS and its programs and activities, write to:

Institute of Jazz Studies
Dana Library, Rutgers, the State University
185 University Avenue
Newark, NJ 07102